New World Choreographies

Series Editors
Rachel Fensham
School of Culture and Communication
University of Melbourne
Parkville, Australia

Peter M. Boenisch
Royal Central School of Speech and Drama
London, UK

This series presents advanced yet accessible studies of a rich field of new choreographic work which is embedded in the global, transnational and intermedial context. It introduces artists, companies and scholars who contribute to the conceptual and technological rethinking of what constitutes movement, blurring old boundaries between dance, theatre and performance. The series considers new aesthetics and new contexts of production and presentation, and discusses the multi-sensory, collaborative and transformative potential of these new world choreographies.

More information about this series at
http://www.palgrave.com/gp/series/14729

Daniela Perazzo Domm

Jonathan Burrows

Towards a Minor Dance

Daniela Perazzo Domm
Department of Performing Arts
Kingston University London
Kingston upon Thames, UK

New World Choreographies
ISBN 978-3-030-27679-9   ISBN 978-3-030-27680-5   (eBook)
https://doi.org/10.1007/978-3-030-27680-5

Cover credit: Jonathan Burrows and Matteo Fargion in *The Quiet Dance* (2005)
© Alastair Muir

This Palgrave Macmillan imprint is published by the registered company Springer Nature Switzerland AG
The registered company address is: Gewerbestrasse 11, 6330 Cham, Switzerland

'*è che questa* dannata *lingua che non so come chiamare* è bellissima,
bellissima... *e io l'amo molto*'
[*This damned language, for which I don't have a name, is beautiful,
beautiful... and I love it dearly.*]
—Tommaso Landolfi, *Dialogo dei massimi sistemi*, 1937

To Valentina and Silvia

Acknowledgements

This book has a long story. In the fifteen-year span from its embryonic conception as an independent project essay during my M.A. Performance and Culture: Interdisciplinary Perspectives at Goldsmiths College University of London, and its present form, a number of people have been instrumental in supporting its development. I am immensely grateful to Jonathan Burrows and Matteo Fargion for creating inspiring work that has fed my curiosity and stimulated my thinking since I first saw them perform in 2003 in Milan. I am indebted to them for making time to engage in conversation and for granting me permission to use their images and allowing me access to their creative process and its documentation. I cannot thank Jonathan enough for his generosity over the years, for his trust in the project and for his patience and solicitude sorting out photographs and archival material and making them available to me.

The monograph has grown out of my doctoral research, funded by the University of Surrey. Sincere thanks go to my Ph.D. supervisor, Janet Lansdale, for her supportive and insightful supervision. Although the present book is a substantial reworking of my 2007 thesis, this initial period of research taught me the importance of rigour and of attentive analysis. I am grateful to Rachel Fensham and Peter M. Boenisch, editors of the Palgrave series *New World Choreographies*, for supporting the project from its conception and through its development. My thanks go to my anonymous readers for providing constructive feedback during the peer-reviewed process: their comments offered useful directions in the reconceptualisation of the research from the original Ph.D. material. The period of research leave I was awarded by Kingston University London, where I have been teaching since 2014, was crucial in allowing me to focus on the writing during the final stages of the project.

Some of the ideas discussed in the book can be traced back to earlier publications: my chapter on *Both Sitting Duet* in Janet Lansdale's edited collection *Decentring Dancing Texts* (2008) and my articles 'Traces of History: Jonathan Burrows' Rethinking of the Choreographic Past' in *Contemporary Theatre Review* (2010) and 'The "Struggle" of the Subject: Productive Ambiguity in Jonathan Burrows' Choreography' in *Choreographic Practices* (2012). These were reworked into the argument of this book and are acknowledged here for offering productive venues for earlier stages of the research. Many perspectives and concepts that underpin this study were tested in the context of conference presentations: most notably, the Society for Dance History Scholars/Congress on Research in Dance conference in Athens, 2015; the 'Deleuze + Art' conference at Trinity College Dublin, 2016; 'Minimalism: Location Aspect Moment' at the University of Southampton/Winchester School of Art, 2016; and the Society for Dance Research conference 'Dance in the Age of Forgetfulness' at Royal Holloway University of London, 2018. I am grateful to the colleagues who, over the years, have engaged in conversation about my research in the context of these and other platforms, but also through their supportive collegiality and friendship: Hetty Blades, Ramsay Burt, Antonio Cerella, Tina Chanter, Laura Cull Ó Maoilearca, Bojana Cvejić, Fred Dalmasso, Diana Damian Martin, Simon Ellis, Vânia Gala, Kélina Gotman, Antje Hildebrandt, Vicky Hunter, Beatrice Jarvis, Celena Monteiro, John Ó Maoilearca, Helen Palmer, Katerina Paramana, Patricia Phillippy, Colin Poole, Efrosini Protopapa, Arabella Stanger, Lise Uytterhoeven, Tamara Tomić-Vajagić, Nik Wakefield. My thanks go also to Kloe Dean, Antonio de la Fe, Hugo Glendinning, Adrian Heathfield and Sarah Whatley for accepting my invitation to take part in a public event on *52 Portraits* at Kingston University London, in 2016, and share their thoughts on the work.

Finally, my deepest gratitude goes to my family for their unwavering support over the years: to my parents, for always knowing that the book would be finished one day; to my sister Valeria, for her long-distance encouragement; and to my husband Lance. My biggest thanks go to my daughters: this book is for them, Valentina and Silvia, for their 'strong questions' and precious laughter.

CONTENTS

LIST OF FIGURES

CHAPTER 1

Dance and/as Poiesis, Poetry, Poetics

POIESIS AS 'NON-MAKING': *WEAK DANCE STRONG QUESTIONS* (2001)

The performance space is a studio theatre with mobile seating, where the spectators are arranged in a semicircle. As they enter, Jonathan Burrows and Jan Ritsema, in everyday clothes and sturdy shoes, welcome the audience, offering information about the title and the duration of the performance and handing out additional chairs or cushions to the latecomers. The house lights are on and are never lowered for the whole fifty minutes of the piece. Almost unnoticed, in keeping with the informal tone of this introduction, they start to move and thus begin their dance. The two men become engaged in movements without creating phrases or recognisable patterns; there is no identifiable rhythm to their manoeuvres, no deliberate relation with the space and with each other, neither at a point in time nor through time. Nevertheless, the overall even distribution of the pace and intensity of the activity and the sense of ease in the lack of formal interaction between Burrows and Ritsema speak of an attentive awareness of their relational presence. They proceed steadily, yet through fragmentary actions, variously inhabiting the space—walking, standing, shuffling, stepping, turning, crouching, hopping, sitting, crawling, pausing. Their movements seem to test balance and the force of gravity, explore unfamiliar qualities and speeds of motion, as though to challenge socially constructed bodily gestures and actions. They look pensive or smile as they bend, hold, tilt, stretch, stiffen,

© The Author(s) 2019
D. Perazzo Domm, *Jonathan Burrows*,
New World Choreographies,
https://doi.org/10.1007/978-3-030-27680-5_1

loosen, flex, jerk, lift, cross, twist, rotate or tangle different body parts: legs, arms, torsos, necks, hands. Possibilities seem endless, yet the range they explore has an ordinary feel: although unusual for a dance performance, their movements do not aim for extremes, do not show off particular skills. The performers present themselves as two of us—even though we admire their focus, their stamina and their seemingly inexhaustible curiosity about movement and its functioning (Fig. 1.1).

I wrote this description of *Weak Dance Strong Questions* (2001) after seeing the performance in September 2003 in Milan, as part of the inaugural programme of 'Uovo Performing Arts Festival', a platform for cutting-edge performance and choreography I collaborated with. It was the first work by Burrows I ever saw and it became the seed for the research that has led to this book. As a theatre and performance researcher and professional, at the time I was already familiar with experimental practices. Dance, however, was fairly new to me and this piece gestured to an idea of it that was significantly different from conventional understandings of this art form. The piece is an improvised duet in which Burrows, a professional dancer

Fig. 1.1 Jonathan Burrows and Jan Ritsema in *Weak Dance Strong Questions* (2001) (Photograph by Herman Sorgeloos)

and choreographer, works alongside the Dutch theatre director Ritsema, who is not trained in dance. As the title suggests, the work is a radical interrogation of dance, of its modes and possibilities. It was described by international reviewers as featuring 'movement combinations which are not normal, either in everyday life or in any dance style' (Staude, 2001) and was depicted as 'a piece which consists only of interruptions', in which 'every movement is taken back just at the moment that it is executed' (Siegmund, 2001). About the choreography, British dance critic Judith Mackrell (2001: 16) wrote that it offered 'no story, no discernible structure and absolutely no virtuoso gloss. [...T]here's no obvious development of the material and no formal linking between the two performers'.

In a published interview, Burrows (2002: 25) defined the piece as being about 'questioning' and 'non-making', about avoiding given formulas and 'coming to the audience with empty hands'. When I met up with him in 2004 to talk about the work (I had, by then, moved to London and started the research that underpins this monograph), he told me that the creation of the piece was organised around three tasks that both performers were to respond to: to move as though in a state of questioning; not to negotiate time and space; to be connected to the other person (Burrows, 2004). In the work, movement is understood as a way of asking questions: it embodies a continuous doubting and looking for possibilities and does not resolve into fixed steps or gestures. Nevertheless, since the constant state of questioning never allows any movement/question to be completed/answered, 'the piece has choreographed itself moment by moment and has also acquired a particular style' (Burrows, 2004). By emptying the dance, through the questioning of given forms and rules, the process allows the work to be filled with new possibilities. A paradox: filling by emptying, a production by subtraction, a way of making—a *poiesis*—by non-making.

In the Aristotelian categorisation of human activity, *poiesis* indicates production, the act of making—from the ancient Greek *poieîn*, to make. As distinguished from *praxis* (practice), which designates an act that is complete in itself, *poiesis* is an activity whose aim exceeds the activity itself: it is a bringing-forth, it invents, it forges, it creates. In this book, I assume the idea of *poiesis* as a starting point to interrogate the paradoxical possibilities of Burrows' invention by subtraction, making by non-making. I engage with the 'practice of simultaneous composition and decomposition' his choreography is predicated upon—to borrow the words that Daniel Heller-Roazen (2005: 193) uses to propose an understanding of poetry.

In fact, as I write elsewhere (Perazzo Domm, 2017),[1] the word *poiesis* is also connected etymologically to the terms *poetics, poetic, poetry*. These concepts become entangled in my discussion of the work—as I ground my analysis in my curiosity for dance and/as language.

Writing about *Weak Dance Strong Questions*, performance theorist and dramaturg Bojana Cvejić (2015: 149–151) premises her discussion of the piece on 'an analogy between dancing and speech', while also acknowledging that 'the sense in dance can't be compared with linguistic meaning' and that such a 'comparison [...] presupposes an approximation between two disparate expressions'. Her perspective is invoked in the discussion of Burrows' po(i)etic(s) (of) dance articulated in this book. In earlier configurations of my research on Burrows (Perazzo Domm, 2007), I moved from the literary notion of poetry and poetic language—drawing on Roman Jakobson, Julia Kristeva and Gérard Genette—to the examination of its philosophical underpinnings—via Hans-Georg Gadamer's thesis on the speculative dimension of poetry. In the present book, as the following paragraphs outline, I engage with Burrows' dance as a po(i)etic practice, while also examining its poetics, its distinctive mode of thinking (about) dance.

A Po(i)etic(s) (of) Dance

This monograph imagines Burrows' work as danced poetry and investigates the performance poetics his choreography has articulated through three decades of choreographing, dancing, collaborating, researching, mentoring and writing. The book argues that Burrows' creative methods—his compositional rigour and interest in clear structures, his collaborative approach and his paradoxical exploration of the possibilities of choreography—mobilise ways of rethinking dance's critical and political positioning in the contemporary moment. I propose that, by challenging the normative grammar of choreography, Burrows' work also resists established artistic and social paradigms, reconceptualising individuation and community through process and performance. As the first full-length monograph on Burrows' choreography, the book also aims to historicise his work in relation to its contexts of reference and to document his pieces through detailed (yet necessarily unexhaustive) commentaries, which draw on an attentive response to the works as well as on extensive archival research and on a substantial corpus of first-hand interview material. The specificities of Burrows' creative approach demand a critical and theoretical perspective that valorises the way in which the significance (artistic, historical and political) of the dance is articulated through the distinctiveness of its aesthetic choices.

The association of dance with poetry and poetics finds compelling and varied articulation in dance and performance scholarship, with important contributions that move between writing and dancing, addressing the creative possibilities of their interaction. It is in the company of these conceptualisations of dance and/as language that I co-imagine Burrows' po(i)etic(s) (of) dance. For instance, Burrows' own dialogical writing with Adrian Heathfield (a series of exchanges in epistolary format published in the journal *Choreographic Practices* in 2013) draws on their extended conversations about the relationship between movement and writing in the context of contemporary dance. Here Burrows and Heathfield interrogate the respective specificities of these practices and question their compositional tools, semantic strategies and affective force; as Heathfield puts it, they attend to the ways in which both dance and poetry produce 'something that is felt and remains in the body of the witness or reader' (Burrows and Heathfield, 2013: 132).

Yet the association of language with choreography, as conceptualised by post-structuralist and deconstructivist positions,[2] has also been wrestled with, on account of the corporeal dimension of movement and its import on the signifying process, often neglected in deconstructivist readings of dance. 'Writing both with and against Derrida', Mark Franko (2008: 241) has argued that the embodied nature of movement troubles the association of dance with writing: insofar as dance involves bodies in their singularity, it occupies and performs specific (social) space and engages in specific (political) action. Nevertheless, an interest in the generative potential of the relationship between dance and language continues to inform both speculative and creative investigations of the possible configurations of this analogy. For instance, Robert Vesty's (2017) edited issue on 'Words and Dance' of the journal *Choreographic Practices* explores poetry and its relationship with dance through an investigation of the creative potentialities afforded by the encounter between movement and language. Engaging with creative processes that play with both language and movement, Vesty foregrounds the spatial and physical aspect of poetry, reflecting on 'how words have dimension, how their geometry can be further understood through somatic awareness, and how they can be produced in the moment with a sensitivity to their material form and corporeal stem' (Vesty, 2017: 4).

In the 1990s, the interrogation of the points of convergence between language and movement gave rise to writings constructing a poetics of dance: Laurence Louppe's (2010 [1998]) *Poetics of Contemporary Dance* and Gabriele Brandstetter's (2015 [1995]) *Poetics of Dance* are two of the most notable examples. While the latter focuses on modern dance and promotes a rethinking of the interrelation between the visual, kinaesthetic and textual dimensions of dance in the historical avant-gardes, the former addresses specifically the tools of contemporary dance. Louppe's contribution is as much a *poetic* (affective) response to the works (and appreciation of the works' *poietic*, transformative, capacity) as a *poetics* intended as an exploration of the mechanisms through which dance produces an encounter with the spectator. Inspired by Paul Valéry's observations of the synergies between poetry and dance,[3] Louppe's poetics, which conceives of dance as 'the body's poetry' (2010: 5), emphasises the perceptual dimension of aesthetics (the *aesthesia*, the experience of the senses) over the critical (analytical, comparative, evaluative) project that a poetics might entail.

Of course, the etymology of the term 'choreography' already combines the idea of dancing with the idea of writing. André Lepecki's (2004b: 124) interrogation of the 'limits between body and text, movement and language' stems from an acknowledgement of this 'shared ground' and a desire to explore the 'spaces of friction' between these two intertwined dimensions. Ric Allsopp (2015) reminds us of this analogy while gathering together several perspectives on poetics and dance with the aim 'to show potential alignments between a poetics of dance and movement, and a poetics deriving from poetic practitioners' (Allsopp, 2015: 7). Considering 'poetics as a creative practice rather than as a critical act' (Allsopp, 2015: 4), he emphasises process and perception over interpretation. Reassessing 'the "textual turn" of the late 20th century, and its implications for dance read as a form of textual practice' (Allsopp, 2015: 6), he pits the textual paradigm against the sensuous dimension of experience. Allsopp reviews Louppe's poetics of contemporary dance, which 'suggests that both poetry and dance are "languages" that operate in excess of the functions of language' (Allsopp, 2015: 4); ultimately, he forgives Louppe for using vocabulary that is reminiscent of post-structuralist analysis (she uses words such as 'reading' and 'inscription') on account of her 'emphasis [...] on the experiential' (Allsopp, 2015: 6).

I am drawn to Allsopp's perspective for how it engages with poetics 'as an approach to creative practices that can propose the possibilities of radical coherence – or how things might hold together without falling into conventional forms and flows' (Allsopp, 2015: 4). Yet, Allsopp's framework appears shaped by a desire to construct the textual and the processual as antithetical models; in this, I see a radicalisation of Louppe's view. Instead, it seems to me that, by focusing on perception and by defining the 'mission' of poetics as that of 'tell[ing] us what a work of art does to us [and] teach[ing] us how it is made' (Louppe, 2010: 4), Louppe's perspective avoids framing the creative and the critical as mutually exclusive. I propose that these two approaches are not antithetical, providing that, on the one hand, we understand creative activity as a form of thinking through practice and, on the other hand, we rethink the role of critical activity within cultural production. In this monograph, I engage with Burrows' dance as a poetic practice—for its interplay of reduction and excess, composition and decomposition—while also constructing a poetics of his work, through both critical and experiential engagement. The next two sections discuss these two perspectives, framing poetics as a creative and speculative practice and as an affective and critical act.

From Poetics to Aesthetics and/as Politics

This book proposes that Burrows' work is also in itself a poetics of dance, in the sense that it is a thinking through practice that generates new horizons for dance—a transformative artistic and reflective practice that is both creative and theoretical. Burrows is a prominent figure in current choreographic debates and his choreographic research finds articulation across practice and theory in a range of contexts: through his own writing, his academic roles, his contribution to debates in the field of dance practice and scholarship, his curatorial and mentoring projects. Burrows (2010) is the author of a widely read choreography handbook, aimed at dance and performance makers, organised as a collection of reflections on choreographic principles and creative approaches. As it has been observed, Burrows' contribution to this field of discourse, alongside those of other choreographers whose writings have been included in dance publications from the last ten years,[4] has 'established a discipline-specific category of the artist-theorist. This reality underscores the muddying of any clear divisions between dance artists and theorists in the early twenty-first century' (Brannigan, Day and Thomson, 2018: 84).

Burrows' pieces are constructed in dialogue with specific dance techniques, everyday movements, the physicality of other art forms (especially music) and explorations into the issues of presence and representation in recent performative practices. In this respect, the research towards new parameters, procedures and structures for dance is at the core of the choreographer's investigation, and the work is a study conducted as much *on* the language of choreography as *through* it. For Genette (1982: 92), a poetics of language concerns 'the innumerable forms of linguistic imagination. For men dream not only with words, they also dream […] about words, and about all the manifestations of language'. Nevertheless, it is Cvejić's conceptualisation of poetics that most directly informs the understanding of its transformative potential that this book promotes. In a recent article, Cvejić (2018: 37) defines poetics as a 'kind of thought' distinguished from others for 'its capacity to ask a curious question: "What is the art I would like to see before I can see it?"' and locates poetics in dialogue with imagination. For Cvejić, 'imagination […] accounts for the ability to think of something not presently perceived, for thoughts without experiential content'. Here Cvejić argues that 'poetical principles direct the thought of creation toward imagination into futurity often leading to a poetic use of language' (Cvejič, 2018: 37).

I suggest that a thought about the future is a socially situated thought, which enables political engagement. In this sense, poetics is taken in this book to mean both artistic and political articulation of ideas. By engaging with a poetics of choreography, I propose to attend to the creative principles adopted by Burrows and his main collaborator, the composer Matteo Fargion, in their artistic processes. I embrace the approach advocated by Cvejić who 'revive[s]' poetics as a way of engaging with 'how [the] principles [of artistic activity] might become instruments for looking past art into society'—a concern which, she maintains, has been 'cannibalized' by today's predominant focus on artistic practice (Cvejić, 2016: 21, 22). Attending to poetics, then, entails a concern with both aesthetic and political aspects of artistic production.

This claim is in alignment with Jacques Rancière's notion of the transformative power of aesthetics and the challenge he makes to paradigms that oppose aesthetics to politics or establish hierarchies between the two. Through the notion of the 'distribution of the sensible', Rancière offers a view of art as inextricably linked to politics: it is through shared experience, whether symbolic or social, that transformation arises. The task of the artist is then to produce creative transformation, which is inevitably also political: the 'principle behind an art's formal revolution is at the same time the principle behind the political redistribution of shared experience' (Rancière, 2004: 17). It is, however, the philosophy of Gilles Deleuze and Félix Guattari that most significantly informs the perspective of this study. In particular, I think of Burrows' symbolic/social transformation in terms of the Deleuzoguattarian notion of 'minor practice', the revolutionary gesture of destabilising major traditions from a minoritarian position. This perspective underpins the argument I construct of Burrows' choreography as a form of 'minor dance', illuminating the entanglement between the linguistic/choreographic and political possibilities that arise from the reworking of conventional forms from within recognised dance environments.

I am suggesting therefore that Burrows creates work that embodies a radical rethinking of the language of dance, by reassessing the scale of bodily movement, reinterpreting its potentialities and renegotiating its strategies of signification. In this book, I will explore the choreographic language he has forged over more than thirty years of creative work as both individual and multiple; I will interrogate how it questions theatricality and representation, problematising historical and disciplinary paradigms by queering the distinction between invention and repetition. Through dramaturgical processes that rethink modes of individualisation and collaboration, his works also reframe the notion of authorship as an inevitably collective process, in the sense that Deleuze and Guattari attribute to the political enunciation formulated by minor cultures. In a Deleuzoguattarian sense, what is distinctive about Burrows' dances is how they question 'major' codes through the mobilisation and 'deterritorialisation' of minor traditions. Drawing on this notion, which highlights the radical potential of the act of critical reworking of major, dominant codes by a dominated minority, I will argue that Burrows' work, while quieter and distinctly less spectacular than many of his contemporaries, nevertheless produces a sustained rethinking of the possibilities of choreographic form and of dance's potential for social critique.

This political framework is further developed in the book through ideas that support an understanding of the singularity of Burrows' work among other transformative voices of the current contemporary dance landscape. My discussion is informed by political theory, particularly by perspectives conceptualised by contemporary Italian philosophers. Engaging with theorists who are perhaps less well known in performance literature, I will investigate the significance of Burrows' work in terms of its minimalist/reductive stance, its capacity to redefine community and the political implications of his 'danced poetry'. Developed as a response to Italy's recent and still ongoing political, economic and identity crisis, Italian political philosophy offers new possibilities for thinking more broadly about the crisis of contemporary society (Calcagno, 2015). The book invokes these forward-looking, radical and often provocative ideas—which deal with questions of nihilism and with the legacy of Michel Foucault's thought and Marxist theory—as a productive framework within which to understand the role of current artistic (and dance) poetics in responding to the contemporary political situation. Drawing on this body of theory is also in itself a gesture of minorisation, which deterritorialises critical discourse through voices that are not widely heard in dominant Anglophone debates.

Specifically, I work with Gianni Vattimo's (2003) notion of 'nihilism as emancipation' to offer an understanding of Burrows' link with the minimalist tradition (Chapter 3). I engage with crucial concepts of Roberto Esposito's political philosophy, building on his deconstruction of modern paradigms of sociality and personhood (Esposito, 2012), in order to question the ways in which relationality is practised and rethought in Burrows' creative exchange with Fargion and in other partnerships (Chapter 5); I also draw on Esposito's (2010) idea of community as a service, a gift which is given, to interrogate the potential of Burrows and Fargion's work to reframe individuation and collaboration (Chapter 6). Finally, I conjure Franco 'Bifo' Berardi's (2012) exploration of the link between poetry and finance to reconnect the political argument with the linguistic perspective of the book and investigate the role of excess (both sensory and semantic) in Burrows' reductionist aesthetics (Chapters 4 and 7).

POETICS AS ENGAGED WRITING

Constructing a poetics of Burrows' dance, the book builds on performance scholarship which reframes critical practice in the light of the transformative potentialities of performance (Fischer-Lichte, 2008) and of the rethinking of models of spectatorship promoted in Western artistic practice since the 1960s (Butt, 2005). As transdisciplinary scholar Gavin Butt points out, since the 1990s a strong tradition of performance writing (by Peggy Phelan, Amelia Jones, Rebecca Schneider among others) has advocated a performative mode of critical address, which abandons descriptive and historical accounts in favour of acts of engagement with the performance event. Refocusing the problem of criticism away from the question of critical distance (seen as evidence of an authoritative, and ultimately transcendental, view of criticism), such modality of critical writing 'does not reproduce the object or event it addresses but instead enacts it through the very practice of writing' (Butt, 2005: 10).

In framing my own response to Burrows' work, I acknowledge, with Butt (2005: 7), the paradoxical position of art criticism, between the need to operate within a consensus and the project of 'frustrat[ing] conventional understandings and received wisdom'. In negotiating my critical position, I want to draw attention to the idea of the unresolved and fluid logic of criticism and advocate for a mode of engagement with the artistic material that combines the 'constative, reportive dimensions of historical enquiry' with a performative, imaginative and affective modality (Butt, 2005: 11). Working with Butt's idea of criticism as torn between reportive writing and engaged response, I position my own writing on Burrows' choreographic work in dialogue with examples of dance criticism that address this trouble. Most prominently, Lepecki (2016: 22) has observed:

> Dance scholarship has been plagued by a crisis set up, on the one hand, by an imperative to describe, and on the other hand, by the frustration [...] that description never, ever, can capture the entirety of the work described. [...] When I say that quite often I linger in description I do not mean I engage in a minute verbal transcription of the works. Rather, I try to offer an empirical account [...] of those moments in the works when something *happens*. [...] Those eventful events must be carefully attended to. Not as a scholastic celebration of hermeneutics, or a recapturing of deconstruction. Attending to the details of performance is the necessary practice of a responsive empiricism that attends to the micro-events that within each work, makes it work, creates its critical-political action, generates a differential movement.

These moments in Lepecki's writing, both detailed and incomplete, as he says, enable the creative practices he reflects upon to be offered to the reader 'performatively', 'in rigorous coimagination' with 'critical-discursive' voices (Lepecki, 2016: 18–19). Similarly, Ramsay Burt's (2017) monograph on recent European theatre dance articulates an engaged response to the works discussed by offering detailed commentaries. In constructing an understanding of the ways in which the dance practices he examines articulate political resistance, Burt attends to the dances by drawing on his own memories of the performances and of collateral events, by gathering archival material and by giving voice to the choreographers' own narratives (or poetics) of their practice. In Burt's approach to dance criticism, a discursive and descriptive modality is integral to the critical and theoretical project of examining how the past is remembered and of 'understand[ing] the affect that these dance works have had and continue to make' (Burt, 2017: 29).

The critical response to Burrows' choreography I articulate in this book takes into account the specificities of the experiences through which I have encountered the works. While for the new millennium pieces, which I saw live more than once, my writing engages experientially and speculatively with the works, for the 1980s and 1990s choreographies I rely on audio-visual recordings, often from Burrows' own archives. For these earlier works, my analysis is offered also as a trace of dances that are not publicly available and that many readers—dance scholars, students and professionals—are unlikely to have seen; here my writing stays close to the artistic material, to the choreographer's own reflections on the creative process and to the critical commentaries that chronicle the reception of the pieces. This is not intended as an authoritative gesture conceiving of my account as a comprehensive rendition of the works; rather, I offer it as a stratified, but always partial, response to the performances, an opening up of material that reveals the complex temporality of the dances and the variety of available perspectives upon them: an act of 'ritual repetition'—as Schneider (2001) calls it—which both acknowledges and interrupts the disappearance of performance by enabling new performative relations (mine and the readers') with the works to emerge.

Furthermore, in line with my engagement with dance and/as poetry/poetics and with my focus on modalities of resistance to normative structures via the Deleuzoguattarian notion of the minor, the book historicises Burrows' choreography in relation to the disciplinary settings and aesthetic paradigms it operates within and against. I engage with his pieces as instantiations of a poetics in which the past lingers into the present, and potentially already prefigures a future. Drawing on contributions in performance theory that reimagine performance history—from Schneider's notion of performance remains (2011) to Gabriella Giannachi, Nick Kaye and Michael Shanks' critical examination of performance presence (2012)—I work with the idea of the present as a queer time that is both a now and an again, a temporality inscribed with the past, which is qualified by its relationship and coexistence with what remains.

In attending to the layering, interrelatedness and dialogical nature of the works, my critical enquiry is concerned with how Burrows' poetic(s) (of) dance constructs signification through processes of recognition, association and displacement. I engage with how it unfolds through exchanges and experiences of coming together—with collaborators but also with the audience. In the book, Burrows' own accounts of the past and personal mappings of the shifting institutional settings he has travelled through form a sort of 'oral cartography', compiled through the numerous interviews, lectures, keynotes and public talks he has delivered over the course of his career (and more frequently in the last fifteen years). These testimonies and reflections are considered alongside, and sometimes intersect with, other (historical, including more traditional) voices on British New Dance, American early postmodern choreography and European contemporary dance.[5] Hence, if Burrows' accounts are not immune to 'revisionist' tendencies— as Burt (2017: 28) notes about the artists he discusses in *Ungoverning Dance*—and may privilege one connection over another, the interplay of his and his collaborators' voices with other historical sources offers the opportunity to reflect on the politics of history. In this respect, Burt's recent contribution to the project of historicising contemporary European choreography provides a compelling framework for understanding the value of the 'cultivation [...] of the past and of memory' including through 'ungovern[ing] canonical histories of dance' (Burt, 2017: 210). From this perspective, an engagement with memories of the past is seen to enable dance practices to fulfil their potential as collective, political experiences.

As the first monograph on Burrows' choreography, it seems important that the book also 'sets the scene', locating his oeuvre within a field of practice and discourse. This kind of contextualisation plays a key role especially in the next two chapters, which specifically address the ways in which Burrows' works interrogate dance's normative paradigms and historical legacies. Burrows' *deterritorialisation* of the language of dance discussed in Chapter 2 (see also below) requires the contours of the 'territories' in question to be sketched. Similarly, Chapter 3 provides an outline of the terms of reference at play in Burrows' paradoxical relationship with the minimalist tradition. Overall, however, the historical research that underpins the project complements the imaginative and political response to the work I articulate in this book. Here Burt's (2017) discussion of the politics of imagining—which invokes conceptualisations formulated by Erin Manning and Brian Massumi— informs my thinking around the affective value of such imagining. Nevertheless, while Burt is concerned with imagining in connection with memory, in my historicisation of Burrows' work I also want to wander in a different direction and interrogate the role that forgetting and loss play in performing a resistance against normative codes. I am inspired in doing so by the fascinating accounts of how a tongue may be acquired or lost, of how an idiom may emerge or vanish offered by Heller-Roazen in *Echolalias: On the Forgetting of Language* (2005). This perspective promotes reflections on forgetting as not remembering/not wanting to remember, on the (political) importance of what is forgotten, on the (im)possibility of differentiating memory and oblivion, on how all language—and dance, as I argue—is 'a simultaneously single yet multiple idiom in which writing and translating, "compos[ing]" and "compos[ing] after", production and reproduction, cannot be told apart' (Heller-Roazen, 2005: 177). This book assumes the idea of loss and incompleteness, of doing and undoing, as a compelling perspective from which to engage with Burrows' *minor dance*—the 'weak', 'cheap', inadequate[6] mode of address through which he performs acts of resistance from within the recognised field of contemporary Western dance.

Finally, to contextualise my claim that my response to Burrows' work is political, as well as imaginative, I want to offer an insight into my own positioning by framing the Deleuzoguattarian concept of 'minor language' and the questions it raises as a perspective of particular resonance for me. Deleuze and Guattari (1986: 19) ask:

> How many people today live in a language that is not their own? Or no longer, or not yet, even know their own and know poorly the major language that they are forced to serve? This is the problem of immigrants, and especially of their children, the problem of minorities, the problem of a minor literature, but also the problem for all of us: how to tear a minor literature away from its own language, allowing it to challenge the language and making it follow a sober revolutionary path?

As an immigrant to the UK who lives in/outside the dominant language, who has forgotten many of the subtleties of her 'mother tongue' (if ever there was one, as Heller-Roazen argues), while striving to learn them in the acquired language; as a mother whose children's 'mother tongue' is their father's; as a dance scholar who was never a dancer in the conventional sense of the term and who started off in a Liberal Arts department before turning to performance studies, and never feels entirely at home in any of these fields; as a European citizen whose residency status in the UK is threatened by the decisions made within our neoliberal democracies: as a minoritarian voice, I connect with the need (as, I argue, is articulated by Burrows and Fargion's artistic practice) to 'tear away' a minor practice from normative codes, to trouble dominant languages from within.

BETWEEN CANONS AND INDIVIDUATION: POSITIONING JONATHAN BURROWS' CHOREOGRAPHY

A former British Royal Ballet soloist and an English Morris dancer, Burrows ventured into the British contemporary dance scene in the 1980s and began his independent career in the early 1990s. He developed his choreographic voice in dialogue with American early postmodern experiments (through their belated introduction to British dance artists and audiences in the 1980s) and with the British and European formalist tradition of minimalist descent.[7] Since 2002, Burrows has created a number of duets with the experimental composer Fargion, embracing limitations of technical and scenographic requirements both as a response to a difficult economic climate and through a close dialogue with the reductionist aesthetics and ontology of the contemporary European dance scene (Lepecki, 2004a).[8] In this book, Lepecki's (2004a, 2004b and 2006) writings on common traits emerging in European choreography from the mid-1990s are put in dialogue with recent conceptualisations of contemporary European dance and performance, from Cvejić's (2015) to Burt's (2017).

As the first dance theorist[9] to write about the emergence, in late twentieth-century European dance, of a desire to rethink 'certain formal and ontological parameters set by modern dance', on the cusp of the new millennium Lepecki (2004a: 171) outlined the main characteristics of this choreographic movement. In the work of artists such as Jérôme Bel, Xavier Le Roy, Boris Charmatz, Thomas Lehmen, Sasha Waltz, Vera Mantero, La Ribot, Meg Stuart and Burrows, he identified common formal, aesthetic and conceptual qualities, including the reduction of 'theatrics', that is, of props and scenic elements (Lepecki, 1999: 129); the critique of the 'isomorphism between dance and movement', whereby dancing does not necessarily mean moving (Lepecki, 2004a: 170); a close relationship with performance art and its focus on the issue of presence; a distrust of the possibilities of representation; the construction of dance pieces according to an inscribed procedure of internal rules; the disregard for formal dance techniques and virtuosity as an end in itself; the critique of the conventional idea of spectatorship and the subversion of audiences' expectations; and an interdisciplinary approach, in dialogue with other arts as well as with performance theory.[10] As well as highlighting the impact of 1960s and 1970s experiments in performance art on this kind of choreographic work, Lepecki (2004a: 171) also recognised a parallel with 'the propositions put forth in the visual arts by minimalism and conceptual art'. Furthermore, he acknowledged the specific legacies of Pina Bausch's Tanztheater, especially for the subtle line it draws between representation and presentation of self, and of the pedestrian and anti-virtuosic dance of the Judson Church choreographers.

In his full-length monograph on experimental choreography in Europe and the USA since the 1990s, Lepecki (2006) builds and expands on his earlier publications, analysing the philosophical underpinnings of the choreographic research of Bel, Le Roy and Mantero, La Ribot, Juan Dominguez and Trisha Brown. As in Lepecki's previous publications, in *Exhausting Dance* Burrows is mentioned as a participant of the European experimental dance movement, but there is no detailed engagement with his work. It is my contention that, although Burrows' work shares with these artists an inquisitive stance towards the canons, modes and functions of dance, it also draws on a different approach to issues surrounding presence and the exposure of the body on stage. In this respect, the inclusion of Burrows within the Western European scene, which finds in the expressionist tradition of Tanztheater an important context of reference, is to an extent uncritical and requires further unpicking. The explicitness in the presentation of the body (Lepecki, 1999), which informs many works produced on continental European stages, does not feature in Burrows' pieces, highlighting a divergence which is to be questioned in relation to the different socio-historical contexts. It is also notable that Burrows is not mentioned in Lepecki's most recent monograph *Singularities: Dance in the Age of performance* (2016), which offers an analysis of current experimental choreography (as presented in Europe, the USA and Brazil between 2003 and 2014), locating the works' critical capacity in their ability to produce strangeness and singularity.

Interrogating the terms of Burrows' relationship with the European scene, I contend that, unlike the works more closely discussed by Lepecki, Burrows' questioning of accepted dance codes does not lead to a dismissal or 'exhaustion' of reference principles, but rather to a different kind of engagement with them: their rethinking implies both remembering and forgetting, doing and undoing—a modulation to a 'minor' key, enacting a gesture of resistance from within. The idea of the exhaustion of dance has already been reviewed by dance scholar and choreographer Efrosini Protopapa (2016), who rethinks Lepecki's proposition through the Deleuzian perspective of 'possibilising'. Protopapa (2016: 168, 169) draws attention to the ability of recent choreographic 'work and discourse' to 'activat[e] a more social space for critical discussion and exchange'. In this context, Protopapa foregrounds the role that Burrows has played over the last decade or so in facilitating such openness within the British contemporary dance landscape: she mentions that in his position as co-artistic director of London's 2012 Dance Umbrella festival (and as director of Sadler's Wells Summer University for emerging dance artists) Burrows has given support and recognition to work characterised by 'intelligence, readability, lightness of touch or humour, generosity towards the audience, connection to the wider culture', and produced on a smaller scale than what British audiences and 'mainstream press' are typically used to (Protopapa, 2016: 169).

I share Protopapa's concerns around the difficult acceptance of experimental work in the British dance scene and frame Burrows' dance as one that generates both aesthetic shifts and a political narrative that interrupt the (often conventional) understandings of contemporary choreography endorsed by audiences and critics in the UK. The role that Burrows has played in questioning Western European contemporary dance's given modes of creation and performance and the international acclaim he has received for his experimental work since the 1980s are at odds with the lack of sustained research on his creative practice in both past and current scholarship. Expanding on Protopapa's contextualisation, in this book I suggest that Burrows, by reframing the possibilities of choreographic form while operating from within the boundaries of traditions and institutions, rethinks the ways through which dance can articulate resistance and social critique.

The Deleuzian lens adopted by Protopapa is also the specific theoretical perspective through which Cvejić (2015) explores recent European dance and performance practices in her monograph *Choreographing Problems*. Focusing on the work of prominent experimental choreographers, Cvejić's book constructs a dialogue between Deleuze's philosophy and aspects of performance practices and their expressive concepts, as they are articulated through processes of 'making, performing, and attending' (Cvejić, 2015: 1). Among analyses of works by other European artists, Cvejić also discusses the piece that opens this chapter: Burrows and Ritsema's *Weak Dance Strong Questions*. Cvejić draws attention to the process of improvisation the performance is based upon and conceptualises how the piece addresses the problem of 'question[ing] movement by movement itself' (Cvejić, 2015: 128). Cvejić's Deleuzian approach is particularly relevant for my own probing of Burrows' work and poetics; more specifically, she coins the terms 'stutterances' to elucidate Burrows and Ritsema's way of creating by posing problems, their approach to 'dancing a question'—or 'dancing in a state of questioning', as Ritsema puts it (Cvejić, 2015: 144)— which results in 'a process of atomization, of dividing each movement into ever smaller and unequal movements' (Cvejić, 2015: 148). The term 'stutterance' makes reference to Deleuze's writings on minor literature, to his discussion of the ways in which revolutionary authors stammer and stutter in language, of how they 'invent a *minor use* of the major language within which they express themselves' (Deleuze, 1998: 109, original emphasis). In Cvejić's argument, the stammering manifests in Burrows and Ritsema's dancing through 'a disjunction between the times of thinking and moving': '[m]ovement stutters because it reaches its limit – in the stops, in the moments of stillness, when the dancer realizes that the movement may yield to the habits' (Cvejić, 2015: 152–153).

Cvejić focuses on the way in which Burrows and Ritsema's approach to dancing operates at the level of the grammar of the language of dance, reinventing its syntax. She also makes reference to Ritsema's theatre poetics and to how he 'embrace[s] a critical distance between what is offered from the stage and the audience' (Ritsema cited in Cvejić, 2015: 151). Significantly, Cvejić's perspective speaks to my own analysis of Burrows' choreography as a project that rethinks the languages of dance and constructs a poetics of the minor. Cvejić positions *Weak Dance Strong Questions* in dialogue with movement practices developed in the 1960s and 1970s, focusing predominantly on improvisational dance, the principles of which are problematised in this duet. Nevertheless, Cvejić's book examines only one of Burrows' choreographies, as a specific instance of a 'method of creation by way of problem-posing' (Cvejić, 2015: 2); in her study, *Weak Dance Strong Questions* is not interrogated in relation to other works in Burrows' repertoire. Considered within the broader context of Burrows' choreographic practice, which typically features pieces characterised by clear structures and set patterns—and often entails the production of written scores—this collaboration with Ritsema, with its exploration of improvised movement, is arguably an anomaly in Burrows' oeuvre. Discussing the piece in an interview I conducted with him, Burrows (2004) commented: 'the work I normally make is […] highly structured and highly musical: even writing the score down. I had never worked before the way I did with *Weak Dance Strong Questions*'. In this sense, Cveijć's insightful reading of the philosophical implications of the practice of thought we see unfolding in the piece requires further contextualisation. This is a gap this monograph aims to address.

In this book, I examine Burrows' body of work in the context of both British and continental European experimental dance of the so-called formalist tradition (also defined as minimalist or post-minimalist), developed from the 1980s onwards. This is a complex legacy that Burrows (2006) himself has acknowledged:

> I grew up in the strongest years of the impact of release technique and contact improvisation, the New Dance scene and the influence of Judson Church through the X6 generation and through Dartington College. I could see all these things going on, but I was a ballet dancer, and also, being the person that I am, I would, on the one hand, be drawn towards working with these very formal ways [...] and on the other hand, I've got a great love of all of the things that came out of that period of time. Formal ways were quite critiqued for a long time, and they still are. In dance there has often been the idea that improvisation and spontaneous physical expression are the richest way to a performance and to a connection with the audience, and the most human and creative. And I see that it can be true sometimes, but I also see that it isn't always true, and it can also be true in other ways. But for me this leads to the inherent contradiction and tension within everything I do.

Interrogating these ambiguities and paradoxes also requires a close engagement with the movement material and its contexts, if the dance is to be examined as a minor use of a major language. A similar approach is adopted by Burt in *Ungoverning Dance* (2017), which offers a rigorously researched analysis and a sociopolitical account of the last two decades of European experimental dance. Burt reads these progressive practices as ethico-aesthetic propositions of ways of making, performing and distributing dance works that resist the dominant logic of neoliberalism.

> [The book] introduces the theoretical perspective underpinning the idea of ungoverning by drawing on recent discussions in European philosophy about responsibility and relationality in the work of such thinkers as Emmanuel Levinas, Maurice Blanchot, and Jean-Luc Nancy. It identifies in recent European contemporary dance the persistence of radical, alternative ways of thinking that should not only be seen as exemplifying avant-garde practices but also enact a political critique in the way they reveal the power relations that disseminate normative values. (Burt, 2017: 7 8)

In Burt's discussion of works by Bel, Le Roy, La Ribot and Burrows, among others, the significance of these artists' practices is found in how they use 'aesthetic means' to 'critique dance as an institution' and to debunk the processes that regulate and normalise the production of dance works, controlling and enclosing common resources (Burt, 2017: 22–23). From a neoliberal perspective, Burt suggests, Burrows' career choices of—for instance—working with non-trained dancers (Ritsema and, especially, Fargion) and of creating what Burrows calls 'out-of-a-suitcase' pieces (Burrows cited in Perazzo Domm, 2005: 7) rather than large-scale productions might be read as a case of 'artistic suicide' (Burt, 2017: 12). Focusing on two of the duets with Fargion (*Cheap Lecture* and *The Cow Piece*, 2009),[11] Burt (2017: 164) proceeds to argue that the radical value of the works lies in how they 'ungovern the conventions and traditions of dance performance' through an ethical engagement that allows them to unmask recognisable aesthetics and reframe them in new ways. For instance, these duos are read as performances of friendship which trouble conventional ideas of interpersonal relationships and rethink, through process and performance, what friendship might mean today.

If the European experimental dance scene is the principal focus of the publications I have so far reviewed, which specifically locate Burrows within this landscape, earlier British critical and scholarly literature highlighted his formative experiences in ballet and his connection with British (and American) postmodern dance. Burrows' links with these contexts are less known to contemporary audiences, both in Britain and overseas. Around the early to mid-1990s, when British New Dance was reaching a turn in its life cycle, opening up to it multiple postmodern declinations, dance critics and scholars in the UK sought to produce accounts of the last thirty years of choreographic experiments, analysing their historical development, stylistic aspects and main figures (Jordan, 1992; Mackrell, 1991 and 1992; Parry, 1996). These writings identify the main points of reference for British contemporary choreographers from the mid-1960s in the movement experimentations by American modern and contemporary dance, and especially in those by the Judson Dance Theater.

Since the late 1980s, British critics have acknowledged and praised Burrows' talent for inventive and creative work, his 'original use of movement' (Percival, 1992: 32), his fresh approach to composition (Mackrell, 1987), his 'controlled, understated' (Percival, 1988) and 'uncompromising' (Crisp, 1996: 15) performances and the humour of his unconventional, challenging and charmingly enigmatic pieces. Nevertheless, within the historical accounts published in the 1990s, the extent of Burrows' contribution to contemporary dance is only partially acknowledged. Jann Parry, in an article on British 'dance at the cutting edge', places him in the variously assorted category of the 'English eccentrics', citing him within an umbrella group of British choreographers that she generically describes as 'different', 'distinctive' and 'original' (1996: 73). Other accounts of the development of contemporary dance in the UK up to the early 1990s only mention him briefly, and mainly for his collaborations as a dancer with Rosemary Butcher (Jordan, 1992; Mackrell, 1991), or leave him out entirely (Mackrell 1992). Furthermore, Burrows' choreographic voice is often portrayed in these accounts as idiosyncratic, if not enigmatic, 'owing nothing to any other choreographer' (Thorpe, 1991: 12), and 'defy[ing] summing up' (Jones, 1998: 84). To this day, Burrows' work is described by some British critics as 'peculiar', 'difficult [...] to relate to' (Roy, 2015) and 'cryptic' (Brown, 2015). In the review of the premiere of Burrows and Fargion's *Body Not Fit for Purpose* at the 2014 Venice Dance Biennale, Mackrell (2014) comments on the 'beguiling mix of the scholarly, the quizzical and the righteously indignant that is unique' to their dances.

Addressing the lack of extensive and sustained engagement with Burrows' artistic oeuvre, this book attends to the contexts, principles and modes of his choreographic practice and poetics, interrogating its aesthetic distinctiveness and political significance. It examines how, through the interplay of expressive methods and compositional devices such as repetition, rhythmical patterning, fragmentation, layering and translation, Burrows pushes the language of choreography towards its limits and engages in a paradoxical, yet transformative, relationship with dance's historical and normative structures. In doing so, the book interrogates how Burrows' po(i)etic(s) (of) dance responds to and takes responsibility for the political questions of the contemporary moment.

ARTICULATION OF CHAPTERS: CROSS-OVERS AND IN-BETWEENS

This monograph offers an examination of Burrows' poetics as articulated through his choreographic works, with particular attention to: the early group pieces *Hymns* (1986–1988) and *Stoics* (1990–1991); the piece for the camera *Hands* (1995); *The Stop Quartet* (1996); several of the duets with the composer Fargion (*Both Sitting Duet*, 2002; *The Quiet Dance*, 2005; *Speaking Dance*, 2006; *Cheap Lecture*, 2009; *The Cow Piece*, 2009; *Body Not Fit for Purpose*, 2014); the online video project *52 Portraits* (2016), created with Fargion and the film-maker Hugo Glendinning, and the collaborative pieces *Any Table Any Room* (2017) and *Music For Lectures* (2018). The book also discusses Burrows' artistic research more broadly, with reference to his writings, curatorial projects and choreographic commissions. Developing the idea of a poetics of choreography that is both individual and multiple, coherent and paradoxical, the next six chapters offer a theoretical reflection on how aesthetic principles and political concerns unfold in Burrows' artistic practice, attending to the complex web of relations between the works.

In the book, I locate Burrows' voice in dialogue with other voices—both practitioners' and theoreticians', whether gathered in these pages or in the space-time around them—and acknowledge them as engaged in forms of 'coimagination': 'co-working theories that are always co-made in the space between artistic-performative practices and critical-discursive ones' (Lepecki 2016: 18, 19). I oscillate between different voices and their different instantiations and engage with the paradoxical (Butt, 2005) task of critically outlining what cannot be but a fluid and fragmentary set of positions: a series of principles and their interruptions. I hope to capture the complexity and plurality of views that make up Burrows' poetics, also by acknowledging its ambiguities and potential contradictions and compromises. My approach to the interrogation of Burrows' reflections on his own poetics and accounts of his own practice is informed by dance and performance scholarship that convincingly foregrounds the importance of engaging with the practitioners' points of view when constructing conceptualisations of performance practices.[12]

Proposing an engagement with Burrows' poetics as an interplay of doing and undoing, remembering and forgetting, invention and repetition, the structure of the book allows for openness and fluidity in the way in which it attends to the choreographic material and the theoretical discourse it embodies. Burrows has often talked about his own work as a continuous attempt to remake the same piece—with each instance conceived as 'unfinished business' to be picked up again at a later date. Adopting a Deleuzoguattarian approach, the book understands the work as 'a rhizome, a burrow' (Deleuze and Guattari, 1986: 3). As in minor literatures, often characterised by fragments and ruptures, each event, each block of Burrows' choreographic oeuvre reveals points of contacts with contiguous segments 'on a continuous and unlimited line' (Deleuze and Guattari, 1986: 73). The affective intensity of the fragments troubles the discontinuity of the 'broken form', of the distinctive pieces, and shows how 'two diametrically opposed points bizarrely reveal themselves to be in contact' (Deleuze and Guattari, 1986: 72, 73).

> We will enter, then, by any point whatsoever; none matters more than another, and no entrance is more privileged even if it seems an impasse, a tight passage, a siphon. We will be trying only to discover what other points our entrance connects to, what crossroads and galleries one passes through to link two points, what the map of the rhizome is and how the map is modified if one enters by another point. Only the principle of multiple entrances prevents the introduction of the enemy, the Signifier and those attempts to interpret a work that is actually only open to experimentation. (Deleuze and Guattari, 1986: 3)

As a result, the next five chapters discuss works from Burrows' repertoire moving between the pieces not in chronological order, but assuming ideas, themes and perspectives from Burrows' poetics as points of entrance. This means that, at times, the discussion returns to a work that has already been introduced, yet approaching it from a different angle or with a different focus. The final chapter attempts to draw these lines of enquiry together, offering a theoretical reflection on the work's political significance. Throughout, the discussion draws on a critical, experiential and affective engagement with the dances; without providing interpretations, it aims to engage with the complex ways through which the works are open to experimentation.

Chapter 2, 'Resisting from Within: Dance Canons and Their Deterritorialisation', examines Burrows' choreography as a paradoxical project which articulates a form of aesthetic and/as political resistance to dominant models of choreographic production 'from within', that is, while operating within recognised artistic frameworks. Attending to the particular kind of choreographic language he creates by engaging with tradition(s) while upsetting established conventions, I draw on the Deleuzoguattarian notion of 'minor literature' to interrogate the transformative potential of Burrows' practice across the thirty years of his dance career. Here I propose that mapping the contexts of Burrows' artistic research is crucial to the examination of the productive tensions and contradictions that characterise his poetics. Such approach foregrounds an understanding of resistance as an (often humorous) interplay between the acknowledgement and the destabilisation of given structures; through this perspective, I attend to the processes of deterritorialisation that are at play in the relationships between 'major' and 'minor' dance languages (and their usage) and begin to interrogate the radical potential of his choreographic choices.

Alongside a critical discussion of the ways in which his choreography might be seen to 'deterritorialise', 'politicise' and 'collectivise' the language of dance, I provide a historical outline of the contexts of Burrows' dance training and choreographic career, highlighting their multiplicity and inherent tensions: his Royal Ballet years (school: 1970–1979; company: 1979–1992); his independent choreographic work from 1986 and his collaborations with Butcher; his move to continental Europe in the late 1990s; and his links with the European experimental choreographic scene. I reflect on how Burrows' work moves to and fro between vernacular and global contexts by calling attention to his engagement with English folk dances alongside his fascination with early postmodern dance practices. I examine works across his career, from the early *Hymns* and *Stoics* to the more recent *Both Sitting Duet* and *Body Not Fit for Purpose*. In this context, I provide detailed descriptions of the dance material so as to attend to the ways in which Burrows' choreographic language, by undoing compositional and semantic paradigms and challenging critics' and audience's expectations, embraces incongruity, disequilibrium and inadequacy as the instruments through which to generate signification through transversal and intensive registers.

Chapter 3, 'Reduction, Repetition, Returns: The Trouble of Minimalism', examines Burrows' relationship with the historical legacy of minimalism working with a notion of history as multi-layered and interrogating the interplay of memory with oblivion. Discussing how Burrows' choreography reconfigures minimalism in pieces such as *The Stop Quartet*, *Both Sitting Duet*, *The Quiet Dance* and *Body Not Fit for Purpose*, I argue that inscriptions of minimalism in Burrows' dances trouble linear notions of time and rethink history as a process in which remembering is entangled with forgetting. These works also shatter the distinction between form and content, exposing the category of purely 'formalist' traditions as one that requires undoing.

Chapter 4, 'Rhythm as Friendship: Movement, Music and Matteo', draws attention to the collaborative nature of Burrows' artistic work. In particular, the chapter focuses on the long-standing collaboration with the composer Fargion. After years of composing music for Burrows' dances, in 2002 Fargion joined Burrows on stage in *Both Sitting Duet*. Since then, they have become a duo, an 'equal partnership', as the artists themselves have often defined their relationship. Their collaboration has become emblematic of a research that rethinks the dialogue between dance and music and inaugurates innovative ways through which the two art forms can communicate, interrupt and reframe one another. In this respect, the chapter interrogates rhythm as a crucial feature of this collaborative relationship, conceptualising how it embodies relationality and friendship through the affective communication it produces. Examining the rhythmical structures of choreographies such as *Speaking Dance*, *Cheap Lecture*, *The Cow Piece* and *Body Not Fit for Purpose*, I consider the poetic, poietic and political potentialities of rhythm.

Chapter 5, 'Duets and (Self-)Portraits: Choreographing the Im/Personal', develops the book's focus on the entanglement of individuation and multiplicity, interrogating how the relationship between singularity and plurality is played in Burrows' choreography. Examining the choreographies of *Hands*, *Both Sitting Duet*, *The Quiet Dance* and the *52 Portraits* project alongside Burrows' writing, especially in *A Choreographer's Handbook* (2010), the chapter conceptualises the ways in which relationality is articulated in Burrows' poetics by embracing the ambivalent and indeterminate space between the personal and the impersonal. This enquiry is taken further in the following chapter, 'Choreographies of Plurality: Rethinking Collaboration and Collectivity', which proposes that the interplay between singularity and plurality that characterises Burrows' collaborative projects mobilises a possible community by troubling accepted understandings of collaboration, consensus and mastery. This chapter considers how Burrows and Fargion's artistic work has played a critical role in creating an international community of dance artists that functions as an alternative to and in dialogue with established circles. Through their teaching and mentoring roles, both in Britain and internationally, Burrows and Fargion have developed knowledge and understanding of the European scene, which they have employed in their curatorial and collaborative projects to facilitate the permeability of institutional boundaries. They have mentored youths, emerging choreographers, hip hop artists and choreographed for older dancers. The chapter continues the discussion of the collective project *52 Portraits*, as well as examining the recent collaborative works *Any Table Any Room* and *Music For Lectures*, suggesting that these works are significant of an interest in escaping the dialectic of the duo and the mirroring that occurs within it.

The emphasis of the critical dimension of Burrows' poetics is foregrounded in the final chapter, 'Towards a Politics of Poetry, Gesture and Humour', which further interrogates the political potential of the work.

Through a series of reflective notes, I take forward my argument about the transformative potentialities of an artistic practice that, by employing rhythmical, dramaturgical and performative approaches that upset accepted models of choreographic composition and performance, breaks with codified modes of exchange and exposes the political significance of pushing against normative limits.

NOTES

1. My article on how the work of British choreographer Charlotte Spencer combines words and dance 'navigates through possible perspectives on the "poetic" […] mov[ing] from Genette's structuralist analysis of poetry to Kristeva's notion of the heterogeneity of poetic language to highlight how poetic texts unsettle signifying processes. While recognizing the value of the metaphors that can be constructed through literary approaches, the article proceeds by arguing that a focus on the ontological dimension of poetry can lead to a notion of the "poetic" that engages with the transformative possibilities of choreographic practices in which movement and words intersect'. Here I '[t]rac[e] a line between Gadamer's and Rancière's discussions of *poiesis* as speculative and productive activity' to argue for the potential of 'poetic' choreographic practices to enact transformation and politicise experiences (Perazzo Domm, 2017: 111–112).

2. See, for instance, Adshead-Lansdale (1999). The post-structuralist approach that constructs dance as a form of (inter)textual practice also underpinned my earlier writing on Burrows: see, for instance, Perazzo Domm (2008).

3. Valéry's oft-cited passage 'poetry is to prose as dancing is to walking' forms the basis of Genette's observations on poetic language. For the modern poet, poetry 'corrects', 'makes use of', 'replenishes, eliminates, and exalts' the 'shortcomings' of language through the 'poetic ambiguity' generated by the 'simultaneous presence' of denotation and connotation in the poetic word and its attempt to overcome the arbitrariness of the sign (Genette, 1982: 90). Genette observes that Valéry 'compared the transitivity of prose with that of walking and the intransitivity of poetry with that of dancing' through an analogy that foregrounds the opposition between 'the essentially transitive, prosaic function, in which we see the "form" eliminated in its meaning' and 'the poetic function, in which the form is united with the meaning' (Genette, 1982: 92). Hence poetic language is thought of not as a 'form' but as a '*state*, a degree of presence and intensity', which is measured against the conventions of ordinary language it infringes (Genette, 1982: 96).

4. Brannigan, Day and Thomson (2018) mention a number of anthologies that feature choreographers' writing, such as Lepecki (2012) and Solomon (2014), both of which include texts by Burrows.
5. Among other accounts of these periods of dance history, see Jordan (1992), Banes (1993), Lepecki (2006) and Burt (2017).
6. These terms echo the titles of some of Burrows' pieces, from *Weak Dance Strong Questions*, to *Cheap Lecture*, to *Body Not Fit for Purpose*.
7. Burrows' ambiguous relationship with minimalism is discussed more specifically in Chapter 3.
8. In my doctoral thesis and in subsequent publications (Perazzo Domm 2007, 2008, 2010 and 2012), I began to unpack the specificities of Burrows' work through an interpretive analysis that proposed to interrogate recurring aesthetic choices and their underlying concerns. Employing a descriptive and intertextual model of dance analysis and drawing on critical and dance theory, I contextualised Burrows' dance oeuvre and examined the distinctiveness of his choreographic language and attitude to performance, arguing that they challenge normative conventions of dance genres and processes of signification.
9. As acknowledged both by Cvejić (2015: 6) and by Burt (2017: 39).
10. Among other choreographers mentioned in this context are: Felix Ruckert, Tom Plischke, João Fiadeiro, Miguel Pereira and Christine de Smedt (Lepecki, 2004a: 171).
11. For a discussion of these works in this book, see Chapter 4.
12. This kind of perspective is underscored, for instance, by Burt (2017) in his recent study of contemporary European dance, in which he provides insights into the artists' theories of praxis and discusses how they locate themselves within historical narratives to negotiate their own position in the present.

REFERENCES

Adshead-Lansdale, Janet (ed.) (1999) *Dancing Texts: Intertextuality in Interpretation*. London: Dance Books.

Allsopp, Ric (2015) 'Some Notes on Poetics and Choreography', *Performance Research*, 20 (1): 4–12.

Banes, Sally (1993) *Democracy's Body: Judson Dance Theater, 1962–1964*. Durham and London: Duke University Press.

Berardi, Franco 'Bifo' (2012) *The Uprising: On Poetry and Finance*. Los Angeles: Semiotext(e).

Brandstetter, Gabriele (2015) *Poetics of Dance: Body, Image, and Space in the Historical Avant-Gardes*. Oxford: Oxford University Press.

Brannigan, Erin, Day, Matthew and Thomson, Lizzie (2018) 'Research as Cohabitation: Experimental Composition Across Theory and Practice', in Hetty

Blades and Emma Meehan (eds.) *Performing Process: Sharing Dance and Choreographic Practice.* Intellect: Bristol: 81–98.

Brown, Ismene (2015) 'The Associates at Sadler's Wells Reviewed', *The Spectator*, 14 February.

Burrows, Jonathan (2002) 'Playing the Game Harder', *Dance Theatre Journal*, 18 (4): 25–29.

Burrows, Jonathan (2004) Unpublished conversation with Daniela Perazzo Domm, London, 7 April.

Burrows, Jonathan (2006) Unpublished conversation with Daniela Perazzo Domm, London, 22 June.

Burrows, Jonathan (2010) *A Choreographer's Handbook.* London and New York: Routledge.

Burrows, Jonathan and Heathfield, Adrian (2013) 'Moving Writing', *Choreographic Practices*, 4 (2): 129–149.

Burt, Ramsay (2017) *Ungoverning Dance: Contemporary European Theatre Dance and the Commons.* Oxford: Oxford University Press.

Butt, Gavin (ed.) (2005) *After Criticism: New Responses to Art and Performance.* Oxford: Blackwell.

Calcagno, Antonio (ed.) (2015) *Contemporary Italian Political Philosophy.* Albany, NY: SUNY Press.

Crisp, Clement (1996) 'Dance Reinvented', *Financial Times*, 10 June: 15.

Cvejić, Bojana (2015) *Choreographing Problems: Expressive Concepts in Contemporary Dance and Performance.* Basingstoke: Palgrave Macmillan.

Cvejić, Bojana (2016) 'A Parallel Slalom from BADco: In Search of a Poetics of Problems', *Representations*, 136 (1): 21–35.

Cvejić, Bojana (2018) 'Imagining and Feigning', *Movement Research Performance Journal*, 51: 36–47.

Deleuze, Gilles (1998) *Essays Critical and Clinical.* Translated by Daniel W. Smith and Michael A. Greco. London and New York: Verso.

Deleuze, Gilles and Guattari, Félix (1986) *Kafka: Toward a Minor Literature.* Translated by Dana Polan. Minneapolis: University of Minnesota Press.

Esposito, Roberto (2010) *Communitas: The Origin and Destiny of Community.* Translated by Timothy Campbell. Stanford, CA: Stanford University Press.

Esposito, Roberto (2012) *Third Person: Politics of Life and Philosophy of the Impersonal.* Translated by Zakiya Hanafi. Cambridge: Polity Press.

Fischer-Lichte, Erika (2008) *The Transformative Power of Performance: A New Aesthetics.* Translated by Saskya Iris Jain. Abingdon: Routledge.

Franko, Mark (2008) 'Mimique', in Carrie Noland and Sally Ann Ness (eds.) *Migrations of Gesture.* Minneapolis: University of Minnesota Press: 241–258.

Genette, Gérard (1982) *Figures of Literary Discourse.* Translated by Alan Sheridan. Oxford: Basil Blackwell.

Giannachi, Gabriella, Kaye, Nick and Shanks, Michael (eds.) (2012) *Archaeologies of Presence*. London and New York: Routledge.

Heller-Roazen, Daniel (2005) *Echolalias: On the Forgetting of Language*. New York: Zone Books.

Jones, Chris (1998) 'Jonathan Burrows', in T. Benbow-Pfalzgraf (ed.) *International Dictionary of Modern Dance*. Detroit, New York and London: St. James Press: 83–84.

Jordan, Stephanie (1992) *Striding Out: Aspects of Contemporary and New Dance in Britain*. London: Dance Books.

Lepecki, André (1999) 'Skin, Body, and Presence in Contemporary European Choreography', *The Drama Review*, 43 (4): 129–140.

Lepecki, André (2004a) 'Concept and Presence: The Contemporary European Dance Scene', in Alexandra Carter (ed.) *Rethinking Dance History: A Reader*. London and New York: Routledge: 170–181.

Lepecki, André (2004b) 'Inscribing Dance', in *Of the Presence of the Body: Essays on Dance & Performance Theory*. Middletown, CT: Wesleyan University Press: 124–139.

Lepecki, André (2006) *Exhausting Dance: Performance and the Politics of Movement*. London and New York: Routledge.

Lepecki, André (ed.) (2012) *Dance: Documents of Contemporary Art*. London: Whitechapel Gallery.

Lepecki, André (2016) *Singularities: Dance in the Age of Performance*. London and New York: Routledge.

Louppe, Laurence (2010) *Poetics of Contemporary Dance*. Translated by Sally Gardner. Alton: Dance Books.

Mackrell, Judith (1987) 'The British Ghetto: Foreign Visitors. Umbrella '86', *Dance Theatre Journal*, 5 (1): 28–31.

Mackrell, Judith (1991) 'Post-modern Dance in Britain: An Historical Essay', *Dance Research*, 9 (1): 40–57.

Mackrell, Judith (1992) *Out of Line: The Story of British New Dance*. London: Dance Books.

Mackrell, Judith (2001) 'Weak Dance Strong Questions', *The Guardian*, 8 October: 16.

Mackrell, Judith (2014) 'Venice Dance Biennale: The Scholarly, the Quizzical, the Indignant', *The Guardian*, 23 June.

Parry, Jann (1996) 'Dance on the Edge', *Dance Now*, 5 (4): 67–75.

Perazzo, Daniela (2005) 'The Sitting Duo Now Walks, or the Piece That Lies Quietly Underneath: Daniela Perazzo Interviews Jonathan Burrows', *Dance Theatre Journal*, 21 (2): 2–7.

Perazzo Domm, Daniela (2007) 'Dancing Poetry: Jonathan Burrows's Reconfiguration of Choreography'. PhD thesis, University of Surrey.

Perazzo Domm, Daniela (2008) 'Jonathan Burrows and Matteo Fargion's *Both Sitting Duet* (2002): A Discursive Choreomusical Collaboration', in Lansdale Janet (ed.), *Decentring Dancing Texts*. Basingstoke: Palgrave Macmillan: 125–142.

Perazzo Domm, Daniela (2010) 'Traces of History: Jonathan Burrows' Rethinking of the Choreographic Past', *Contemporary Theatre Review*, 20 (3): 267–282.

Perazzo Domm, Daniela (2012) 'The "Struggle" of the Subject: Productive Ambiguity in Jonathan Burrows' Choreography', *Choreographic Practices*, 3: 99–117.

Perazzo Domm, Daniela (2017) 'The "Making" of Movement and Words: A Po(i)etic Reading of Charlotte Spencer's *Walking Stories*', *Choreographic Practices*, 8 (1): 111–130.

Percival, John (1988) 'Dance: Onward Christian Soldiers. Hymns, The Place', *The Times*, 25 June.

Percival, John (1992) 'Moving Beyond Dance', *The Times*, 30 October: 32.

Protopapa, Efrosini (2016) 'Contemporary Choreographic Practice: From Exhaustion to Possibilising', *Contemporary Theatre Review*, 26 (2): 168–182.

Rancière, Jacques (2004) *The Politics of Aesthetics*. Translated by Gabriel Rockhill. London: Continuum.

Roy, Sanjoy (2015) 'Jonathan Burrows & Matteo Fargion: *One Flute Note, Body Not Fit for Purpose*', *The Guardian*, 3 February.

Schneider, Rebecca (2001) 'Archives Performance Remains', *Performance Research*, 6 (2): 100–108.

Schneider, Rebecca (2011) *Performance Remains: Art and War in Times of Theatrical Reenactment*. London and New York: Routledge.

Siegmund, Gerald (2001) 'Really Strong This Weak Dance' (translated from the German), *Frankfurter Allgemeine*, 10 May.

Solomon, Noémie (ed.) (2014) *Danse: An Anthology*. Dijon: Les Presses du Réel.

Staude, Sylvia (2001) 'The Routine Breakers' (translated from the German), *Frankfurter Rundschau*, 7 May.

Thorpe, Edward (1991) 'Talking to an Enigma: Edward Thorpe Interviews Jonathan Burrows', *Dance and Dancers*, June–July: 12.

Vattimo, Gianni (2003) *Nihilism and Emancipation: Ethics, Politics and Law*. Edited by Santiago Zabala, translated by William McCuaig. New York: Columbia University Press.

Vesty, Robert (2017) 'Editorial: Words and Dance', *Choreographic Practices*, 8 (1): 3–8.

CHAPTER 2

Resisting from Within: Dance Canons and Their Deterritorialisation

A key player of the British and European choreographic scene, Jonathan Burrows has occupied a paradoxical place within the socio-historical space of contemporary dance. Since the mid-1990s, when he received high-profile commissions to choreograph for Sylvie Guillem's television series 'Evidentia' (*Blue Yellow*, 1995) and for William Forsythe's Ballett Frankfurt (*Walking/music*, 1997), his notoriety has led to his identification as one of the main protagonists of the Western European dance scene. In the last two decades, he has enjoyed significant international following and has been programmed by large-scale venues and as part of world-renowned platforms in major capital cities and cultural hubs.[1] In parallel to this, he has been advocating resistance to the dominant logic of choreographic production, questioning creative processes and performance frameworks and taking part in the construction of a counter-narrative that acknowledges the ongoing expansion and productive re-framing of the notion of dance. Burrows is known for engaging with venues that support innovative research and emerging or marginalised artists and with projects that foster links with local communities[2]; he has also contributed to current choreographic debates across practice and theory.[3] Of significance, in relation to the interplay between experimentation and institution that characterises Burrows' profile is also his long-term commitment to mentoring younger generations of dancers and artists.[4] More recently, Burrows has engaged

© The Author(s) 2019
D. Perazzo Domm, *Jonathan Burrows*,
New World Choreographies,
https://doi.org/10.1007/978-3-030-27680-5_2

directly with performance research, through his academic posts[5] and his writings.[6]

This chapter probes and articulates the idea of resistance by interrogating the positioning of Burrows' dance between the experimental scene and established choreography. It attends to the tensions, questions and contradictions inherent in such a distinctly dialogical presence in relation to the contemporary British and European dance scene, proposing to consider the political potential of choreographic work that entangles the marginal and the mainstream. In addressing these concerns, I construct an argument around the reconfiguration of the languages and conventions of dance that Burrows' work enacts, by proposing an understanding of his dance as a 'minor practice'. As indicated in Chapter 1, I engage with Gilles Deleuze and Félix Guattari's (1986) notion of the minor to interrogate the critical positioning of a body of work that destabilises creative processes and signifying strategies, while operating from within recognisable traditions and established contexts.

The Deleuzoguattarian notion of the minor offers an understanding of the ways in which artistic practices articulate resistance; it highlights the radical potential of the act of critical reworking of major, dominant codes by a minority. Minor practices draw on local and vernacular forms, manipulate codes and often use humour to reject dominant conventions and invent new processes, thus embedding the political potential of the work in their engagement with both 'dissent' and 'affirmation' (O'Sullivan, 2005). The notion is notably conceptualised in relation to Franz Kafka's deterritorialised use of the German language—not the standard high German, but the Prague dialect, a stripped-down language spoken by a dominated minority, which achieves intensity through its 'dryness' and 'willed poverty' (Deleuze and Guattari, 1986: 19). Deleuze and Guattari (1986) identify three characteristics in minor literatures: the deterritorialisation of major codes they actualise by operating from a minoritarian position; their political nature; and their collective value. I invoke this tripartite notion as a critical framework for the discussion of the ways in which the 'minor' is articulated in Burrows' choreography. In this chapter, I reflect on how aesthetic choices—the entanglement of traditional, vernacular or idiosyncratic movement idioms with the stripped-down vocabulary and reduction of scenic elements of recent European dance—become vehicles of a personal stance that is emblematic of a collective voice and is inextricably linked with his sociopolitical positioning.

As I begin to discuss in Chapter 1, the question of the ways in which recent choreographic practices, including Burrows', might resist established ways of conceiving and making dance is at the core of both pioneering and more recent writings that examine contemporary European choreography. These invaluable contributions to the discourse on experimental European dance draw on the philosophy of Deleuze—either predominantly (Cvejić, 2015) or alongside other critical and theoretical voices (Lepecki, 2006; Burt, 2017)—to construct arguments around its aesthetic, ontological, philosophical or political significance. In positioning my contribution in dialogue with these writings, I underscore the question of resistance as central to my critical response to Burrows' work. In addition, however, I also aim to open up the idea of resistance itself. The concept of the minor then becomes an instrument for troubling unambiguous understandings of resistance and for questioning the relationship between dissent and affirmation in the destabilisation of dominant canons. It also foregrounds the role of humour, which is so emblematic of Burrows' choreographic voice, as a strategy for the deterritorialisation and politicisation of normative codes. As art theorist Simon O'Sullivan (2005) writes, 'we might see humor as a form of affirmative violence: violence against typical signifying formations'. While I attend to the questions raised by the interplay between respect of and resistance to tradition, the notion of dissent will be examined more closely later in the book (especially in Chapter 6), also in the light of Jacques Rancière's theorisation of dissensus as 'a difference between sense and sense: a difference within the same, a sameness of the opposite' (2011: 1), in order to interrogate the contradictions and paradoxes of collaborative processes. In the present chapter, the analysis focuses on the minorisation at play in Burrows' choreography, attending also to the use of humour in the interruption of representational signifying paradigms and in the engagement with an 'intensive, affective' register (O'Sullivan, 2005).

I suggest that the terms of reference of Burrows' 'minorisation' of the language of choreography are to be found in the dance idioms he has crossed through his own training and practice: these include his ballet background, English folk-dance styles and his contemporary dance training and connections—notably with Rosemary Butcher (1947–2016), Anne Teresa De Keersmaeker, the American avant-garde of the Judson Church choreographers and, from the 1990s, Forsythe and the European 'post-dance' scene. Framing Burrows' movement practice as 'minor dance' does not imply the identification of a fixed distribution between major and minor: while as Bojana Cvejić (2015: 152) writes, 'the minor/major opposition indicates power relations in representation, where the literary canon is the major, normative language', the terms of this relationship are subject to shifts according to spatio-temporal conditions and to perspective. 'We might as well say that minor no longer designates specific literatures but the revolutionary conditions for every literature within the heart of what is called great (or established) literature' (Deleuze and Guattari, 1986: 18). An awareness of how the contexts of Burrows' dance career have been shaped over the years, and of the artist's perspective on their shifting equilibria and on his own place within them, will provide an understanding of how his choreographic practice has dealt with the tensions between canon and experiment, institutional structures and independent artistic production, renegotiating the terms of this relationship and acknowledging the fluidity of the power relations involved.

It should be noted, with O'Sullivan (2005), that '[d]eterritorialization is always accompanied by reterritorialization [...]. A minor practice must then be understood as always in process, as always becoming – as generating new forms through a manipulation of those already in place'. Kafka's idea of a minor literature is the 'purification of the conflict that opposes father and son and the possibility of discussing that conflict' (Kafka cited in Deleuze and Guattari, 1986: 17), in the sense of a political struggle, rather than a psychoanalytical issue. I suggest that, for Burrows, the dominant tradition has assumed a plurality of forms, in and through the institutional contexts his practice has inhabited. From British ballet to British New Dance, to the European 'post-dance' scene, I see these frames and canons as some of the major codes that Burrows' dance practice has deterritorialised, politicised and collectivised through the minor uses of recognised forms across his field of works.

In order to discuss Burrows' aesthetic and political positioning within the Western European dance landscape over the three decades of his artistic oeuvre, the next section provides a contextualisation of his choreographic career. My primary focus here is on Burrows' early years, from his dance training to his first works, to offer a background to his more recent encounter with the European scene emphasised by the literature I discussed in Chapter 1. The overview that follows draws on archival research on Burrows' early years conducted at the National Resource Centre for Dance (University of Surrey), on an examination of the dance works, on early reviews and critical literature[7] and on a number of detailed interviews I conducted with Burrows (2004, 2005a, 2005b, 2005c, 2006a, 2006b, 2006c, 2006d and 2008)[8] about the contexts and references of his movement language. Necessarily, they reflect the choreographer's subjective perspective, his selective memory of the past and his interpretation of events and situations. Equally, interviews have been shaped and framed according to my own curiosity and interests; hence, this account of Burrows' career also wants to challenge assumptions of a singular historical narrative (Hammergren, 2004). The subjective component of this account is also consistent with the conceptualisation of Burrows' choreography as minor practice, insofar as 'the question of the spectator's investment in, and participation with, a particular practice becomes crucial, which is to say, his or her specific production of subjectivity and propensity for deterritorialization' (O'Sullivan, 2005).

BALLET, ENGLISH FOLK, ROSEMARY BUTCHER AND JUDSON CHURCH: A HISTORICAL ACCOUNT

Although Burrows' style and movement vocabulary have progressively moved further and further away from classical dance, ballet has always been present as a source for his dances: it is on this technique—as well as in reaction to it—that he shaped his dancer's body and built his understanding of movement and of its physical, structural and aesthetic rules. Burrows joined the Royal Ballet School in 1970 and trained at White Lodge for nine years. In 1979, he was invited by Royal Ballet director Norman Morrice to join the company in Covent Garden, with the unusual role of 'apprentice choreographer' (Burrows, 2005c).[9] As early as 1978, he had started to choreograph for Royal Ballet School performances (*Kaleidoscope, Songs of Travel, Nemeton*) and his potential had already been acknowledged by the Ursula Moreton Award granted in 1978 for his student piece *Three Solos*. In the early 1980s, he began to create works both for classical dance companies, such as Sadler's Wells Royal Ballet (*Catch*, 1980 and *The Winter Play*, 1983), and for modern dance groups, such as Extemporary Dance Company (*Listen*, 1980) and Spiral Dance Company (*Cloister*, 1982). These first experiments, and the solos he created for himself (e.g. *With a Gaping Wide-mouthed Waddling Frog*, 1980), received good critical reviews, which praised his creative gift and unconventional compositional choices (Clarke, 1981 and 1983; Dromgoole, 1983; Goodwin, 1981 and 1983; Macaulay, 1985; Percival, 1978and 1980; Smith and Agis, 1982). In particular, *Cloister*, a contemporary work presented at Dance Umbrella 1982, is described by Stephanie Jordan and Howard Friend (1982: 192) as a suggestive and dynamic dance, in which the 'entanglements and upward striving movements' of the dancers in the group scenes, together with the energetic solo sequences that intersperse them, evoke a 'desire for escape from confinements of place and people'. In *The Winter Play*, critics applauded the way in which Burrows brilliantly orchestrated different kinds of movement materials, blending together the various dance forms of his background to create an original ballet:

> the means he uses are so diverse that the unity of the piece is remarkable; so is the excitement he distils from a mixture of old myth, the tradition of the mummers' plays, English folk and popular dances and straight ballet. [...] It is gratifying to see Burrows, whose inventiveness and originality were never in doubt, find a strong and theatrical use for his gifts. (Percival, 1983: 9)

In 1986, Burrows was promoted to soloist, having built his reputation mainly on his choreographic potential and on his talent for character roles. He is remembered especially for bringing 'the shy sister poignantly to life' in *Cinderella* (Levene, 1996: 23) and for 'the bossy Widow Simone in *La Fille Mal Gardée*' (Levene, 1991: 22), both performed in 1986. Burrows often belittles his performances as a ballet dancer and ascribes his relative success in the Royal Ballet to favourable circumstances:

> at the Royal Ballet, I mainly ran around in drag or as some comic character with a large beard. It wasn't the same as being in a pair of white tights dancing Balanchine. And I only got a job at the Royal Ballet because it was the time when they were interested in new choreographers. [...] I didn't get given the job because they loved my dancing. (Burrows, 2005a)

Nevertheless, the critical literature demonstrates that he also created interesting and captivating roles. In 1991, for example, John Percival (1991a) welcomed his debut as Drosselmeyer in a *Nutcracker* performed by the Royal Ballet at Covent Garden, with the following comment: 'his is a particularly well-conceived interpretation, wry and sharp at once, with a sad, twisted smile'. When asked about his success in this context, Burrows (2005a) comments: 'I did eventually end up doing much more dancing because the choreographer Kenneth MacMillan kind of liked me. So I ended up doing quite technical things'.

Burrows has also claimed that he was 'a terrible ballet dancer' that he 'spent quite a number of years standing around carrying spears' and has talked about the difficulties he had when choreographing for ballet companies (Burrows, 2005c) and the 'feeling that [he] didn't belong' in that world (Burrows, 2005a). Nevertheless, he has also acknowledged the impact that ballet has had on various aspects of his work. The humour of some of his dances bears the influence of the numerous character roles he played for the Royal Ballet—the 'small funny people', as Burrows (2005c) defined them in an interview. The methodical accuracy of his movement language reflects his fascination for the precision and rigour of classical technique:

> the principles of ballet make extraordinary physical sense and are extraordinarily complex. There are very few physical systems in the world that are as complex as that, to do with coordination of mind, eyes, arms, legs, head, gravity and anti-gravity. (Burrows, 2005a)

There is one aspect of this ballet legacy that Burrows has tried but found difficult to eradicate, which has to do with the attitude to performance: 'as much as I like to be cool, at the end of the day there is something that comes from ballet, which is about "mugging it up"', by which I think he means working hard to show your skills (Burrows, 2005c). At times, this 'played-up' approach resurfaces even in his most restrained dances, despite his efforts to resist any form of amplification, in favour of a more matter-of-fact manner.

> I'm a ballet man still, really, under the skin, that's where I came from. And I have within me still that kind of visceral experience of performing all those ballets which are giving, giving, giving to the audience in a marvellous way. And of course I also react against that, not least because I did it for thirteen years, so I earned the right to find other ways. (Burrows cited in Perazzo, 2005: 6)

Another dance form that has had an impact on Burrows' style is Morris dancing. In this respect, Burrows (2005a) has stated: 'a physical influence that has constantly been as strong as ballet for me has been English folk dance. [...] There's hardly a thing I've made that doesn't have that somewhere in the heart of it'. Its traces can be seen mainly in the physicality and cadenced patterns of some of his works, where rhythmic jumping and lilting arm moves and steps feature among the essential elements of the vocabulary of his pieces, often lending them a cheerful and light tone. Burrows studied it at White Lodge, where folk-dance classes were introduced for the purpose of fostering a national style of ballet; he recounts: 'it was Ninette de Valois's idea that, since the Russian ballet schools all learned Russian folk dance, the English ballet school should learn English folk dance' (Burrows, 2005c).

The folk-dance classes Burrows attended at the Royal Ballet School were taught by Ron Smedley and Bob Parker, about whom he talks with great affection (Burrows, 2005a and 2005c). He often quotes Smedley's description of the fundamental principle of Morris dancing: 'it's a jump that doesn't go up, it goes down' (Burrows, 2005c). Burrows has talked about his fascination with this distinctive physicality, its peculiar use of weight and gravity, its unusual movement quality ('it's heavy, but at the same time it has this kind of strange, ugly grace to it') and its pragmatic, matter-of-fact attitude that he finds 'deeply moving' (Burrows, 2005a). He has also remarked on the rigour and precision that this and other forms of folk dance require, as well as on the element of ritual they entail, which is not about showing off one's individual virtuosity but rather about achieving an overall effect: 'it's very fast, very skilled. It's extraordinary, you are part of a machine in which you lose sense of self completely, and that's something that I still love about it' (Burrows, 2005c). Although a relationship with English Morris dance is mostly evident in his early pieces, and especially in *Hymns* and *Stoics*, traces of the physicality and repetitive structure of folk dance, based on the concatenation of segments, can be found throughout Burrows' oeuvre. In the early 1990s, Louise Levene quoted the choreographer as saying:

> people look at what's on the outside, but what I'm talking about is the actual technique of it. It's a wonderful technique to do with dropping into the ground and bouncing off it. It's something that appears to have evolved over a long period of time and it makes great physical sense. It's unlike any other way of dancing. It's not evident when you look at what I'm doing from the outside but from the *inside*, dancing it, the connection is there. (Burrows cited in Levene, 1991: 22)

In Burrows' more recent pieces, traces of this peculiar dance form may also assume the form of 'quotations'. In *Both Sitting Duet*, for instance, the movement sequence contains a section that in the choreographer's own score of the performance is called 'Bampton', which includes an arm pattern drawn from Morris dancing. The name comes from Bampton-in-the-Bush, a village near Oxford, where Burrows goes every year on Whit Monday to see the traditional all-day session of folk dances (Burrows, 2005a). In

The Quiet Dance, an arm pattern consisting in bouncing one's fists on the knees and then lifting them up to one's ears is also a citation of a folk-dance element.

In the mid-1980s, Burrows also started to work as a dancer for the Rosemary Butcher Dance Company. He was invited to take part in Butcher's 1986 ten-year retrospective (including *Landings, Space Between* and *Traces*); he also danced in *Flying Lines* (1985), *Touch the Earth* (1987), *After the Last Sky* (1995) and *Scan* (1999) (Butcher and Melrose, 2005; Burrows, 2005a). On Burrows' commitment to Butcher's work, Percival observed that the choreographer

> used to take time off from the Royal Ballet to dance for her, and has appeared with her recently even since starting his own company. His explanation of her achievement is: 'it's a matter of her perseverance – she really has gone on following her clear vision in a very courageous way'. (Percival, 1997: 6)

Butcher's 'minimalist simplicity' and 'reduced movement' (Jordan, 1992: 160, 161) are traceable in Burrows' own physical vocabulary, which mainly plays with a limited range of movements and gestures at a time through the repetition of patterns. It has informed his rigorous attention to detail and his fragmented, non-climactic and open-ended treatment of the dance material. Other aspects of Burrows' practice that recall Butcher's approach to choreography are the importance he attributes to structural elements such as time and space and to their relationship with the other components of the performance, his concern with structural devices and his interest in collaborations with other artists. Above all, however, Butcher's constant research into the possibilities of dance and movement seems to have inspired Burrows' working method and especially his relentless questioning of the direction and principles of the work. This approach was shared during the Friday evening classes that Butcher taught at the Riverside Studios, which Burrows began to attend in 1985:

> we did a lot of contact work, but we did many other things as well. We were, in some ways, researching with Rosemary whatever she was researching. And then, once I did start to work with Rosemary, we went on doing a lot of different kinds of that research. (Burrows, 2005c)

Moreover, Burrows recognises her legacy in the way he perceives the job of the choreographer, that is, an activity that is bound by a sense of responsibility towards the work that is being created:

> this was something that Rosemary Butcher taught me a long time ago. You may find one way or another to make [a piece], but basically that's the piece that you have in you and the job that you have is to uncover that, or discover it. (Burrows cited in Perazzo, 2005: 3)

In a recent talk on practice given at Doch, School of Dance and Circus, in Stockholm, with dancer Chrysa Parkinson, Burrows (2018) reflects on how working with Butcher has shaped his understanding of movement as a layered and richly elusive process in which the material is experienced as simultaneously close and distant:

> Dancing for Rosemary Butcher was a process whereby she slowly and persistently disturbed each moment and with it any possibility of ownership of gesture, even as you were busy embodying the gesture. Your body distanced by procedures, by practices, which diverted what you thought you were doing, splitting each impulse down other or multiple routes. Rosemary liked the movement that had been rendered archaeological, that had become an artefact altered by time and chemical, call them alchemical processes. Traces of resonant experience. Dug up, exposed again to the air but worn out, all surfaces unreliable. Everything changed.

In the early 1980s, the Dance Umbrella festival played a key part in making British experimental choreographers (and their audience) aware of the new territories and ideas being explored on an international level. As Bonnie Rowell (2000) illustrates in her account of the first two decades of the festival and of the contexts of its development, post-Cunningham choreographers who had been involved in the Judson Church movement in the 1960s, as well as those who had subsequently developed the dance language of contact improvisation, were invited to perform at several editions of the festival right from its opening in 1978—thus contributing to shaping the choreographic language and style of many British New Dance choreographers. In this respect, besides the connection with Butcher's aesthetic choices, Burrows' use of pedestrian movement, of simple gestures and actions belonging to the everyday and defying conventional classifications of genres and styles can be linked also to the work of American postmodern choreographers such as Steve Paxton, Yvonne Rainer, Douglas Dunn, David Gordon, Trisha Brown and Lucinda Childs, whom he saw perform at the Riverside Studios in the 1980s, often as part of the Dance Umbrella programmes (Burrows, 2005c).

Affinities between American early postmodern choreography and Burrows' movement language can be identified in aspects such as the incorporation in the dance of pedestrian activities and of different styles and qualities of movement, the inclusion of stillness, the non-hierarchical involvement of every part of the body, the use of everyday clothes, a reduced stage décor and a close spatial proximity with the audience. Furthermore, similarities can be found also in more specific traits of contact improvisation techniques, such as the exchange of weight and the orientation of the dancer's focus inwards or on the other dancer(s), in a non-expressive fashion. Burrows has acknowledged more than once the impact that the Judson Church choreographers had on his artistic development (Thorpe, 1991; Duerden, 1999). He has referred, in particular, to Paxton as an important source of inspiration for his investigations of movement and the body. Besides seeing his performances, he took part in one of his contact improvisation workshops in the early 1980s, developing further dialogue with him in more recent years (Burrows, 2005c).

In 1988, while still performing for the Royal Ballet and, on a project basis, for Butcher, Burrows founded his own dance company, the Jonathan Burrows Group. In 1992, after four years of juggling his ballet commitments and the creation, rehearsals and touring of his own pieces, he left the Royal Ballet to become an independent choreographer. This move was also helped by the choreographic awards he had recently been granted (Frederick Ashton Choreographic Award, 1991; Digital Dance Award, 1991). Thus, like other British choreographers of his generation, from Matthew Hawkins to Russell Maliphant, from Michael Clark to Matthew Bourne, Burrows left a world towards which he held mixed feelings (Burrows, 2005a), following his desire to experiment with movement beyond the codes of ballet:

I wanted to keep my horizons as open as possible. I've always thought of myself as a choreographer simply of dance, not as a choreographer with a particular attachment. What is important to me is the ability to look at all the possibilities and explore them. (Burrows cited in Meisner, 1996: 19)

Burrows and his group were invited to perform in the main UK dance venues, events and platforms for contemporary experimental dance, with the Dance Umbrella festival playing a key role in the distribution of his work. There he premiered the first version of *Hymns* (1986), an extract from *Stoics* (1990), followed by the complete piece (1991), and *Very* (1992) (Rowell, 2000). In the early 1990s, he started to tour internationally and his work enjoyed wider success, both in Britain and abroad. During this period, he also established closer contacts with the contemporary European dance scene, and with Belgium in particular, where he became associate artist at the Kunstencentrum Vooruit, Gent, between 1992 and 2002 and started his involvement as guest teacher and mentor at PARTS, the Performing Arts Research and Training Studios directed by De Keersmaeker. He also lived in Brussels full-time between 2000 and 2003 (and then again between 2008 and 2011).

Despite the recognition Burrows continued to receive from British institutions (*Time Out* Award, 1994; Prudential Award for Dance, 1995; Choreographer in Residence at the South Bank Centre, 1998–1999; Arts Council of England Dance Fellowship Award, 2000–2002, nomination for a 2003 South Bank Show Award), his move to continental Europe in the late 1990s affected his relationship with the British dance scene, where his already idiosyncratic position was interpreted at times as a sign of distance and isolation. On the other hand, it widened his popularity abroad, especially in Europe and the USA, where he started to tour extensively and receive considerable support (New York's Foundation for Contemporary Performance Arts Award, 2002; Bessie Award for Choreography, 2004). This shift in Burrows' fortune started to attract the attention of British critics. Ismene Brown, for instance, wrote an article titled 'The Vanishing Man of British Dance', whose subtitle reads: 'European audiences love Jonathan Burrows' latest piece, a duet performed in silence. So why isn't he a big noise in his home country?' (Brown, 2003: 19). Here she compares the increasing success in the UK of European-based choreographers such as Forsythe with Burrows' progressive disappearance from British stages. Brown (2003: 19) wrote of Burrows that he was 'probably Britain's cleverest, most stimulating choreographer', calling herself 'baffle[d] and trouble[d]' by the fact that he was 'so little seen' in his home country. Brown also reported Burrows' strong views on the matter, with regard both to his choice to move to continental Europe and to the reasons behind Britain's limited interest in his work:

he has been based in Belgium for three years, which he believes gives him a better view of the waves of innovation that constantly break in European dance and art. London, with its 'island mentality', is 'resolutely isolated.' Britain, he says forcefully, is addicted to hype, which is intensely discouraging for choreographers not keen to replay old familiarities. (Brown, 2003: 19)

At the beginning of the new millennium, Burrows disbanded the Jonathan Burrows Group and began creating work in close collaboration with other artists from different disciplines. Although Burrows does not currently receive regular funding, German and Belgian art institutions (Joint Adventures, Munich; Kaaitheater, Brussels; PACT Zollverein, Essen; BIT Teatergarasjen, Bergen) have since supported his work, some of which to this day, alongside old and new British producers and sponsors (Sadler's Wells, Dance Umbrella, Dance4, British Council). Burrows has been sharing contexts of exposure and lines of investigation with continental European choreographers. Despite significant differences in training, background and creative outcomes, in the early 2000s Burrows recognised a 'mutual curiosity' (2004), which he identified mainly in a questioning attitude towards the boundaries of dance, in the enquiry into its codes and structures and in the clarity and coherence of the principles governing a piece.

Paradoxically positioned between tradition and experimentation, Burrows' choreography has reworked disciplinary codes and performative approaches from within. In the next sections of this chapter, I discuss his experimental and idiosyncratic approach to composition as a mode of resistance to dance canons, making reference to specific pieces, from the early *Hymns* to the 2014 Venice Biennale commission *Body Not Fit for Purpose*. Attending to the linguistic and compositional strategies adopted in the dances and the shifts of syntactical and semantic paradigms and audience's expectations they imply, I examine how the fluidity of the reference codes 'allow[s ...] the possibility of invention' (Deleuze and Guattari, 1986: 20). Engaging further with Deleuze and Guattari's readings of minor literatures, I reflect on Burrows' (political) reworking of the language(s) of dance, providing an analysis of structural and expressive elements from selected pieces. My attention is directed to the entanglement between form and content, aesthetic and political significance in Burrows' rethinking of the language of choreography. To this end, the following sections offer close examinations of dance material alongside theoretical reflections.[10]

The Paradox of the Familiar in *Hymns* (1986–1988)

As the historical account provided in the first part of this chapter illustrates, from the late 1970s Burrows experimented with solo and group works, from ballet choreographies to contemporary dance commissions. These first attempts were informed by both his classical training and the contemporary dance vocabulary he had been eager to investigate with frequent visits to the Riverside Studios and Dartington (de Marigny, 1994; Burrows, 2005c). About his first ballet choreographies *Catch* (1980) and *The Winter Play* (1983), Burrows (2005c) noted in an interview: 'both were really really difficult experiences for me. I made ballets which were not right for me and were a real struggle. And then I just gave up, I didn't choreograph anything for two years'. The next piece he created was *Hymns*, which is considered his debut work (Constanti, 1994): in this choreography, he negotiated his position between different artistic territories. Burrows worked on *Hymns* at different stages between 1985 and 1988, thus the piece is known in different versions: parts 1 and 2 of the duet (1985, approximately seven minutes); the duet in three parts (1986, approximately twelve minutes); and the complete version, including a trio, the duet and an epilogue (1988, approximately forty-five minutes).[11] The core of the work, which is also the section that appears most closely related to the theme suggested by the title, is the duet, danced by Burrows and Simon Rice to Anglican hymn tunes. In the final version, the piece begins with a twenty-minute work for three other male dancers, performed to six bossa nova pieces, and the central duet is lengthened by adding a coda danced to a Bach chorale and a Chopin nocturne (Percival, 1988).

The piece plays with unfamiliar combinations of aesthetic and expressive registers. In the initial trio, the Royal Ballet dancers Jeremy Sheffield and William Trevitt and the Royal Ballet School student William Tuckett perform a choreography combining ballet-derived leaps and spins with social dancing steps, cha-cha moves and pedestrian gestures. The musical accompaniment is a selection of charismatic songs by the Brazilian Wilson Simonal, and the costumes are sky-blue striped pyjamas. In the following section, Burrows and Rice, who at that time were both soloists with the Royal Ballet, dance to hymn tunes. In most versions of the duet, the dancers wear simple everyday clothes: t-shirts tucked inside classic trousers and black shoes. The movement vocabulary ranges from dance steps drawn from ballet, contact improvisation, social dancing and English Morris dancing, to everyday gestures and movements with inscribed connotations.

These can be located between Christian traditions and schoolboys' social behaviour—respectively, in the praying postures and gestures interwoven in standing physical sequences and in the chasing and wrestling patterns of the interaction between the two dancers (Fig. 2.1).

Burrows has acknowledged the significance of this work for his choreographic career: 'it was a real attempt to define something for myself in relation to all these new experiences of dance, and I was really conscious of that' (2005c).[12] The piece blends traces from different dance forms, while also bringing personal and vernacular suggestions into the composition. Commenting on the choice of hymn tunes for the duet, for instance, Burrows, whose father was a vicar, said: 'it was [...] music that kind of belonged to me' (Burrows, 2005c). The level of closeness and familiarity transpiring from the relationship with his dance partner in the duet, the easiness with which they play and fight with each other like two schoolmates speak of the fact that Burrows and Rice 'did go to school together, [...] did have that relationship' (Burrows, 2005c). Discussing the characteristics of minor artistic practices, O'Sullivan (2005) writes of the attention to the personal, the everyday and the 'local' as a strategy through which minor art might destabilise expectations generated by global forms: 'A minor practice might then involve itself in deterritorializing – stammering – the global language of contemporary art production, for example in a focus on the local (a turn to the vernacular) or in the use of specifically non-artistic materials'.

What strikes the viewer about the work considered as a full evening of dance is the apparent incongruence of its structure, in which two seemingly unconnected parts and a coda are placed beside each other and under the same title. Significantly, on some occasions, Burrows had to resort to a visual solution to create a link between the different sections of the piece and had the duo wear brown striped pyjamas to establish a continuity with the preceding trio (Burrows, 2005c). The disparity of the compositional elements of the different parts of the performance, most evident in the choice of three unrelated and yet strongly distinctive musical accompaniments, reflects the stratified process of creation of the piece.[13] Nevertheless, the work is given a sense of unity by the movement vocabulary, the recurrence of compositional patterns (involving a well-studied alternation between solo and partnered work, as well as frequent physical contact), and especially an attitude to performing which is relaxed, understated, matter-of-fact. Burrows (2005c) describes this attitude as dry and tough, 'deadpan' but not of the 'played-up' type, as if the dancers' stance was, 'we are just going to do this and we are just going to go on doing this'. In a review of

Fig. 2.1   Jonathan Burrows and Simon Rice in *Hymns* (1988) (Photograph by Chris Nash)

the work, dance critic Judith Mackrell (1988: 15) comments: 'what makes *Hymns* so seductive as dance is Burrows's control over the rhythms and inplications [*sic*] [of] movement and the dancers' drily understated performances'. The piece is also performed by an all-male cast, which speaks of the gendered environments the work was conceived within, both in terms of the religious and educational traditions it is shaped by and in terms of the dance styles (ballet and folk dance) it draws on.

The personal and local references inscribed in the movement vocabulary are filtered through compositional devices such as fragmentation and juxtaposition, which undo the distinction between congruence and incongruence; such strategies are a nod to narrative structures, while also enacting a resistance to representational paradigms. O'Sullivan (2005) reflects that

> A minor art pushes up against the edges of representation; it bends it, forcing it to the limits and often to a certain kind of absurdity. This is not to say that a minor art cannot itself work through representation (or at least through fragments of representation). Indeed affective ruptures – which themselves utilize existing materials – are the fertile ground for new forms of representation, new signifying regimes.

Signification emerges then from the sense of accumulation and interruption that differently connoted elements produce by being assembled together: an 'intensification' created by their 'assemblage' (Deleuze and Guattari, 1986: 23, 22). The individual elements that are combined in the work allude to distinctive sociocultural contexts, which the movement language (both gestural and dance-specific) evokes but also resists. Yet, each of these elements is not a point of arrival, but rather indicates a possibility, a horizon of sense, through its collective aggregation with other distinctive elements. While the Anglican hymns would have been familiar to a greater or lesser extent to a British audience, their use in the piece is not figurative: not only because the tunes are not accompanied by songs, but also through the way in which the religious narratives intersect with multiple other images. As in the minor languages described by Deleuze and Guattari (1986: 22), '[t]here is no longer a proper sense or figurative sense, but only a distribution of states', which make visible the potentialities of the language. The pedestrian gestures and costumes show us these five young men as ordinary individuals; however, the choreography moves away from representation and the intersection of dance movements and phrases borrowed from different dance styles—from English Morris dancing to contact improvisation, to ballet—generates sequences of intensifications and interruptions that suggest the struggle of the new dance language to emerge, between normativity and rebellion. Deleuze (1998: 112) writes that '[i]t is no longer the formal or superficial syntax that governs the equilibriums of language, but a syntax in the process of becoming, a creation of syntax that gives birth to a foreign language within language, a grammar of disequilibrium'. I suggest that the piece's paradoxical use of dominant canons allows a critical, inventive and ultimately poetic voice to emerge.

Burrows' incorporation of everyday gestures in *Hymns* sits in a dialectical relationship with previous and contemporary choreographic investigations into the pedestrian, as well as being in tension with his balletic background. Both in the trio and in the duet, references to contact improvisation are found in postures and phrases in which the dancers lean against each other or carry one another's weight. However, Burrows' resistance towards balletic normalisation draws also on the vernacular element of English folk dancing. In this sense, the piece deterritorialises the dominant dance languages by manipulating them through the use of singular, local elements. Throughout the choreography of *Hymns*, Morris dance elements can be traced in partnering sequences and in lilting and hopping patterns. One of the most significant of these phrases occurs in the second part of the duet, between the third and the fourth stanza of *Eternal Father, Strong to Save*, when Burrows and Rice execute a repeated hopping step, holding each other's right hand. Here, a five-second background silence makes the light stomps of the feet audible, highlighting the connection they establish with folk dance and the intermixing operation Burrows is attending to.

The piece's treatment of the religious hymns oscillates between the critique of the establishment ideas they are associated with and a certain fondness for the familiarity they inspire through the childhood memories they bring back. The evocation of ballet is equally paradoxical: Burrows' use of balletic language calls attention to the contradictions and tensions of his relationship with its normative codes. Ballet-like steps and figures occur throughout the choreography, but they are most frequent in the third part of the duet and in the coda. The last hymn tune to which the duet is danced, *The Day Thou Gavest, Lord, Is Ended*, brings the piece to a close with an evening prayer, before 'darkness falls'. Here, the lyricism of certain phrases of the tunes creates the ground for balletic steps and turns. These are performed very gracefully, in an exaggerated fashion and with deliberate affectation. Burrows rushes in different directions and spins around, fluidly, while Rice stands upstage, raises his arms with equally lyrical movements and eventually sits down elegantly. Towards the end of the stanza, the roles are inverted and Rice spins around while Burrows lies down, until they are both moving from one end to the other of the stage, leaping and spinning.

By overemphasising balletic traits and attitudes to performing, *Hymns* underlines Burrows' ambiguous connection with classical dance. Since the piece was created only a few years before Burrows' departure from the Royal Ballet to become an independent choreographer, the choice of a composite movement language figures as an attempt to sanction his role and position outside the institution of ballet through reference to his established classical background. Significantly, as a political and collective enunciation, a minor practice, even when 'produced by [...] an artistic singularity, [...] occurs necessarily as a function of a [...] social community, even if the objective conditions of this community are not yet given' (Deleuze and Guattari, 1986: 83–84). Looking back on the choreography for the third hymn, Burrows concedes that it may have been influenced by what he thought were the expectations of audiences and critics. He felt pressure to incorporate some more traditional dance, in contrast with the larger freedom with which he composed the first minutes of the work. 'It's like I was thinking, "we'd better do something!" [...] We made a finale, because that's the background we came from' (Burrows, 2005c).

The oblique and contradictory nature of the relationship between (unsung) lyrics and movements pushes the dance language to the limits of codified signification and towards an intensive register that allows the humorous voice of the choreographer to emerge in the tensions between system and individuality, deference and rebellion. The near-absurdity resulting from the deterritorialisation of the dominant language can be read as a poetic gesture, which is also parodic, in the Kristevan sense of the term: it pushes towards contradictory and paradoxical signification in which the poetic voice troubles the normative codes of the language of reference and generates multiple, heterogeneous positions. Kristeva locates such a creative, transformative act in relation to its history and contexts, noting that 'the only way a writer can participate in history is [...] through a process of reading-writing; that is, through the practice of a signifying structure in relation or opposition to another structure' (Kristeva, 1980: 65). I suggest that this conceptualisation of poetic language can be productively put in dialogue with Deleuze and Guattari's notion of the minor: a Deleuzoguattarian perspective points to the political implications of such expressive choices; it illuminates the transformative, and potentially collective, possibilities afforded by the unconventionality and marginality of a creative practice that, by assembling multiple idioms—'a blur of languages', rather than a new 'system' (Deleuze and Guattari, 1986: 24)—produces ruptures and a kind of (often humorous) stammering of the dominant language.

ABSURDITY AND DE-/RE-TERRITORIALISATION IN *STOICS* (1991)

The humorous and collective potentiality of such reworking of the language of ballet from within continues to characterise the 1991 production *Stoics*, which earned Burrows recognition inside and outside the British ballet world—signalling that an experimental dance community founded on the deterritorialisation of dominant styles (such as ballet and contemporary dance) was now closer to taking shape in the UK. I suggest that, in this group piece, established dance and musical conventions are 'appropriate[d] for strange and minor uses' (Deleuze and Guattari, 1986: 17) and signification is reinvented by pushing the narrative register towards absurdity.

As highlighted in critical reviews of the piece, the movement vocabulary of *Stoics* 'is a combination peculiar to [Burrows]' (Mackrell, 1991), blending ballet, folk dancing and contact improvisation, whose basic principles are employed to construct an unusual choreography made of intricate compilations of curious moves, with dancers' bodies handled and manipulated in extravagant yet seemingly careless and matter-of-fact ways: 'individuals are lifted and supported in all kinds of impossible positions and combinations like choreographic jigsaws' (Meisner, 1992a: 29). The movement sequences feature patterns of stomping feet and swinging arms with the distinctive Morris dancing quality already found in *Hymns*. Although the performers' ballet background is revealed in the skilled lifts, spins and jumps and in the overt characterisation of roles, the manner of the piece is 'decidedly unclassical' (Constanti, 1990: 24): twists, angled positions, blunt movements, deliberately clumsy-looking steps, awkward poses and deadpan performance were read by critics as a sign of 'Burrows's [...] quiet, personal revolt against the spectacle of ballet and the amorphousness of much modern dance' (Constanti, 1990: 24).

The musical arrangement is equally eclectic, featuring Felix Mendelssohn's *Songs Without Words* and two Bach *Chorales* alongside Curly Putnam's country song *Green Green Grass of Home* (made famous in Britain by Welsh country singer Tom Jones), *Piece for 2 Pianos* by Burrows' collaborator Matteo Fargion and Johann Strauss' *Blue Danube Waltz*. Adding to the heterogeneous character of the aural accompaniment, the piece was performed in different versions, with changes made to musical choices, to include sections danced in silence. Such composite history is reflected in the fragmented structure of the piece. The complete version of the work was performed by Burrows and four other dancers, all members of the Royal Ballet; it lasted approximately forty minutes and was composed of seven parts: two duets, danced by Burrows and Lynne Bristow; a trio performed by Bristow, Deborah Jones and Natalie McCann; a solo danced by Luke Heydon; a third part starting with a solo danced by Burrows, who was subsequently joined by Heydon and Bristow to form, in turn, a duet and a trio; a section danced by Burrows, Bristow and Jones; and a final quartet with Burrows, Heydon, Jones and McCann (Fig. 2.2).

The performances of *Stoics* produced decidedly humorous effects; in the two live recordings of the performance of the *Stoics Quartet* and of the complete piece held in the choreographer's personal archives (Burrows, 1991 and 1992), the audience can be frequently heard bursting into raucous laughter. Humour is achieved in the piece through unfamiliar compositional choices that wrong-foot expectations, through caricatured movement language or through the representation of incongruent or absurd social and behavioural patterns. The two opening duets performed by Burrows and Bristow, for instance, provide numerous examples of humorous treatment of gender power relations. The action-reaction arrangement of the choreography mimics the pattern of a contest: while the man performs a phrase, the woman stands and watches and vice versa. The sequences, danced to Mendelssohn's lyrical notes, are made of fast, energetic, blunt movements—flinging and slicing arms and purposeful steps and jumps—which appear to be making firm statements, as in a showdown between two quarrelling partners. Towards the end of the first duet, Burrows turns upstage and crouches down; when Bristow sits on his back, facing the audience, resting her legs comfortably and elegantly to the left, the spectators understand that she has won the battle and respond with laughter. Burrows gets up and turns around carrying Bristow on his back, while she sits properly and upright, looking out with a solemnly unperturbed expression,

Fig. 2.2 Luke Heydon in *Stoics* (1991) (Photograph by Rosy Sanders)

her hands composedly joined on her lap. The absence of drama in the performance tone gives the 'argument' a matter-of-fact, almost understated quality, placing its humorous effects in the physicality of the movement, beyond signification.

A crucial quality of Burrows' dance poetics, humour is also typical of minor practices, where it does not signal 'the irony of "postmodern" practice with its emphasis on parody and pastiche, but something more affirmative, celebratory even – and something that works on an intensive rather than a signifying register' (O'Sullivan, 2005). Significantly, writing of laughter and humour in Kafka's literature, Deleuze and Guattari identify its affective register in a strong connection with 'life', in 'a micropolitics, a politics of desire that questions all situations' (Deleuze and Guattari, 1986: 41, 42). By analogy, I consider how Burrows' choreography is also founded on an interplay between life and art. As already in *Hymns*, the starting point for *Stoics* is his personal experience. In a BBC video documentary (MacGibbon, 1992), Burrows explains that the choreography of the final quartet 'was inspired by a visit to an aunt in hospital and the handling of patients'. Through the use of movement, rather than facial expression or other stage effects, the piece reproduces the dynamics of interpersonal and social interaction, dwelling on attitudes and conditions such as competitiveness and stubbornness (a certain 'stoicism'—hence the title), aggressiveness and passivity, transgression and diligence, isolation and mutual incomprehension, cruelty and humiliation. The dance is therefore at times vehement and tough and features frequent, often forceful, manipulation of bodies and body parts.

> The work is not stagey: there are no starry leaps and glossy leg lifts. Emotions are conveyed [...] through the body, which is required to put itself in danger by being walked on or slung over someone's shoulder like a laundry bag, or even to hang upside down. (Sacks, 1992: 20)

The resulting effect is ambivalent and the element of risk and physical effort generated by the acrobatic passages of the choreography adds another perspective to the predominantly playful character of the piece. This produces an element of uncertainty in the narrative register of the piece, troubling its signifying process. While the composite structure of the piece generates interruptions in its expressive regime, the vocabulary and syntax of the dance are organised around the continuous friction between opposing expressive elements, which are pushed towards each other, creating intensive moments. These clashes may resolve at times in legible contrapuntal juxtapositions that reterritorialise the manipulated dance languages into a newly found equilibrium; nevertheless, this balance is elusive as the choreography constantly tries to move away from easily recognisable solutions. In the all-female trio, for instance, humorous effects are produced by the pairing of rough, unscrupulous movements with fluid, rhythmical patterns. Performing in silence for the most part, Bristow and Jones handle McCann (the smallest and lightest of the three) matter-of-factly, grabbing her, lifting her and carrying her like a dead weight. Yet, business-like actions are followed by cadenced, graciously flowing sequences, including a pretty line dance performed in unison.

Through the fragmentation of the scenes, posed stances, alternation of qualities in the movement patterns and the dancers' deadpan interpretation, the comic side of the portrayal of human relationships prevails over more serious readings. As Duerden summarises,

> audiences have perceived *Stoics* as funny rather than menacing [...] because the dynamic shaping of the movement, whether it be aggressive, violent, or threatening, is somehow channelled differently so that it is never focused one person on the other – though dancers may stop to watch or contemplate each other from time to time. (Duerden, 1999: 49)

The section of the piece in which the humorous effects of seemingly careless and pragmatic manipulation of bodies are exploited to the full is the final quartet. The choreography for this section is based on the close interlocking of unusual acrobatic passages that resolve into each other. Whether danced to the *Blue Danube Waltz*, as in its original version, or mostly in silence, as it was later rearranged, the quartet reaches peaks of 'overt comedy' (Meisner, 1992a: 30). Humour is generated through the use of excess, absurdity and caricature of an almost graphic quality; the images are so vivid that they resemble those of comic strips. One of the dancers in particular (McCann again) is constantly and deliberately manoeuvred by the other three (Burrows, Heydon and Jones). She is guided, surrounded, slammed, thrust around, lifted in the oddest ways, passed from one to the other and dumped on the floor with apparent indifference; she is carried head-down, or horizontally like a ladder, pushed up and thrown in the air in a frog-like posture, with an absurdity of behaviour that generates hilarious effects. Her impassivity and composed acceptance of these impositions add to the comedy, as does the unemotional performance of the other three dancers, who execute such unceremonious gestures without signalling to underlying intentions.[14]

In a different context, such vigorous handling of a female dancer would raise questions surrounding the gender politics of the piece. In this instance, the pragmatic focus of the manipulation and the matter-of-fact execution of the movements direct the attention to the politics of aesthetics, rather than to identity politics. The jerky patterns and angular shapes bear traces of the folk-dance element at the basis of the movement language, contributing to the wrong-footing of the audience and the cartoon-like character of the quartet. Moreover, the distinctive, almost caricatured roles that the dancers perform in *Stoics* are in dialogue with classical aesthetics: on the one hand, they appear to stage a reaction to the gracefulness of ballet, while, on the other hand, they also intensify the exaggerated qualities of ballet character parts. In particular, these are roles that Burrows used to play—and was still playing at the time—in the Royal Ballet, reminiscent of the music-hall slapstick comedy of the mid-twentieth century. Reflecting on it in the context of an interview, Burrows observed that, in ballet, the 'overt humour' and greater freedom of movement of these roles are only experienced by male dancers, whereas 'with *Stoics*, it was about trying to find a way that we could all, but especially the women, feel confident to move in a different way' (Burrows, 2006a).

In the extensive coverage of the piece, the freshness and unconventionality of the movement language were specifically praised: '*Stoics* is quiet in presentation, yet stunningly inventive and original' (Meisner, 1992b: 2); 'amazing contortions, explosive invention and almost deadpan dancing reveal wild emotions, despair, determination and comic effects all mixed in' (Percival, 1991c). Critics commented that Burrows had 'certainly invented a strong and extraordinary style with inventive and impossible looking lifts' (Bayston, 1992: 1156);

> he uses many everyday, naturalistic movements, poses and gestures that are recognisable as common body language, supercharged with a strange assortment of sudden stampings, falls, twists, flurried and angled limbs together with deliberately awkward lifts – humping sacks come to mind – and moments of stasis, very often in a prone position, to create an elaborate dance structure that is continually fascinating to watch even without trying to impose narrative ideas upon it. (Thorpe, 1991: 12)

With *Stoics*, British dance and ballet reviewers saluted Burrows as one of Britain's most gifted choreographers: 'Jonathan Burrows is the most impressive talent to come out of the Royal Ballet since Kenneth MacMillan' (Meisner, 1992a: 29); 'this is the best new choreography the Royal Ballet has shown in a long while' (Percival, 1991c). The press also reported very enthusiastic audience responses, including at the Royal Opera House: '[Burrows'] young dancers borrowed from the Royal Ballet toured so successfully that a hilarious extract was transferred triumphantly to Covent Garden' (Percival, 1991d).

Several critics initially wondered how the *Stoics Quartet* would be received at the Royal Opera House, especially in a programme dominated by two major works by Balanchine: 'it will be fascinating to see what a Covent Garden audience makes of Burrows's unpredictable choreography: will they sit in baffled silence or break into guffaws of laughter?' (Parry, 1991: 57). Indeed, the matching was audacious, as one critic clearly pointed out: 'I found it [...] provocative to have *Agon* followed by the *Stoics Quartet* from Jonathan Burrows' (Goodwin, 1992: 18). But the warm reaction at Covent Garden dissipated all fears that the piece would not appeal to a ballet audience: 'when a quartet from that piece was announced for inclusion in Wednesday's Covent Garden programme, I imagined that it would look out-of-place on this stage; but not so' (Dougill, 1991); 'I feared the Opera House audience might not take it, but they did' (Percival, 1992: 22). Some critics went as far as describing the piece 'the hit of the evening' (Dougill, 1991), 'the joy of the programme' (Percival, 1992: 22) or the 'surprise hit of the last Opera House season' (Mackrell, 1992: 6). The success was also marked by an official recognition: as Angela Kane (1991) points out, soon after the performance of the piece at The Place Theatre in 1991, Burrows was presented with a Frederick Ashton Choreographic Award. Through invention and reinvention of given dance vocabularies, the movement language of *Stoics* redefines the territory of contemporary dance, engaging with varying degrees of deterritorialisation and reterritorialisation—resisting fixity and opting instead for heterogeneity and ambivalence.

Similarly, fluctuation between and across territories characterises the treatment of the musical accompaniment, which unsettled expectations by traversing different genres and styles: critics described it as 'witty and original' (Levene, 1991: 22), 'imaginative' (Percival, 1991b), 'irreverent' (Constanti, 1990: 24) and 'anarchic' (Crisp, 1990: 17). Continuing the approach already identified in *Hymns*, *Stoics* generates surprise by juxtaposing widely popular musical scores with choreography of mismatched character. The most evident example is the use of the lyrical notes of the

Blue Danube Waltz to accompany the final quartet, where the movements are at their most pedestrian and manic—Burrows 'cleverly us[ed] some well-worn Johann Strauss music to underpin every point' (Dromgoole, 1990). As the quartet develops and it becomes easier to anticipate the comical moments, the blur of deterritorialised languages seems to be settling into a new equilibrium and reterritorialise, regain figurative sense, through the contrapuntal treatment of classical references that work to produce humorous effects. Yet, the stratified process of creation of the piece, which never settled into one final version, allows a new degree of deterritorialisation: when the quartet was presented at the Royal Opera House, Burrows decided that the choice of Strauss was 'much too ironic' and 'corny' (Burrows, 2006a) and had the piece performed in silence for the most part, with just a few notes from Mendelssohn's *Songs Without Words* played towards the end. As a critic recounts:

> one section of Burrows's 1991 *Stoics* [...] was first performed to the *Blue Danube Waltz*. The familiar Strauss music aroused expectations of a lyrical style – typical of English dancing – that were wittily contradicted by Burrows's blunt, end-stopped, deadpan, everyday movement. But when the traditionalist Royal Ballet took the already offbeat piece into its repertoire, Burrows decided that 'there are fresher ways of working than taking well-known music and counterpointing yourself against it' – and insisted much of the work be performed in silence. (Hunt, 1993: 52)

In this sense, invention is a central principle of Burrows' choreographic process and precedes the organisation of content. Choreographing becomes a way of reworking modes of expression; the ideas that are being expressed are formed through the dance-making process itself. As such, this creative practice distances itself from established choreographic languages, which, as major literatures, start from content to arrive at expression. The analogy with the notion of major/minor literatures seems particularly productive here, as Deleuze and Guattari (1986: 28) write:

> A major, or established, literature follows a vector that goes from content to expression. Since content is presented in a given form of the content, one must find, discover, or see the form of expression that goes with it. That which conceptualizes well expresses itself. But a minor, or revolutionary, literature begins by expressing itself and doesn't conceptualize until afterward. [...] Expression must break forms, encourage ruptures and new sproutings.

This radical approach pushes a language—movement-based or written—towards its limits. As I discuss in the following section, it does not simply move beyond figurative sense: through the use of an intensive register, a minor usage of language moves from signification to asignification.

INTENSIVE (A)SIGNIFICATION IN *BOTH SITTING DUET* (2002)

Since 2002, shortly after disbanding the Jonathan Burrows Group, Burrows has worked in a close partnership with the composer Fargion, with whom he has devised ten duets, as well as other collaborative artistic and mentoring projects.[15] Fargion is a long-time collaborator of Burrows and, by the early 2000s, he had already composed musical accompaniment for many of Burrows' works. However, with the 2002 piece *Both Sitting Duet* the relationship between choreographer and composer changed from the more traditional 'vertical' model (reflecting a hierarchy between dance and music) to a 'horizontal' configuration, in which Fargion and Burrows became performance partners. In an earlier publication (Perazzo Domm, 2008), I analysed their inaugural duet as a work that rethinks the relationship between dance and music and their signifying strategies: for this piece, the duo meticulously translated a score for violin and piano by the minimalist composer Morton Feldman into a gestural choreography, which they performed in silence and mainly from a seated position. My earlier writing offers a detailed examination of the movement material of the work, in terms of both vocabulary and structure. My argument there highlights how the choice of a stripped-down movement vocabulary adopted in this piece embodies a radical attitude towards codes and conventions. I call it a 'degree zero' of dancing, invoking a Barthesian (Barthes, 1968) expression and concept, in order to draw attention to the idea that the apparent disengagement of the movement from identifiable connotations can be read as a form of engagement and critical positioning with regard to institutional codes.

> With the house lights still on, Burrows and Fargion walk into the performance space and sit down on the two chairs placed in the middle, slightly turned towards each other. On the floor in front of them lie two open notebooks. The two men, both in their forties, wear everyday clothes – jeans, a shirt or t-shirt and boots. After a short pause, just enough to adjust their position on the chairs and focus their concentration, they begin the execution of

their choreography. From the first minute, the performative elements (lights, silence, ordinary clothes, middle-aged performers, seated position, pausing, back-stage-like actions) deny expectations conventionally associated with a dance duet with regard to scenic elements, age of the dancers, and the kinetic dimension of the piece. (Perazzo Domm, 2008: 129)

Further discussion of this well-known piece—which remains part of Burrows and Fargion's repertoire to this day—is offered in the following chapters, through an analysis of the piece's compositional procedures (Chapter 3), of its treatment of rhythmical patterns (Chapter 4) and of its rethinking of relationality (Chapter 5). In this chapter, my focus is on continuing to draw a parallel with minor languages and on moving the analysis towards a consideration of how the piece's syntactical invention opens the movement to 'unexpected [...] intensities – in short, an asignifying *intensive utilization* of language' (Deleuze and Guattari, 1986: 22). In these terms, the creative process and performance event of this dance signal the questioning of vertical, 'arborescent' collaborative principles and a move towards a 'rhizomatic' approach through a horizontal search that proceeds in multiple directions, defying hierarchies and binary oppositions. The final piece advocates a kind of partnership that expands the limits of creative expression.

> The score is converted to movement by transposing each acoustic and rhythmic combination into a particular physical pattern. [...] The variations of rhythm, emphasis and colour of the 'disappeared' musical accompaniment are recreated in the dance through the exploration of the various combinations of movements of different types, qualities and intensities and by the interplay of simultaneous, alternate and overlapping modes of gestural execution by the two artists. (Perazzo Domm, 2008: 127–128)

Valerie Briginshaw (2009) also develops a Deleuzian reading of the work, identifying notions of repetition and difference in the gestural sequences, where the potential for signification and individuation is rediscovered through the musical concept of counterpoint. Binary oppositions between dance and music, dance and non-dance, trained and non-trained dancer, representation and presentation are challenged through the horizontal, non-dichotomous approach the work employs towards the terms of the relationships it establishes. From a similar perspective, I suggest that, on the plane of signification, the piece jeopardises the binary relationship between signified and signifier, content and expression by employing movements and gestures that acknowledge varied and multiple relationships with meaning. In doing so it opens generative thresholds and invites the transformation of signifying registers.

This openness to multiplicities and potentialities is crucial to the minorisation of the language of choreography which, I am arguing, is at play in Burrows' dances. As already discussed by Cvejić (2015) in relation to Burrows and Ritsema's *Weak Dance Strong Questions*,[16] the idea of the minor is further articulated by Deleuze (1998) in the essay 'He Stuttered', in relation to literary examples of minor uses of major codes, in which writers stutter a dominant language, challenging its conventions and stretching it beyond its limits. Here Deleuze (1998: 108–109) discusses cases of literary language that 'trembles from head to toe'; if language ventures into a state of 'perpetual disequilibrium', it is 'stretched', it 'vibrate[s] and stutter[s]'. The stuttering of language is for Deleuze (1998: 109) the condition of its 'poetic comprehension', of its potential for greatness and 'progress'. Language achieves greatness by embracing multiplicity, by exceeding its own boundaries and attaining variation and intensity. Among other authors, Kafka is again given as an example here, alongside Samuel Beckett: 'a Czech writing in German, and [...] an Irishman (often) writing in French' (Deleuze, 1998: 109). What Deleuze points to is not their bilingualism, the mixing of two languages, but rather their 'minor use' of a major code: '[t]hey are great writers by virtue of this minorization: they make the language take flight, they send it along a witch's line, ceaselessly placing it in a state of disequilibrium, making it bifurcate and vary in each of its terms, following an incessant modulation' (Deleuze, 1998: 109).

The result is often a language that is not identifiable with the code it shakes up and brings to the point of explosion. Burrows and Fargion's reformulation of the language of choreography in *Both Sitting Duet* pushes the system out of balance, makes it stutter and allows for multiplicity and otherness to be expressed within the choreographic idiom, so that unexpected possibilities are awakened through the dance itself. Their choreographic language stumbles so dangerously that it may fail to be recognised as such. In Deleuzian terms, this is a necessary risk rather than a concern or element of weakness, as '[w]hat better compliment could one receive than [...] this is not English' (Deleuze, 1998: 110)? The movement language of the piece is characterised by a 'strange poverty': an 'accumulation of stereotypical' or basic gestures through repetitions and patterning produces an intensification of expression, away from 'proper sense' (Deleuze and Guattari, 1986: 22–23) and towards an affective register, which calls the viewer to engage with the work on an imaginative, instinctive, even hypnotic level. The opening sequence prefigures the approach to signification of the whole piece:

> The choreography opens with gestural phrases performed alternately and repeated six or seven times: Fargion rubs the back of his hands on his thighs, from hips to knees, and then bluntly brings his hands to his ears, as if to stop them, but without touching them; Burrows starts with his hands resting on his knees, gestures towards the right, with his hands joining and the middle fingers touching, then reaches down for the floor with his right hand. After approximately twenty seconds, Burrows picks up Fargion's phrase and both performers repeat it four times in unison and five times alternately, before Burrows goes back to his first pattern. After just over a minute, a new phrase is introduced, which they repeat successively, Burrows leading: the right hand reaches for the left hand, slides on its palm then up to the forearm and down again to rejoin the left hand and over, ending with only the fingers touching. About thirty seconds later, they synchronise their movements and continue in unison, with a pattern that looks like a smaller version of the previous one, where the movement stops at the hands, without going over the wrists and up to the forearms. The next few minutes are a combination of repetitions of patterns already performed, with variations of the speed, rhythm, succession, duration, energy, size, quality and details of the movements. (Perazzo Domm, 2008: 129)

Nevertheless, the choreography also clearly engages with dance and its recognised territory. In this respect, attention should be called to transversal connections with images that exist outside of the work, expanding the potential for asignifying intensification. These include traces, corporeal memories and aesthetic signs, which locate the piece within a personal and collective choreographic field. The most obvious instances are a sequence with ballet arm positions executed by Burrows to Fargion's rhythmic clapping and the overall idea of a seated dance that recalls (among other examples) De Keersmaeker's piece *Rosas Danst Rosas* (1983). In these images, we recognise some of the major codes that compose Burrows' choreographic language: ballet technique and the contemporary dance tradition are mobilised and their claim to singularity is exposed. Their most recognisable attributes are stripped bare, made ambiguous and expanded—including by foregrounding the musician as performer alongside the dancer. In *Both Sitting Duet*, Burrows and Fargion deterritorialise these dominant languages by simplifying them 'to the point of sobriety' (Deleuze and Guattari,

1986: 19). Deleuze and Guattari (1986: 16) argue that 'a minor literature doesn't come from a minor language; it is rather that which a minority constructs within a major language'. *Both Sitting Duet* has been performed over 300 times in more than thirty countries; it has been presented at major venues and has been awarded prestigious prizes.[17] In this sense, Burrows has challenged the language of choreography from within; he is a foreigner within his own world, rather than an outsider. As a non-trained dancer, Fargion performs in a language that is not his own; Burrows, on the other hand, draws on this relationship with a 'non-dancer' to become 'a nomad and an immigrant and a gypsy in relation to [his] own language'; he makes dance 'follow a sober revolutionary path' (Deleuze and Guattari, 1986: 16). While, over the last decade and a half, the piece has been operating within dance's institutional system, the work is not offered as a monument, a masterpiece. At each occurrence, it exists through its live variations, despite the rigorous score, and in its capacity to exceed the form of the duet: at every performance, the arrangement and principles associated with a dance duo are questioned, again and again.

INADEQUACY AND URGENCY IN *BODY NOT FIT FOR PURPOSE* (2014)

In close collaboration with Fargion, Burrows has constructed a choreographic language that, while continuing to engage with recognisable codes and parameters, stumbles and stutters, exposing accepted formats to 'strange and minor uses' (Deleuze and Guattari, 1986: 17). A reference to an inadequacy to meet expectations is made in the title of Burrows and Fargion's most recent stage duet, a 2014 Venice Biennale commission: *Body Not Fit for Purpose*. Similarly to *Both Sitting Duet*, the piece is constructed around movement sequences exploring detail and variation within precise limits, largely determined by the range of gestures and patterns that can be performed by hands and arms. However, this more recent work combines these gestural elements with spoken, chanted or shouted references to the immeasurable world outside of the dance, whose absurdities and idiosyncrasies from both the public and the private domain are exposed, named or spelt out. I suggest that, following the approach to composition established in the earlier duets, the language of *Body Not Fit for Purpose* draws even further on extra-choreographic signs that generate transversal signification by reaching beyond the language of dance.

Arranged in a series of similar yet discrete sections, each introduced by a title, this expanded web of references causes the tapestry of movement, music and moods that forms the grid of the piece to brim over its own rigorous outline and generate ambivalence through an overload of content that appears to be incongruously married to the dance. The performers, casually dressed, sit at a table: Burrows frontally to the audience, Fargion sideways, on the left. Two microphones are arranged on stands. As in *Both Sitting Duet*, and in several of the other duets they have created since, both performers refer to their notebooks, which lie open in front of them. Following the titles, which Burrows—or, occasionally, Fargion—announces introducing each section, Burrows' hands dance on and over the table to Fargion's mandolin melodies. In some sections, Fargion sings, in others Burrows plays the mouth organ; in some sequences, Burrows stands up and waves his arms more widely, or steps forwards to address the audience more directly. There are pauses as well as moments of joint performance, whether gestural or musical; occasionally, Fargion puts down his instrument and joins in the gestural phrases. The underlying mood is the duo's signature combination of overt humour and deadpan performance.

The piece openly acknowledges its intrinsic inadequacy to create clear correspondences between content and expression. The title itself declares this lack: *Body Not Fit for Purpose*. The *body* in question or the bodies, rather, are those of the two middle-aged artists who, aside from a few exceptions, limit their performances to their respective comfort zones: sat at a table, Burrows, the dancer, makes hand dances, and Fargion, the musician, makes music on a mandolin. The *purpose* is 'express[ing] that which is of concern', as the programme notes for the show read (Burrows, n.d.). Repetition and difference and their ability to support individuation are again at play here. However, what distinguishes this work from previous duets is the open denunciation of political concerns through the extended use of the spoken word. According to the programme notes, this is Burrows and Fargion's 'first overtly political work'. Throughout this chapter, I have made reference to aspects of the deterritorialisation in Burrows' choreographic language and have argued that his works demonstrate a critical engagement with the institution of dance, which is ultimately symptomatic of a radical, political positioning. In *Body Not Fit for Purpose*, the turn to the political becomes more explicit. The titles that introduce the brief dances, which are performed in steady succession, are often topics of powerful impact and make reference to conspicuous names and concerns of international politics. They include: 'One: The Arab-Israeli conflict'; 'This dance is called

George W. Bush'; 'Fear of immigrants'; 'Special interrogation techniques'; 'This dance is called bank bailout no. 3'; 'The war on drugs'; 'Vladimir Putin'; and many more.

Or this one: 'This dance is called: Silvio Berlusconi'. As an Italian, I brace myself as I hear this title. However, as is customary for Burrows and Fargion, who in this respect follow creative principles that can be traced back to Merce Cunningham and John Cage (as I discuss more specifically in Chapter 3), the movement patterns were not devised to illustrate or convey the content expressed in the titles. As Burrows explained in a post-performance talk with Kingston University Dance students in 2015,[18] the matching between titles and gestural sequences was done later in the creative process, which means that the text was devised independently of the movement material. Burrows also writes about this random process of pairing in an article published in *Performance Research*. Referring to himself in the third person, he says: 'Writing "The Arab Israeli conflict" on one piece of paper and "A curse on bankers" on another. Folding the papers into his pocket and pulling them out as he improvised the order. Holding them up, like titles, to see where the dramaturgical jolt would happen' (Burrows, 2015: 85). Any associations we may read between the mimic qualities and symbolic potential of the gestures and the themes referred to in the titles are the result of our inclination to read narrative in what we see.

Yet, watching Burrows' fast hammering gestures, the shuffling and reshuffling of invisible objects, the tapping of fingers on open hands and the quick moving of the hands under the table, the dextrous fingers travelling to and fro across the table, the rubbing of a hand against the other, I think about a magician's tricks, a poker dealer: I think of corruption, money laundering, of Tangentopoli, of 'Mani pulite' ('clean hands')—the frauds and judicial investigations that have plagued Italy's political history. The political reference is conveyed through an accumulation of basic gestures, through the tensions between opposing directions, through quick changes in chains of repetitions. When the music comes in, with Burrows' mouth organ and Fargion's mandolin, it is fast, too manic to be jolly. The melodies are based on the structure of La Folia, an old European musical form that originated as a peasant dance, a folly of tumultuous character, dating back to the Renaissance (Hudson, 1973). The dancers' bodies are inadequate expressive instruments, unfit for representation: in this piece, folly—the extreme intensive, which pushes expression to unrecognisable limits—is what bridges the gap between the mundanity and unpretentiousness of the delivery and the vastness and urgency of the concerns evoked by the words.

In *Body Not Fit for Purpose*, Burrows and Fargion employ shouting and manic gesticulation to engage with political content. What I find of significance is that, by resorting to folly and to the frantic intensity of popular and folk forms, they deterritorialise the choreographic language predominantly associated with political content: that is, Western (European and American) experimental choreography, whose works openly perform dissensus and are uncontestedly labelled as political in recent critical and academic discourse, through authoritative perspectives (Joy, 2014; Lepecki, 2016). Significantly, these writings often exclude or marginalise Burrows' dance. Towards the end of the piece, Burrows stands up and recites, loudly and clearly: 'This dance is called: the purpose of this performance is to demonstrate how arm waving and laughter cannot tell you that we don't tour to Israel, that we recycle our plastic, glass, paper, cardboard, batteries, food waste including bones, garden waste and clothing, and that we have marched against the war and against those whose neoliberal policies have allowed the rich to inherit the earth'. I am once again struck by the analogy with Deleuze and Guattari's (1986: 42) reflections on Kafka: 'Everything leads to laughter [...]. Everything is political'. What is brought to our attention is a 'micropolitics' that emphasises the intrinsic connection between 'art and life'—which are conceived in opposition 'only from the point of view of a major literature' (Deleuze and Guattari, 1986: 41–42).

For Deleuze and Guattari, it would be 'grotesque' to 'oppose' life and art, to think of art as a 'refuge' sought 'out of some sort of lack, weakness, impotence, in front of life'—since artistic 'enunciation is always historical, political, and social' (Deleuze and Guattari, 1986: 41, 42). I suggest that, perhaps not so paradoxically, the political message of *Body Not Fit for Purpose* is conveyed most effectively by interventions of a private nature. Examples, alongside the references mentioned above, are titles such as Burrows' 'Artist, 54, happy to help gentrify your city; no pension at all'; or Fargion's 'Sometimes I wish I lived a simple life in a community of loving people with low carbon emissions'. Once more, as highlighted in this chapter in relation to Burrows' early works, it is the personal, the lived experience that opens possibilities for an intensive register to push expression against the limits of signification. In a minor practice, the personal is what foregrounds the collective. According to Deleuze and Guattari (1986: 17), while in major literatures 'individual concerns' function as 'mere background', in minor literatures they 'connect immediately to politics': 'the individual concern thus becomes all the more necessary, indispensable, magnified, because a whole other story is vibrating within it'. In a minor literature, 'what each author says individually already constitutes a common action' (Deleuze and Guattari, 1986: 17).

It is my contention that Burrows' choreographic practice has been about 'setting up a minor practice of major language from within' (Deleuze and Guattari, 1986: 18), where the terms of this act of resistance, of the revolutionary project of 'creat[ing] a becoming-minor' (Deleuze and Guattari, 1986: 27) have shifted as a response to the spatio-temporal (sociopolitical) variations of the terms of reference. By engaging with the critical and creative reworking of accepted codes and practices, Burrows and Fargion operate at the intersection between tradition and radical dissent. Through the manipulation of heterogeneous dance and musical languages and territories, they formulate a poetics of choreography in which the personal and the political are not conceived in opposition: rather, they articulate a micropolitics that feeds on the interdependence of the private and the collective. Their work 'becomes all the more collective because an individual is locked into it' (Deleuze and Guattari, 1986: 18). These two dimensions are negotiated and mobilised in their practice and poetics in transversal ways.

In the next chapter, I discuss more specifically how Burrows and Fargion's compositional procedures engage with dance and music traditions, and especially with minimalism, through a 'microhistorical' attention to their traces and layers (Chapter 3). The discussion of processes of deterritorialisation offered in the present chapter thus supports further conceptualisation of how Burrows' dances rethink tradition and memory, as well as the role of the individual within the plurality of history and politics.

NOTES

1. Among the programmes, he has been invited to or commissioned by are the Venice Biennale (2014), December Dance 16 (Bruges, Belgium, 2016, supported by the British Council and showcasing the 'best of the British dance scene'), London's Southbank Centre and Dance Umbrella festival. He also has an ongoing relationship with London's Sadler's Wells, Brussels' Kaaitheater and Essen's PACT Zollverein, which regularly co-produce his works (Burrows, n.d.).
2. For instance, New York's The Kitchen, 2004, and Danspace, 2011; Philadelphia's Pew Centre, 2014; 'Parallel Voices', a series of talks and events on contemporary dance guest-curated for Siobhan Davies Dance, London (2007); *The Elders Project* with older dancers, co-directed with Fargion at Sadler's Wells, London (2014).

3. Among his most prominent addresses are his keynote for the DanceHE conference 'Resilience: Articulating "Knowledges" Through Dance in the 21th Century', The Montfort University, Leicester, April 2015, and for the 'Post Dance' conference, Stockholm, October 2015, as well as his talk at Inventur#2 'Contemporary Dance and Performance' conference at Tanzhaus NRW Düsseldorf, June 2017.

4. Since 1992 he has been a visiting tutor at PARTS, the Performing Arts Research and Training Studios directed by Anne Teresa De Keersmaeker; since 2010 he has collaborated with Sadler's Wells as director of their Summer University and as mentor in Breakin' Convention's 'Back To The Lab', a training project for hip-hop choreographers led by hip-hop theatre artist Jonzi D.

5. Burrows is currently a Senior Research Fellow at the Centre for Dance Research, Coventry University, and holds an Honorary Doctorate from Royal Holloway University of London.

6. Burrows' publications include, among other writings: Burrows (2010 and 2015), Burrows and Ritsema (2003) and Burrows and Heathfield (2013).

7. The sources on Burrows' early career are relatively scarce. The biographical and bibliographical notes compiled by Chris Jones (1998) in the *International Dictionary of Modern Dance* and by Rachel Chamberlain Duerden (1999) in Martha Bremser's guide to contemporary choreography are two chronological and critical summaries of his early work. Another useful overview, including a brief list of references, a biographical note and company information, is Duerden's 2001 article in *The Dancing Times*, which nevertheless does not review any of the late 1990s pieces. A more detailed chronology, a bibliography and list of works up to 1993, was also compiled by Sarah Harris in her MA dissertation (1993). Burrows' (n.d.) official website has a list of works and collects important bibliographic and interview material.

8. Extracts of some of these interviews—on *Hymns* (Burrows, 2005c), on *The Stop Quartet* (Burrows, 2006c) and on reviving it (Burrows, 2008), on *Weak Dance Strong Questions* (Burrows, 2004), on *The Quiet Dance* (Burrows, 2005b) and on *Speaking Dance* (Burrows, 2006d)—can be found on Burrows' website (Burrows, n.d.).

9. As highlighted by Burrows (2005a, 2005c) in interviews, Morrice played a crucial role in the development of modern dance in Britain, especially through his choreographic and directorial roles at Ballet Rambert (see, for instance, Craine and Mackrell, 2004).

10. It should be noted that my conceptualisation of Burrows' choreography as minor dance stems from a different kind of enquiry from the one underpinning the analogy that Cvejić (2015) draws between Burrows' (and Ritsema's) improvised dance mode and Deleuze's writings on minor literature.

As already mentioned in Chapter 1, Cvejić (2015: 152) focuses on the stuttering of language/movement as a 'disjunction between the times of thinking and moving' to conceptualise how Burrows' and Ritsema's practice of improvised movement in *Weak Dance Strong Questions* diverges from phenomenological understandings of dance improvisation. The pieces I examine in this chapter are not based on improvisational processes; instead, they follow precise scores.

11. My reconstruction of the development of the piece differs slightly from the one proposed by Duerden (1999). Whereas she identifies as the first version an *Hymns, Parts 1–3*, dated 1985, to my knowledge, the third part of the duet was not choreographed until 1986. The only documentation of the 1985 version is a rehearsal video shot in a studio of the Royal Ballet in January 1986, and this only comprises two parts (Burrows, 1986). The complete duet and the final version of the piece had their premiere respectively at the Riverside Studios, London, in October 1986 and at The Place Theatre, London, in June 1988. They are documented by reviews and critical accounts, by a rehearsal video including both the trio and the duet (Burrows, 1988) and by a BBC documentary featuring the *Hymns* duet alongside other works by Burrows (MacGibbon, 1992). The analysis constructed in this chapter is mainly based on the 1988 rehearsal video (from Burrows' personal archives), which provides the most complete documentation of the piece.

12. On the period of time preceding the creation of *Hymns*, critic Jann Parry reports: 'he became so dissatisfied with his experiments that he stopped choreographing for almost two years. "I waited until I was driven to make something really personal," he says. "Then I started again, very slowly and meticulously, not moving on until I was satisfied I'd got it right"' (1991: 57).

13. Burrows explains that it was in order to present it as a full-length performance that the duet was extended and the trio was added at the beginning (Burrows, 2005c).

14. Both the victim and the tormentors, though, seem aware of their respective conditions, as it is shown for instance in the passage in which Heydon, after sandwiching McCann between the other two dancers in a pile of human bodies, turns around to stare at the audience, as if to gauge their reaction, or when McCann attempts to escape and rebel against her oppressors. Talking about the unorthodox handling of the dancers' bodies, Mackrell comments: 'these lifts and balances produce some of the work's funniest moments where the contrast between preposterously undignified positions and polite teatime expressions is deliciously absurd' (1991).

15. 'Burrows is currently engaged with an ongoing body of work made with composer Matteo Fargion, which began in 2002 with *Both Sitting Duet*, followed by *The Quiet Dance* (2005), *Speaking Dance* (2006), *Cheap Lecture*

(2009), *The Cow Piece* (2009), *Counting To One Hundred* (2011), *One Flute Note* (2012), *Show and Tell* (2013), *Rebelling Against Limit* (2013), *Body Not Fit for Purpose* (2014), *52 Portraits* (in collaboration with Hugo Glendinning 2016), *Any Table Any Room* (2017), *Music For Lectures/Katye Coe* (in collaboration with Katye Coe and Francesca Fargion 2018), *Music For Lectures/Mette Edvardsen* (in collaboration with Mette Edvardsen and Francesca Fargion 2018). The two men have given performances across 34 countries' (Burrows, n.d.).

16. See Chapter 1.
17. Including a 2004 New York Dance and Performance 'Bessie' Award (Burrows, n.d.).
18. The talk was given in the context of a module I teach and followed Burrows and Fargion's performance of *Both Sitting Duet* and *Body Not Fit for Purpose* (Kingston University London, 2 February 2015).

References

Barthes, Roland (1968) *Writing Degree Zero*. Translated by Annette Lavers and Colin Smith. New York: Hill and Wang.

Bayston, Michael (1992) 'Dance on Television', *Dancing Times*, 82 (984): 1156.

Briginshaw, Valerie A. (2009) 'Affective Differences and Repetitions in *Both Sitting Duet*', in Valerie A. Briginshaw and Ramsay Burt (eds.) *Writing Dancing Together*. Basingstoke: Palgrave: 183–203.

Brown, Ismene (2003) 'The Vanishing Man of British Dance', *The Daily Telegraph*, 13 October: 19.

Burrows, Jonathan (1986) *Hymns: Parts 1 & 2*, video-recording of rehearsal, 23 January, London: Royal Opera House studio.

Burrows, Jonathan (1988) *Hymns: Trio, Duet*, video-recording of rehearsal, London.

Burrows, Jonathan (1991) *Stoics Quartet*, video-recording of performance, 20 November, London: Royal Opera House.

Burrows, Jonathan (1992) *Stoics*, video-recording of performance, 2 February, London: Southbank Centre, Purcell Room.

Burrows, Jonathan (2004) Unpublished conversation with Daniela Perazzo Domm, London, 7 April.

Burrows, Jonathan (2005a) Unpublished conversation with Daniela Perazzo Domm, London, 26 May.

Burrows, Jonathan (2005b) Unpublished conversation with Daniela Perazzo Domm, London, 28 July.

Burrows, Jonathan (2005c) Unpublished conversation with Daniela Perazzo Domm, London, 26 November.

Burrows, Jonathan (2006a) Unpublished conversation with Daniela Perazzo Domm, London, 22 June.

Burrows, Jonathan (2006b) Unpublished conversation with Daniela Perazzo Domm, London, 13 August.

Burrows, Jonathan (2006c) Unpublished conversation with Daniela Perazzo Domm, London, 7 September.

Burrows, Jonathan (2006d) Unpublished conversation with Daniela Perazzo Domm, London, 9 November.

Burrows, Jonathan (2008) Unpublished conversation with Daniela Perazzo Domm, Brussels, 10 September.

Burrows, Jonathan (2010) *A Choreographer's Handbook*. London and New York: Routledge.

Burrows, Jonathan (2015) 'Body Not Fit for Purpose', *Performance Research*, 20 (5): 81–86.

Burrows, Jonathan (2018) 'What Would Be Another Word for It?', Unpublished text written for a talk with Chrysa Parkinson at Doch Stockholm.

Burrows, Jonathan (n.d.) *Jonathan Burrows.* http://www.jonathanburrows.info/. Accessed 20 December 2018.

Burrows, Jonathan and Heathfield, Adrian (2013) 'Moving Writing', *Choreographic Practices*, 4 (2): 129–149.

Burrows, Jonathan and Ritsema, Jan (2003) 'Weak Dance Strong Questions', *Performance Research*, 8 (2): 28–33.

Burt, Ramsay (2017) *Ungoverning Dance: Contemporary European Theatre Dance and the Commons*. Oxford: Oxford University Press.

Butcher, Rosemary and Melrose, Susan (eds.) (2005) *Rosemary Butcher: Choreography, Collisions and Collaborations*. London: Middlesex University Press.

Clarke, Mary (1981) 'Sadler's Wells Royal Ballet', *Dancing Times*, 71 (848): 540–541.

Clarke, Mary (1983) 'The Winter Play', *Dancing Times*, 73 (872): 615.

Constanti, Sophie (1990) 'Riverside Studios: Jonathan Burrows', *The Guardian*, 12 July: 24.

Constanti, Sophie (1994) 'Spring Loaded: Restless Dissidents of the Mainstream', *Dancing Times*, 84 (1005): 905.

Craine, Debra and Mackrell, Judith (2004) *Oxford Dictionary of Dance*. Oxford: Oxford University Press.

Crisp, Clement (1990) 'A Good Do: Riverside Studios', *Financial Times*, 12 July: 17.

Cvejić, Bojana (2015) *Choreographing Problems: Expressive Concepts in Contemporary Dance and Performance*. Basingstoke: Palgrave Macmillan.

de Marigny, Chris (1994) 'Burrows: Our Thoughts', *Dance Theatre Journal*, 11 (2): 6–9, 48.

Deleuze, Gilles (1998) *Essays Critical and Clinical*. Translated by Daniel W. Smith and Michael A. Greco. London and New York: Verso.

Deleuze, Gilles and Guattari, Félix (1986) *Kafka: Toward a Minor Literature*. Translated by Dana Polan. Minneapolis: University of Minnesota Press.

Dougill, David (1991) 'Dancing a Party Piece: Drama', *Sunday Times*, 24 November.

Dromgoole, Nicholas (1983) 'Ballet: Six of the Best', *The Sunday Telegraph*, 17 April: 19.

Dromgoole, Nicholas (1990) 'Dim Delights Under the Umbrella', *The Sunday Telegraph*, 14 October.

Duerden, Rachel Chamberlain (1999) 'Jonathan Burrows', in Martha Bremser (ed.) *Fifty Contemporary Choreographers: A Reference Guide*. London: Routledge: 47–51.

Duerden, Rachel Chamberlain (2001) 'Jonathan Burrows: Exploring the Frontiers', *Dancing Times*, 91 (1086): 551–557.

Goodwin, Noël (1981) 'London', *Ballet News*, 3 (1): 36–37.

Goodwin, Noël (1983) 'Spirited and Unconventional', *Dance and Dancers*, July: 27–29.

Goodwin, Noël (1992) 'Sound and Sight: Marginal Comment', *Dance and Dancers*, January/February: 18.

Hammergren, Lena (2004) 'Many Sources, Many Voices', in Alexandra Carter (ed.) *Rethinking Dance History: A Reader*. London: Routledge: 20–31.

Harris, Sarah (1993) 'Ambiguity in Jonathan Burrows' Choreography: The Paradox of Humour and Violence'. MA Dissertation, University of Surrey.

Hudson, Richard (1973) 'The Folia Melodies', *Acta Musicologica*, 45 (1): 98–119.

Hunt, Marilyn (1993) 'Jonathan Burrows: Laughter of Recognition', *Dance Magazine*, 67 (10): 52–55.

Jones, Chris (1998) 'Jonathan Burrows', in Taryn Benbow-Pfalzgraf (ed.) *International Dictionary of Modern Dance*. Detroit, New York and London: St. James Press: 83–84.

Jordan, Stephanie (1992) *Striding Out: Aspects of Contemporary and New Dance in Britain*. London: Dance Books.

Jordan, Stephanie and Friend, Howard (1982) 'Dance Umbrella 1982', *Dancing Times*, 72 (867): 190–192.

Joy, Jenn (2014) *The Choreographic*. Cambridge, MA: The MIT Press.

Kane, Aangela (1991) 'The Jonathan Burrows Group', *Dancing Times*, 81 (969): 868.

Kristeva, Julia (1980) *Desire in Language: A Semiotic Approach to Literature and Art*. Edited by Leon S. Roudiez. Oxford: Blackwell.

Lepecki, André (2006) *Exhausting Dance: Performance and the Politics of Movement*. London and New York: Routledge.

Lepecki, André (2016) *Singularities: Dance in the Age of Performance*. London and New York: Routledge.

Levene, Louise (1991) 'By Royal Assent: Jonathan Burrows Tells Louise Levene That He Has No Plans to Give up His "Day" Job', *The Independent*, 13 April: 22.

Levene, Louise (1996) 'Dance: Cinderella; City Ballet/Royal Ballet, London', *The Independent*, 19 December: 23.

Macaulay, Alastair (1985) 'The Royal Ballet: The Next Choreographers', *Dance Theatre Journal*, 3 (1): 36–40.

MacGibbon, Ross (1992) 'The Far End of the Garden', in the video documentary series *Dancemakers*. Beaulieu Films/BBC2/Arts Council.

Mackrell, Judith (1988) 'The Sound and the Furry', *The Independent*, 27 June: 15.

Mackrell, Judith (1991) 'Country Manners', *The Independent*, [n.d.] April.

Mackrell, Judith (1992) 'Is New Ballet Old Hat?', *Dance Now*, 1 (2): 5–9.

Meisner, Nadine (1992a) 'Jonathan Burrows, Julyen Hamilton', *Dance and Dancers*, January/February: 29–30.

Meisner, Nadine (1992b) 'Seasonal Movements', *The Times*, 5 February: 2.

Meisner, Nadine (1996) 'Pointe of Extinction: Dance', *Sunday Times*, 1 September: 19.

O'Sullivan, Simon (2005) 'Notes Towards a Minor Art Practice', *Drain: Journal of Contemporary Art and Culture*, 2 (2). Available at http://drainmag.com/index_nov.htm. Accessed 15 January 2017.

Parry, Jann (1991) 'Living on Spare Time and Borrowed Dancers', *The Observer*, 27 October: 57.

Perazzo, Daniela (2005) 'The Sitting Duo Now Walks, or the Piece That Lies Quietly Underneath: Daniela Perazzo Interviews Jonathan Burrows', *Dance Theatre Journal*, 21 (2): 2–7.

Perazzo Domm, Daniela (2008) 'Jonathan Burrows and Matteo Fargion's *Both Sitting Duet* (2002): A Discursive Choreomusical Collaboration', in Lansdale Janet (ed.) *Decentring Dancing Texts*. Basingstoke: Palgrave Macmillan: 125–142.

Percival, John (1978) 'Reviews: London', *Dance Magazine*, 52 (12): 119–121.

Percival, John (1980) 'Reviews: London', *Dance Magazine*, 54 (11): 92–97.

Percival, John (1983) 'Boldness Rewarded: The Winter Play, Hippodrome, Birmingham', *The Times*, 16 April: 9.

Percival, John (1988) 'Dance: Onward Christian Soldiers. Hymns, The Place', *The Times*, 25 June.

Percival, John (1991a) 'The Nutcracker', *The Times*, 1 January.

Percival, John (1991b) 'Stoics; Plain Song', *The Times*, 18 April.

Percival, John (1991c) 'Royal Ballet; Dance', *The Times*, 22 November.

Percival, John (1991d) 'The Year We Nearly Forgot Mozart: Best of British', *The Times*, 31 December.

Percival, John (1992) 'Sylphides/Present Histories/Symphony in Covent Garden; Sylphides/The Burrow, Birmingham Hippodrome', *Dance and Dancers*, January/February: 22–25.

Percival, John (1997) 'Trace Elements: Rosemary Butcher Is a Choreographer Who Rarely Lets Her Dancers Tread the Same Ground Twice—Which Is Why They Always Come Back for More', *The Independent*, 18 February: 6.

Rancière, Jacques (2011) 'The Thinking of Dissensus: Politics and Aesthetics', in Paul Bowman and Richard Stamp (eds.) *Reading Rancière: Critical Dissensus*. London: Continuum: 1–17.

Rowell, Bonnie (2000) *Dance Umbrella: The First Twenty-One Years*. London: Dance Books.

Sacks, Anne (1992) 'Adventures in Body Language', *The Independent on Sunday*, 18 October: 20.

Smith, Owen and Agis, Gabrielle (1982) 'An Evening of New Choreography', *New Dance*, 22 June: 22.

Thorpe, Edward (1991) 'Talking to an Enigma: Edward Thorpe Interviews Jonathan Burrows', *Dance and Dancers*, June–July: 12.

CHAPTER 3

Reduction, Repetition, Returns: The Trouble of Minimalism

Jonathan Burrows' choreography has often been defined in critical literature in terms of its relationship with minimalist dance and music traditions. In particular, in his formative years, Burrows developed a dialogue with the explorations of pedestrian movement of the Judson Church choreographers and worked closely with British and continental European artists interrogating formalist practices (especially Anne Teresa De Keersmaeker in Belgium and Rosemary Butcher in the UK). Moreover, throughout his career, he has collaborated with composers associated with the post-minimalist movement (Kevin Volans and, primarily, Matteo Fargion). These connections and partnerships provide the background for the analysis of traits such as the scenographic reduction and compositional clarity of his dances and the ways in which these modalities rethink representation and figuration.

While the narrow usage of the term 'minimalism' refers specifically to a movement developed in the 1960s in North American visual art and sculpture, in a broader sense the category has also been applied to other art forms, from music to architecture to dance. Although minimalist movements in music and dance do not necessarily adhere to the same principles of minimal art, they nevertheless share its choice of limited materials, repetitive and modular patterns and simple structures, as well as its rejection of expressivity and emotional display. From the mid-1960s, American composers such as Philip Glass and Steve Reich substituted harmonic development with repetitive patterns: they created static pieces whose reduced

© The Author(s) 2019
D. Perazzo Domm, *Jonathan Burrows*,
New World Choreographies,
https://doi.org/10.1007/978-3-030-27680-5_3

scope for variation and 'deliberate technical limitations' gave the compositions a calm and serene mood (Brindle, 1987: 195). Similarly, a minimalist
aesthetic was embraced in dance by the artists of the Judson Dance Theater in New York, who in the 1960s became interested in the exploration of
the everyday, through the use of pedestrian movements, street clothes and
functional objects (Banes, 1987). This genre of performance is commonly
known as 'task dance' and, in its 'anti-illusionist' attitude, it 'shares a set of
recognized aesthetic preoccupations with contemporary fine art. [...] That
is, it attempts to close the gap between artworks and real things' (Carroll
and Banes, 1982: 38).

Early on in Burrows' career, critics and reviewers identified a distinctive
minimalist style in his dances, mainly due to their simplified movement
vocabulary, use of patterns and limited technical and scenographic requirements.[1] This chapter questions the productivity of these categorisations
and draws attention to the generative ambiguity of the formalist dance
tradition's engagement with content. It interrogates to what extent the
resistance to representational and narrative modes might in itself facilitate
an affective regime of communication, which, I argue, signals a curiosity
for the (a)signifying potential of formalist and abstract aesthetics. Examining Burrows' choreographic language and focusing on devices such as
repetition and rhythmical patterns and on his concern for structure and
process, I point to an understanding of the relationship between form and
content that acknowledges plurality and ambivalence. I suggest that content is expressed in Burrows' work through an unconventional use of form
which reframes strategies of signification and opens an intensive register.

Crucial to minimalism is its rethinking of the relationship between art
and object, which was the focus of a well-known critical debate from the late
1960s: on the basis of the encounter it orchestrated between an object and
a viewer, minimal art was labelled as 'theatrical' by American critic Michael
Fried (1968), an interpretation later rejected by readings that emphasised
minimal art's anti-illusionistic engagement with the real (Foster, 1996).
Addressing the concerns of this debate, this chapter reflects on the terms
of the relationship between Burrows' choreography and the real, with particular attention to the ways in which Burrows' dances are composed of
physical memories of past dances—memories which I understand as bodily traces of real things. I suggest that Burrows creates work that speaks
of the present moment by threading the peculiarities of microworlds into
its weave—a sort of choreographic micronarrative, which gestures towards
wider issues by focusing on 'minutiae' and 'close-ups' (Ginzburg, 2007).

In this respect, the microhistorical perspective of (among other historians) Carlo Ginzburg offers a productive framework through which to draw out the larger significance of the 'small things' that Burrows' choreographic practice concerns itself with and presents in performance. It also operates on a scale that, I suggest, is analogous to the 'micropolitics' of minor practices (Deleuze and Guattari, 1986: 42), in which—as I discuss in Chapter 2—art and life are intertwined. In this sense, a concern for the 'minor' positioning of Burrows' artistic work—that is for how his choreography destabilises signifying strategies while operating within recognisable traditions—resonates in the analysis of its microhistorical approach I offer in this chapter.

An interest in the 'micro' is evident in Burrows' works through their distinctive focus on the minute details of movement, in the personal references that compose the fabric of the dance and in a certain fondness for the odd and the old-fashioned. Attending to 'the anomalous, not the analogous' is in itself the project of microhistory (Ginzburg, 1993: 33). It presupposes the potential richness of its atypical object and the heterogeneity of its relationship with its larger context; in valuing individuality, it reduces the scale of observation and concerns itself with the 'exceptional typical', with the link between the peculiar and its wider significance, between the micro and the macro (Peltonen, 2001). Through the attention they pay to minute physical details, which, as Burrows (2017) writes, is the outcome of a negotiation between 'familiar movement' and detours to untravelled 'backroads', his choreographies are emblematic of a critical concern with the historicity of the dance medium, which is both a curiosity for the generative potential of the simplest, oddest, most improbable bodily traces and an understanding of choreography as 'an archival-corporeal system', a 'dynamic system of transmission and transformation' (Lepecki, 2010: 37).

A Foucauldian idea of the archive as a constant dialectic of past, present and future—as articulated in *The Archaeology of Knowledge* (1972) and as invoked in André Lepecki's (2010) conceptualisation of 'the body as archive'—underpins the discussion constructed in this chapter, which proposes to approach Burrows' relationship with the historical legacy of minimalism from the perspective of thinking history as archaeology, considering how the complex relationship between past and present is articulated through 'inscriptions of the past into the present' (Giannachi, Kaye and Shanks, 2012: 1). I argue that traces of minimalism in Burrows' dances, as both lingerings and re-doings of an artistic tradition, unsettle the temporal dimension of the 'newer' dances and reveal the complicated structure of time—constructing, in turn, a specific understanding of history (and of dance history). It is worth noting that, in Burrows' case, these re-framings are not formulated as re-enactments or reconstructions of dance works, but rather as a travelling through memories of movement as corporeal traces of his own dancing or recollections of a witnessed dance, which remain or intervene semantically and affectively in the making and reception of the work.

This discussion acknowledges important writings in performance and dance scholarship on the question concerning the presence and ephemerality of dance and the notion of the body as archive: the above-mentioned publication by Lepecki, but also Ramsay Burt's (2003) article on the critical potential of bodily memory and the politics of repetition in contemporary dance, as well as Peggy Phelan and Rebecca Schneider's influential contributions to performance studies.[2] Nevertheless, in this chapter I propose to interrogate the idea of memory and 'afterlife'[3] of dances by considering what Peter Osborne (2013) calls the 'distributive' character of contemporary artworks, which, by conceptualising their temporal 'malleability', specifically illuminates their historicity. Thus, in offering my thoughts on Burrows' critically and historically situated rethinking of minimalism, I work with Osborne's philosophy of contemporary art, invoking in particular his theorisation of its postconceptuality as the condition of being 'premised on the complex historical experience and critical legacy of conceptual art' via a shift in its ontology towards relationality and malleability, to account for the plurality of instantiations, media and relations it travels through (Osborne, 2013: 48). Under this conceptual gaze, the relationship of Burrows' dance with formalist traditions is construed through a questioning of its self-referentiality and an interrogation of its critical and affective engagement with the historicity of the form.

More broadly, I am interested in interrogating how dance performance might upset dominant historical discourses and actualise different versions of its artistic and political past. Inspired by Daniel Heller-Roazen's reflections on forms of linguistic forgetfulness, the analysis I propose draws attention to the ways in which Burrows' choreography articulates a dance poetics that problematises the complex interplay of remembering and forgetting through which dance and its history are constructed. In *Echolalias: On the Forgetting of Language*, Heller-Roazen offers fascinating accounts of how a tongue may be acquired or lost, of how an idiom may emerge or vanish. Reflecting on how all language (and dance) is 'a simultaneously single yet multiple idiom in which writing and translating, "compos[ing]" and "compos[ing] after", production and reproduction, cannot be told apart' (Heller-Roazen, 2005: 177), I seek to investigate the role of dance performance as a site of disappearance/reappearance of historical traces and to engage with the political significance of affective re-framings and re-imaginings of history. In constructing a parallel between the stratified nature of language and that of dance, it is not my intention to disavow the bodily dimension of dance; instead, I am drawn to language as a material phenomenon, lived and moulded through the experiences of communities of speakers.

The structure of this chapter is organised around the themes and issues outlined above. More specifically, the first section is devoted to a reassessment of Burrows' relationship with minimalism. To elucidate the problems inherent in categorisations based on traditional critical labels, I examine the critical debate provoked by an early piece, *The Stop Quartet* (1996). This work also offers a pertinent case for a detailed analysis of Burrows' rethinking of minimalist compositional principles, which constitutes the focus of the second part of the chapter. Consideration is then given to the issue of minimalism's relationship with the real, which supports a discussion of Burrows' choreographic language as distinctly personal, yet historically situated and politically concerned. Here I construct an understanding of Burrows' engagement with the real as a creative attention to 'small things' that, I propose, is 'microhistorical' in method. This line of thinking is developed also through an interrogation of Burrows and Fargion's duet *Body Not Fit for Purpose*, which expands the analysis of this piece offered in Chapter 2. Finally, the argument moves on to consider the stratified dimension of Burrows' approach to choreography, which entails the labour of layering remembered and/as forgotten material: a series of other works are considered here, albeit only briefly, to illustrate how the act of repeating and restaging material productively queers the temporal dimension of the dances and foregrounds their stratified historicity.

Burrows' Minimalist Label: A Critical Divide

There are a number of reasons that compel me to explore the question of minimalism in relation to Burrows' choreography, troubling the usage of the term, while at the same time reaffirming its productivity (providing that the notion of minimalism is afforded some rethinking). One such reason is the recent re-emergence of scholarly debate on the place of minimalism in the arts, which is indicative of a desire to explore its paradoxes and question accepted critical, historical and geographical understandings of its scope and significance. In October 2016, for instance, a conference devoted to minimalism, organised at the University of Southampton/Winchester School of Art by Sarah Hayden, Paul Hegarty and Ryan Bishop, set out 'to expand our conception of what minimalism was, where it happened, who was making it, why, and how it extends through time until now'— beyond the 'unifying vision' that locates it in New York, in the 1960s, in conjunction with a handful of white male American artists (Donald Judd, Robert Morris, Dan Flavin, Carl Andre) or that traces a single important link between the visual arts and the music of Glass, Reich or John Adams.[4] In the opening remarks, Hegarty raised the question of 'why minimalism now?' and offered a vision of minimalism as a different, less recognisable mode through which to deal with the political, alternative to the overuse of trauma of much contemporary artistic production.

Another reason for rethinking the relation of Burrows' work to minimalism is my contention that the minimalist tag that critics and reviewers have assigned to Burrows since the 1990s has contributed to Burrows' paradoxically minoritarian place within the contemporary European dance scene. While Burrows has not been alone in championing creative methods that emphasise clarity of structure and compositional principles, this positioning has often come with associated issues, of which he has clearly been aware (as already discussed in Chapters 1 and 2).

I suggest that the limited attention Burrows has received in academic discourses (as I discuss in Chapter 1) is connected to some extent to his interest in the formal aspects of choreographing, insofar as the contextualisation and conceptualisation of minimalist and formalist dance has not been at the centre of dominant critical and theoretical debates in twenty-first-century dance and performance scholarship.

A further reason to interrogate the question of minimalism is that Burrows himself has often challenged the characterisation of his work as 'minimalist', which some reviewers have identified as one of the traits that started to emerge distinctively in his choreographic language from the 1990s, especially with *The Stop Quartet*. References to his compositional method found in the literature point out that his 'careful, piecemeal approach' and the resulting 'spare, intense choreography' are 'often dubbed minimalist but Burrows seems uncomfortable with the term. "I don't think the dance piece is minimalist: it's just economical"' (Anon, 1997). Here Burrows appears to make a distinction between the economy of ingredients and instruments on the one hand and the sophistication of the creative process and general effect of the work on the other. This is a position that he has championed in more than one occasion, including in a public talk with Tim Etchells, moderated by Adrian Heathfield, in which Burrows discussed the idea that the clarity of structure and process of his works is often mistaken for minimalism and argued that by choosing 'clear means', he aims instead at generating 'the richest possible communication' (Burrows and Etchells, 2004). In one of our interviews, he elaborated on this further, with reference to the creative process for *The Stop Quartet*:

> I never want to call it minimalism because I always think that, physically, I'm always trying to do something as rich as possible [...]. I've always wondered if the fact that people feel that what I'm doing is minimal is more to do with how I want to concentrate on the thing itself and not dress it. But at the same time, I do love things which you don't question and which seem to be very effective, but which are made of simpler ingredients. [...] When we started to work on *The Stop Quartet* we were using really simple elements, and in a way you couldn't break movement down more than we broke it down. So in a way that gives it a certain feeling of something stripped back which then arrives at a flight via a different route. But the idea of 'less is more' doesn't really underpin my way of thinking. (Burrows, 2006b)

As already mentioned above, in historicising Burrows' minimalist label, two important convergences need to be taken into account: with the so-called analytic line of American early postmodern choreography and with minimalist and post-minimalist music. This consideration requires a brief contextualisation. In the 1960s, a generation of artists based in New York, most of whom had trained with Merce Cunningham, developed Cunningham's enquiry into the medium and function of dance, questioning accepted techniques and codes of choreographic composition. They advocated the democratisation of dance movement, which they freed from stylistic prescriptions, spectacular effects and emotional content. This collective—of choreographers, dancers, composers and visual artists—included artists such as Steve Paxton, Yvonne Rainer, Deborah Hay, David Gordon and Robert Dunn, among others. They became known as Judson Dance Theater as they gave their first public performances at the Judson Memorial Church in Greenwich Village in New York.[5] Their agenda was explicitly and effectively summarised in Yvonne Rainer's 1965 'No Manifesto', which rejected 'spectacle', 'virtuosity', 'glamour', 'style', 'seduction of spectator', 'eccentricity', 'moving and being moved', among other codes and frameworks. In a later text from 1968, examining her 1966 work *Trio A*, Rainer draws a parallel between her artistic project and minimalist sculpture, advocating the removal from dance of the equivalent of those aspects which had been eliminated in minimal art objects: these include 'phrasing', 'development', 'variation', representation and virtuosity.[6] Such traits were to be substituted with the repetition of singular task-like actions, neutrally performed.

As already mentioned in Chapter 2, Burrows' encounter with the work of the Judson Church choreographers took place both through attendance at workshops led by members of the New York collective in London in the 1980s and through his participation in dance and installation works choreographed by Butcher, whose dance aesthetics was often characterised as 'minimalist' (Jones, 1998; Jordan, 1992). A key figure of British experimental dance, Butcher (1947–2016) was known for her improvisational processes, use of everyday movement, and for her interest in visual arts and architecture through the exploration of site-specific performance.[7] As Stephanie Jordan argued, discussing her 1980s and early 1990s works, 'counter[ing] … [the] noisy, strongly coloured theatre' of much postmodern dance, Butcher 'retains strong formal interests', which locate her work within the modernist agenda, as a demonstration of the minimalist belief that 'less can still be more' (Jordan, 1992: 160, 180, 181).

In the 1990s, Burrows also established closer contacts with the contemporary European dance scene, and with Belgium in particular, where he started his involvement as guest teacher and mentor at PARTS, the Performing Arts Research and Training Studios directed by De Keersmaeker in Brussels. De Keersmaeker is also known for her minimalist tendencies, both through her links with the New York dance avant-garde and through her interest in minimalist music. Her first choreographic success, for instance the work *Fase* (1982), was a danced interpretation of Reich's music (Bräuninger, 2014). The 1990s were also the years when Burrows intensified his collaborations with post-minimalist composers: Volans wrote the music for three of Burrows' pieces,[8] and Fargion, who studied composition with Volans, became Burrows' regular collaborator.

Significantly, Volans and Fargion co-wrote the music for *The Stop Quartet*. Burrows choreographed it during the time when he was living and working between the UK and Belgium, where he held positions as associate artist and was awarded choreographic residencies. The piece opens as a male duet between Burrows and Henry Montes and, only in its second half, turns into a trio and then into a quartet, with two subsequent additions of a female dancer, Fin Walker and Kate Gowar. A music score consisting of piano notes, dissonances, natural sounds and silences is combined with Michael Hulls' geometrical lighting, characterised by perpendicular beams creating a glowing grid on the dark floor. The choreography is made of simple pedestrian material—jerky movements and gangly steps—composed in patterns and performed in a casual manner. The language of the piece dissects the most basic movements that legs, arms, torso and head can execute. The found movement, the repetitions and the neutral performance could be said to follow Rainer's chart mapping the features of minimalist dance.

The existing literature on *The Stop Quartet*[9] offers strong yet often divergent opinions. Two conflicting comments, by a choreographer and by a dance critic, may be juxtaposed to sketch the contours of the reception of the piece. William Forsythe spoke of the work as a 'masterpiece' by which he 'was deeply moved and changed' (Brown, 2003: 19). Observing that 'it's when the choreography is indivisible from the dancers that you have something', Forsythe (cited in Brown, 2003: 19) praised the way in which the dancing was seamlessly integrated within the piece's choreographic principles.[10] Conversely, Judith Mackrell's *Guardian* review lamented the loss of the broader variety of movement and other choreographic elements that Burrows had displayed in earlier works, claiming that 'compared to Burrows's dark and comical *Stoics*, the piece feels meagre in its material, and over-fastidious in its methods' (Mackrell, 1996: 14). She also criticised the piece for abandoning the narrative dimension through which his previous choreographies had constructed a now humorous, now harsh world, sacrificing subject matter in favour of structure. In her evaluation, which she rehashed in a later article, Mackrell appears to reinstate the form/content opposition on which conventional criticism is based, reaffirming its validity as a canon for contemporary dance:

> Burrows has a much wider palette of movement than he lets himself play with in the *Quartet*, and it makes you nostalgic for earlier works like *Stoics*. Here the choreography pursued an uncompromising logic yet it still took a dark and comic look at the foibles of human behaviour. As a poised, confident and richly satisfying balance between narrative and form, it was an exemplum of what new British dance is doing best. (Mackrell, 1996–1997: 58)

With this comment, Mackrell questions how far the expressive and narrative dimension of Burrows' early choreographies, developed through the use of pedestrian elements, continues to inform later works. However, a

critical reading of her perspective suggests the need for further interrogation of the modalities through which the movement material informs the
mode of address of a work, destabilising codified signification and moving
towards an affective register (see also Chapter 1). Forsythe's and Mackrell's
statements exemplify two distinctly different viewpoints not only on Burrows' piece, but on approaches to choreography. On the one hand is the
idea of an organic combination of method, aesthetics and performance, and
on the other hand is a dichotomous vision of dance in which the physical
arrangement is seen as functional to the telling of a story. While Forsythe's
personal remark, by its very nature, does not investigate the aspects underpinning the uniqueness of the dance, Mackrell's critical account arguably
fails to understand the significance of *The Stop Quartet* within the larger
picture of Burrows' artistic practice and of the critical discourse articulated
by contemporary dance.

The piece enjoyed considerable success with audiences and critics, who
described it as a 'revelational work' (Constanti, 1996b: 959), 'his most dar-
ing and most uncompromising piece to date' (Crisp, 1996: 15), a 'stun-
ning dance piece' (Brown, 1997: 74), 'so intriguing, so consummately
structured' (Meisner, 1997: 34). A number of reviewers were fascinated
by the complexity of the composition, the intricacy of the patterns and
the unconventionality of the combinations; Clement Crisp, for instance,
depicted the work as 'odd. Odder than odd, it is difficult, very far out,
and insidiously rewarding' (Crisp, 1996: 15). However, other critics—
Mackrell, but also Ismene Brown—objected that it was far too elaborate
and excessively demanding on the attention even of experienced viewers,
resulting in dryness, since 'its intelligence is formidable but in the end,
unlovable' (Mackrell, 1996: 14); 'it is an awesome achievement, but my
admiration was frayed, in the end, by mental exhaustion' (Brown, 1996a).
From an audience's point of view, the piece could come across as exceed-
ingly difficult and inscrutable. Jennifer Dunning (1997: E3) observed that
'Burrows proceeded to test the outer limits of boredom and exhaustion'
and George Dorris (1997–1998: 47) commented that '*The Stop Quartet*
[...] tested the audience's attention quotient'. The piece was deemed so
uncompromisingly obscure that it was seen to call into question the need
for an audience altogether: as Nadine Meisner (1996: 4) pointed out, 'a few
spectators criticised the dance for being insular and making the audience
feel dispensable'; and Mackrell (1996–1997: 58) went as far as claiming
that 'it's a work that virtually ignores its audience'.

The response from British critics focused on the meticulousness of the movement language, which explored endless possibilities of basic combinations. Its articulation was described as an in-depth investigation of 'the mechanics of the human body' (Brown, 1996a) and was often illustrated in very concrete terms, emphasising the materiality of the movement and the intense physicality of the work: 'its flat-footed, chaining steps, its arms slicing like broken-sailed windmills, its abrupt animal crouches' (Meisner, 1997: 34); 'the elements are neolithic – stamping, treading, walking, crouching, squatting, bodies bent, arms extended in semaphore line' (Crisp, 1996: 15); and 'it is beauty on a new, instinctive level' (Brown, 1996c). To the extent that they attend to both the structural and the embodied qualities of the dance, these descriptions offer a productive starting point for a critical reappraisal of conventional criticism's binary view of the relationship between form and content. Moreover, the critical debate summarised above provides a useful preamble for an analysis of the aesthetic and historical relationship of Burrows' work with late twentieth-century art practices and suggests that an exploration of the conceptual foundation and philosophical implications of minimalist artistic stances may support a more meaningful interrogation of Burrows' response to formalist traditions.

While similarities between these aesthetic and conceptual approaches and Burrows' work can be found in his use of repetitive patterns and of pedestrian movement, a detailed analysis of these practices and of their underlying principles leads to a more complex picture. The next section of this chapter examines the compositional process and the choreography of *The Stop Quartet* in order to interrogate Burrows' connection with minimalism. Attending to the stratified character of the piece, the category of purely 'formalist' traditions is exposed as one that requires undoing, in the sense that returns of the form imply and uncover the complex interrelationality of time, of places, of disciplines and of experiences. The analysis I construct is based on the 1996 film version of the piece, directed by filmmaker Adam Roberts.[11] It is worth noting that, in his collaborations with Burrows, Roberts' intervention does not aim to produce neutral documents of the dance works, as if recorded by an invisible hand.[12] Especially in the case of *The Stop Quartet*, with its complex texturing of dance, music and lighting, the video editing adds a further layer to the choreographic text; the distinctiveness of the cinematic language arises from a dialogue with the other elements of the choreography and with the compositional principles of the piece.

RECONFIGURATIONS OF MINIMALISM IN *THE STOP QUARTET* (1996)

I maintain that Burrows' engagement with minimalism is only one aspect of an approach to choreography which, as this chapter argues, is intrinsically relational and historically open. By this, I mean that Burrows' dances exist as processes which happen and unfold through layers of activity and in constant dialogue with the stratified nature and historicity of the medium. In this sense, focusing on Burrows' work as an instance of 'minimalist' dance is reductive and does not take into account the interplay of composing and recomposing that characterise processes of creation as well as the simultaneous coexistence of multiple traces within the same artistic idiom. Writing about the complex and paradoxical historicity of language, Heller-Roazen (2005: 177) foregrounds the idea that the notion of an original 'first' language, of a 'mother tongue', should be troubled and questioned: 'no language may justly lay claim to the title of being a "first" language, acquired purely by imitation and so untouched and untouchable by rules and writing, schools and grammatical consciousness; every language [...] is "first" and "second" at once'.

Hence, while in rethinking the art form of dance Burrows draws on minimalist ideas and examples, I posit that an interrogation of his choreography ought to abandon traditional critical categorisations based on genres and styles and take into account the ontological shift that characterises contemporary artworks—the works of postconceptual art, in Osborne's definition.[13] Such works, as well as being founded on the dialectic interplay between their conceptuality and their materiality, articulated through a critical stance towards their aesthetic dimension and an expanded notion of their material means, are also defined by their 'radically distributive – that is, irreducibly relational – unity [...] across the totality of [their] multiple material instantiations, at any particular time' and by the 'historical malleability of the borders of this unity' (Osborne, 2013: 48). As such, contemporary artworks come into being through layers of activity, diverse formats and multiple occurrences and are available to enter into future relations which might modify their unity—they have an 'afterlife' which gives them a *'retroactive* ontology' (Osborne, 2013: 50, original emphasis). In this sense, interrogating the relation of Burrows' choreography with minimalism means being attentive to the work's historicity—to its open, stratified, malleable ontology.

This perspective appears particularly pertinent for an analysis of the choreography of *The Stop Quartet*, which, as I wrote elsewhere, 'is a piece composed by accumulation' (Perazzo Domm, 2012: 107).[14] The architecture of the dance, its physical language and its interrelation with the musical score, with the lighting design and with the film editing are the result of a process of interrogation of the compositional fabric of the piece and of consequent additions and subtractions of material. In interviews, Burrows pointed out that the piece started off as a duet with Montes, focusing on the exploration of simple movements, performed at a given pace and in constant relationship with each other (Fig. 3.1). The process of creation involved using a metronome, working with counterpoint and 'building basic blocks of movements which then, when they are combined, become something completely different from what you would have imagined' (Burrows, 2006b). Burrows also explained that the piece began as a continuation of *Hands* (1995), a short choreography for the camera,

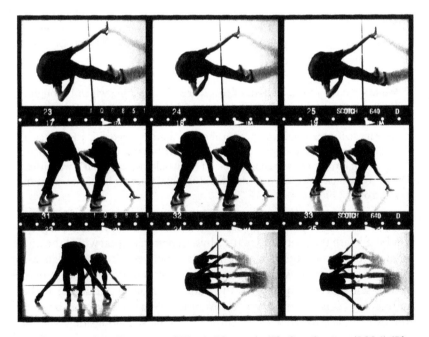

Fig. 3.1 Jonathan Burrows and Henry Montes in *The Stop Quartet* (1996) (Photograph by Richard Dean)

and as a reaction to the earlier group work *Our* (1994). *The Stop Quartet* resumed and expanded the investigation of the principles behind patterns of simple hand gestures executed in counterpoint between the right and the left hand, on which *Hands* was based (see also Chapter 5). Conversely, it rejected the quest for 'interesting' and 'virtuosic' movements aiming at the 'physical expression' of images and ideas that can be found in *Our* (Burrows, 2006b). The making of the duet started from breaking down the physical material to basic elements, which were then composed together in complex phrases; the patterns were visualised on paper on two parallel lines, representing the two dancers (Burrows, 2006b). It was Fargion who taught Burrows how to observe movement in time, using a form of notation of rhythm and counterpoint employed in African music: producing a score of the physical sequences allowed him to visualise time and become aware of the intersections between the dancers also on a temporal level.[15]

In terms of the concept of the piece, when composing the movement phrases, Burrows deliberately rejected narrative elements. Discussing the creative process in interviews, he explained that he began to feel the need to step outside and, for a period of time, Gowar replaced him in working with Montes. This enabled him to distance himself from the choreography and identify its dynamics.

> We worked for a week and out of that there was one thing which I thought, 'this is very interesting'. The one thing is the very beginning of the piece, which I tried with Kate and Henry: it's the relationship between one person moving half speed and one person moving double speed. [...] But then I decided that the one thing I didn't like was it being a man and a woman, because it introduced a narrative which I felt would be lessened if it was either two women or two men. So I decided that I had to come back into it again. (Burrows, 2006b)

The elimination of potentially narrative elements from the choreography, combined with the simplicity of the physical material upon which the movement sequences are built, highlights a link between Burrows' dance and minimalist aesthetics. As already noted, reviewers of the piece commented on the self-reflective quality of the dance and on its reduction to basic ingredients (Boxberger, 1996; Constanti, 1996a). Hence, on one level, Burrows' choice to work from simple elements sits alongside a key characteristic of minimal art. The visual and sculptural works of artists such as Judd, Flavin and Morris employed basic elements, often of industrial origin, composed according to rigorous geometrical patterns of extreme simplicity. As it has been observed, 'the ambition they shared was to create works of maximum immediacy, where the whole is more important than the parts, and where relational composition is suppressed in favour of an arrangement of simple ordering' (Gablik, 1994: 246).

However, on another level, the intricate interweaving of elements and parts of *The Stop Quartet* breaks with minimalism's structural immediacy. As Nick Kaye (1994: 27) maintains, 'the "minimalist" objects [...] rejected not only representation, reference and symbol, but the very idea that the art-object should be composed of inter-related parts'. Modular patterning was one of the most frequent organisational principles and the rationality, predictability and 'outstanding [...] clarity' of its repetitiveness made the work self-explanatory and, according to the American art critic Gregory Battcock, totally unambiguous (1968: 32).

The extension of the duet into a quartet, via the intermediate trio section, was the result of a contingent rather than premeditated decision. According to Burrows' account, when he and Montes concluded that they had exhaustively explored the possibilities of movement and its combinations in the duet, they decided to expand the variables of the piece by adding two more dancers, Walker and Gowar:

> I had the idea that if we had a twenty-five-minute duet – and we had already been talking about asking Fin Walker to join us for a trio – it would be great if we had a trio which was shorter than the duet, and finally a quartet which was shorter than the trio. So, just arbitrarily, I thought: if the duet is twenty-five minutes, then use all the fives, so make the trio fifteen minutes and make the quartet five minutes, and it would make for a really interesting shape: you get this huge activity at the end, but it only lasts a very short time. (Burrows, 2006b)

The compression of the dance material in the last part of the piece also entailed the addition of new elements and therefore the expansion of the range of 'ingredients' used. Changes and alternations in the ways in which the movement was condensed and extended were also applied to other components of the choreography and especially to the arrangements of the music and of the lighting.

The collaboration between choreographer, composers and lighting designer began in the early stages of the creation process and each artist contributed to the structural and conceptual coherence of the piece (Burrows, 2006b). In the first ten minutes of the duet, in which the choreography begins its exploration of movement and spatial and temporal dynamics from simple elements and small changes, treated almost individually, the music is made of slow and soft piano notes with frequent pauses and long silences. Through this gentle, subdued opening, the music allows the dance to affirm its voice and make a first connection with the audience. In the second part of the duet, the dance becomes more 'choreographed' and single elements are organised together in phrases; the dancers travel more widely through the space and move faster than in the first part. Here the music breaks in with renewed strength, with louder and more vigorous sounds, employing multiple pianos to create a score of staccato notes and blunt breaks and changes.

In the trio, the dance begins with a slower pulse, although the addition of one more performer balances the reduction of the speed by enhancing the complexity of the choreography; in contrast, towards the end of the section, multiple changes of direction and the mechanical and brisk quality of the movements generate a sense of tension. This progression from a more meditative mood to an increasing nervousness is paralleled in the music, which begins with piano lines of quiet, deep notes, frequent silences and sparse sounds and ends with the addition of screeching and metallic noises and birds' chirruping, which turn progressively louder. This direction is developed further in the quartet, where the dance and the music concur in enhancing the overall feeling of increasing pressure: a faster pulse and the addition of a fourth dancer match the intensification of the sound volume and the insistence of the piercing noise continuing from the previous section. However, on a compositional level, choreography and soundscape follow conflicting principles in the final quartet: a new freedom in the organisation of the phrases, in the spatial and temporal relationships between the dancers and in the treatment of unison and counterpoint (Burrows, 2006b) increases the variety of the physical arrangements and is developed in opposition to the uniformity of the musical score, based on a single sound.

Battcock (1968: 26) wrote of minimalism that it is 'extremely complex': 'The artist has to create new notions of scale, space, containment, shape, and object. He must reconstruct the relationship between art as object and between object and man'. Nevertheless, in minimal art these notions were addressed individually, since 'composition is a less important factor than scale, light, colour, surface or shape, or relation to the environment' (Gablik, 1994: 252). Moreover, the relations between these elements were determined rationally, not experientially, seeing that 'the Minimalists shared with Mondrian the belief that a work of art should be completely conceived by the mind before its execution' (Gablik, 1994: 245). In contrast, Burrows' piece is the result of a laborious compositional process, of a negotiation between the different parts of the choreography and between the dance material and the other artistic media. Hulls' lighting, for instance 'a carpet of chequered light beams' (Brown, 1996b: 20), gives visual consistency to the idea underpinning the organisation of the movement and the overall choreographic arrangement. The geometrical light patterns projected on a black floor are an optical translation of the intersections between the other media. The lighting also creates correspondences with the dancers' foot patterns which are often organised in grid-like diagrams. Whereas in the filmic rendition the lighting design was static, in live performances the relationship between the bright lines and the darker background was constantly changing (Burrows, 2006b). In Roberts' film version, the dynamism of the lighting is replaced by frequent cuts and blackouts and by the movement of the camera, which 'pans left to right in a similar structure to the choreography' (Burrows, 2006b). Blackouts may coincide with pauses in the dance or in the music, but usually, these moments give the audience the chance to concentrate on the soundscape (or they give the sounds the opportunity to intervene more forcefully) and often the noise of footsteps can still be heard when the scene is blacked out, indicating that the dance is continuing in the dark, unseen.

In *The Stop Quartet*, minimalist concerns with rethinking the relationship between art and object and the self-referential and self-explanatory nature of the artwork are echoed in the way in which Burrows' stripped-down dance vocabulary triggers a re-mapping of movement in terms of shape, size, space and presence. The movements have a seemingly casual quality, while also intersecting with studied precision. Yet what comes across most clearly is the experiential dimension of dancing, its tangibility and materiality. The result is a finely textured dance, the complexity of which is enhanced by the interplay of media: *The Stop Quartet* is constructed around strata of movements, sounds and lighting patterns—and also camera framings in the film version of the piece. There is also a compelling attention to composition in the piece, which rearranges the focus that minimalism placed primarily on the whole, as made of simple, self-evident units, and transfers it to the intricacy of the relations that are created between the parts.

I suggest that in this work, Burrows returns to questions and principles of minimalism, while readdressing them and directing attention to the space in, around and beyond the whole of the dance—namely to the web of relations the dance entertains with the music, the lighting and the filming. In this sense, through its irreducible relationality and 'transcategoriality', the piece turns to what Osborne (2013) identifies as postconceptual concerns, which represent the condition for contemporary art. Discussing how the cultural and social situatedness of art is at the basis of art's critical potential as a practice capable of engaging with and distancing itself from the 'historical present', Osborne argues for a conceptualisation of contemporary art that '*activate[s]*' (Osborne, 2013: 113, original emphasis) the relationship with its critical premises: the 'object-based and medium-specific neo-avant-garde practices' that characterise minimalist and conceptual artworks (Osborne, 2013: 19).

The attention to the correlation between the parts of the composition and their coherence in *The Stop Quartet* signals both an engagement with and a critical distancing from minimalist approaches. In minimal music, for instance, strategies such as repetition and patterning, that is 'the repetitive use of short cells' (Mertens, 1983: 15), are not functional to the development of a consistent arrangement, but draw attention to individual notes and the effects that their (repeated) occurrence has on the listener. As the musicologist Wim Mertens (1983) argued, the use of reduced means, which can be read as an influence of ethnic music from India, Bali and West Africa, is one of the main attributes of minimal music. Here repetition is to be interpreted in opposition to how it is employed in classical music, where it 'is used in a pre-eminently *narrative* and *teleological* frame [...] so that a musical perspective emerges that gives the listener a non-ambivalent orientation and that attempts to inform him of *meaningful* musical *contents*' (Mertens, 1983: 16–17, original emphasis).

In the context of American minimalist works, which reject traditional musical principles of linear development, mimesis or expression of emotions, the use of repetitive patterns 'can be described as non-narrative and a-teleological' (Mertens, 1983: 17). Repetition presents and reiterates sounds as discrete entities, in a non-dialectical fashion in which 'the concept of *work* has been replaced by the notion of *process*, and [...] no one sound has any greater importance than any other' (Mertens, 1983: 88). In minimal music, dramatic substance, when perceived, emerges from pitches and rhythm, which are experienced as the sole event, thus resolving the form/content duality. As a consequence, 'structure is secondary to sound':

'with the removal of logical causality sound becomes autonomous, so that [...] no structure exists before sound: *it* is produced at each moment' (Mertens, 1983: 89, original emphasis). Within this framework, the listener plays an essential role in the production and experience of the music, and perception becomes 'an integral and creative part of the musical process' (Mertens, 1983: 90).

Burrows' *Stop Quartet* is instead held together by the precisely studied relationships between the elements of the choreography, which captures the attention of the spectator through its ordered, yet unpredictable, changes. Dichotomies, such as movement and stillness, music and silence, light and dark, are explored and deconstructed, challenging the viewers' perception of interruptions and continuities, chaos and order. This in-betweenness appears to be mirrored in the visual composition of the filmic images as well, where the dancers' figures are often dissected by the camera framing, which leaves parts of the bodies out of sight. This compositional choice implies an awareness of the impossibility of making sense of the work in its entirety and suggests that the arrangement of the different fragments and the discernment of the mutual effects that one element has on the others and in relation to the whole destabilises conventional patterns of signification and point to an affective register. While minimal music offers the listener an immediate experience of perception, Burrows' *Stop Quartet* engages the viewers in the paradoxical process of reception: the careful layering and progressive addition and subtraction of material imply the possibility of signification, which is nevertheless always eluded.

In interviews (Boxberger, 1996; Burrows, 2006b), Burrows refers to Gerhard Richter's paintings as a source of inspiration for the compositional method and conceptual rationale behind *The Stop Quartet*. In the German artist's abstract works created in the 1980s and 1990s, a technique consisting in applying cumulative layers of paint and then scraping off quantities of the pigment reveals the texture and history of the work. Similarly, in *The Stop Quartet*, the individual elements of the choreography—dance, music and lighting, with the addition of the film in the case of Roberts' version—expose each other through the gaps in the mesh created by their interlacing, like intersecting and overlapping brushstrokes. As Burrows explains,

it was Kevin Volans' idea to cut holes in the thing through which you can see or hear the work of the others. [...] You've got a fabric in which you cut holes. Through the holes in the dance you hear the music, see the lighting. The same thing goes for the music: through its gaps you see the dance and the lighting. And it's just the same with the lighting. (Burrows in Boxberger, 1996: 49)

Hence, the composition of the piece revolves around the intersection of the different media and the use of pauses, silences and blackouts in the choreographic, musical and visual sequences, creating a grid through which the other media are exposed. As Burrows describes it, the

> dance consists of various strata of activities, and over that there's the music which also presents a strata [*sic*] of activity within which there are further smaller levels, and then there's the lighting, yet another layer of activity that can be subdivided. Dance, music and light inhabit their own space-time continua and dance and music especially meet at the intersections, where the material alters. (Burrows in Boxberger, 1996: 48)

Correspondences between dynamic, acoustic and visual arrangements can be read throughout the piece. In the first part of the duet, for instance, moments of suspended activity and held poses in the choreography are as frequent as short pauses in the score of gentle piano notes and blackouts in the camera shots. This well-orchestrated alternation between movement and its suspension, sound and silence, vision and its absence generates a finely composed texture conveying an impression of overall balance between the different elements of the choreography. In the second part, the composition presents stronger accents and the impact of the different media on each other is sharper. Connections are never obvious, and the intersections between the shifts in the dynamic modes of the choreographic, musical and filmic sequences often generate indistinct moments in which the relationships between the different media fluctuate between intensification, dissonance and complementariness.

I contend that Burrows' engagement with processes of layering signals an understanding of the semantic openness of each and every work of dance, which stems from an attention towards the material and bodily relationality of choreography. Moreover, working with strata of activity, as Burrows describes above, implies a critical appreciation of choreography as an 'archival-corporeal system' (Lepecki, 2010: 37) and of the interplay of memory and forgetting that characterises artistic practice. Examining processes of linguistic persistence and disappearance, Heller-Roazen reflects on the inevitable mutability of language, drawing attention to how 'the present invariably contains the stratified residues' of the past (Heller-Roazen, 2005:

77). For Heller-Roazen, languages are composed of strata and move in a 'continuum' in which 'repetition and difference [...] grow indistinct' (Heller-Roazen, 2005: 87). In the archaeological complexity of languages, 'the obsolescent and the incipient, conservation and innovation, inevitably coexist' (Heller-Roazen, 2005: 86), with phenomena extending beyond the geographical and temporal boundaries of a community of speakers, to the extent that '[i]t is always possible to perceive in one form of speech the echo of another' (Heller-Roazen, 2005: 99). In historical terms, 'every language, moved by a music that resonates beyond its borders, translates itself "of its own accord" and passes "into another"' (Heller-Roazen, 2005: 177).

The idea of how an understanding of the archaeological condition of choreography may support the actualisation of an artistic community and contribute to a rethinking of the notions of collaboration and togetherness will be developed in Chapter 6. In the remainder of this chapter, I will discuss how, through an engagement with dance's physical traces, Burrows' choreography articulates a critical rethinking of minimal art's relationship with the real. In this sense, I contend that this kind of choreography offers a compelling vision of what minimalism might mean in twenty-first-century dance performance, through a po(i)etic practice that articulates a critico-historical response to its own artistic (aesthetic, ontological and political) premises.

DANCE AND THE REAL: OR THE PO(I)ETIC POTENTIAL OF 'SMALL THINGS'

A crucial function that minimalism fulfilled in twentieth-century art was to challenge conventional principles of conception and reception in order to expose the circumstances and conditions of the work. Critics of minimal art at the time of its development and affirmation saw in the conceptual shift it promoted a corruption of modernist art's strive towards the purity, separateness and absoluteness of its formal essence. Fried condemned minimal art for adopting a 'literalist' approach and thus showing the conventional nature of art. In his essay 'Art and Objecthood', Fried (1968) famously argued that minimal art exposed the 'objecthood' of the artworks, which modernist painters and sculptors had been trying to defeat by creating art that responded solely to its own internal rules. Minimalist works were thus essentially affected by an 'incurably theatrical' condition (Fried, 1968: 130). This turned the experience of art into a temporal event in which the viewers were lucidly aware of their position, of their relationship to the work and of the work's terms of presence.

However, the charge of theatricality was argued against by critics who emphasised instead the anti-illusionistic character of minimalist objects. Specifically, the American art critic and historian Hal Foster (1996: 37, 38), who sees in minimalism the genealogical antecedent of postmodernism, argues that 'minimalism breaks with the transcendental space of most modernist art' and places art 'among objects', thus redefining its place. For Foster (1996: 40), interpretations of minimalism that focus on its reductive attitude to materials and on its idealist, conceptual and abstract nature are a 'misreading' of its key principles. These were aimed at challenging modern art's dichotomies of abstract and real, subject and object, by drawing attention to the conventional nature of art and of its reception. Minimalism's self-reflectivity 'tends toward the epistemological more than the ontological, for it focuses on the perceptual conditions and conventional limits of art more than on its formal essence and categorical being' (Foster, 1996: 40). Examining the complex relationship of minimalism with reality and abstraction, Foster (1996: 38) observes: 'not only does minimalism reject the anthropomorphic basis of most traditional sculpture [...], but it also refuses the siteless realm of most abstract sculpture'. For Foster, what minimalism rejects is the illusionism intrinsic in both traditional and avant-garde art, which can be found in realist tendencies as much as in abstract ones.

The 'impulse to abandon illusion' is again the focus of Christian Grüny's more recent discussion of how contemporary art, from minimalism onwards, has been moved by a 'promise of reality'—a discussion which is still articulated in response to Fried's seminal argument:

When Michael Fried accused minimal art (or 'literalist art', as he called it) of theatricality because it created a situation in which artwork and spectator inhabited the same space, he failed to the [*sic*] see that this is not the situation of theater at all. Inevitably, theater is illusion and representation just like a picture or a sculpture, and to arrive at the immediacy of a real situation theatricality had to be abandoned as well. Tony Smith, Robert Morris and Donald Judd's objects were not theatrical but real, or in Judd's terms specific. From here it was a logical next step (of course there are always innumerable logical next steps, and their obviousness and necessity are only noted ex post) to get rid of objects and their stubborn permanence as well and resort to action plain and simple: no text, no pretext, no repetition, no permanence.

The immediacy of contact could be intensified by its fleetingness. (Grüny, 2017)

In this sense, Burrows' attention to the smallest units of movement and rejection of narrative elements evoke minimalist concerns. In *The Stop Quartet*, these are even more minute, raw elements than the task-like movements employed in minimalist dance: they are trajectories, shifts and rotations of parts of the body, with no literal reference to everyday activities. The piece troubles compositional strategies employed in previous works, where movement patterns more clearly exposed themes and subject matters—from the religious references in the early *Hymns* to the strongly connoted behaviour in *Stoics* (as discussed in Chapter 2). As Burrows explains, 'in *The Stop Quartet* I made a clear decision not to use any functional movements with a verbatim basis' (Burrows in Boxberger, 1996: 48). From the perspective of the creative process, the final structure of the work is not determined by an a priori concept but is arrived at through a continuous questioning of the choreographic material and the performers' physical experience of it. The smallest moves, from steps (the piece's most widely exploited physical element)[16] to arm trajectories, head rotations, simple gestures and yoga positions, were composed together by applying floor grids or constructing sequences based on changes of the level of the body in space, in random or chance-derived order (Burrows, 2006b). Furthermore, while the beat was determined by a metronome, the speed at which each dancer moved was often diversified, 'from single speed to double speed, to sometimes four times faster, to sometimes syncopated speed, and sometimes combinations of those' (Burrows, 2006b).

Yet the project of pursuing immediacy through the materiality of physical presence is inevitably confronted with the cultural particularity of the human body: 'the body is so overdetermined that anything you do to it or with it evokes a plethora of meanings, and references into all possible directions' (Grüny, 2017). The analysis of *The Stop Quartet* I have constructed in this chapter points to the inextricable tension between the promise of reality of a stripped-down movement vocabulary and the inevitably representative, yet ultimately impenetrable, character of embodied performance. More than that, what I suggest here is that Burrows has worked with this paradox to produce not only a critical rethinking of the minimalist model but also a choreographic language capable of engaging with the corporeal archaeology of dance—of tracing its microhistory. From the point of view of the bodily language of *The Stop Quartet*, if simple, basic elements are chosen as a starting point, this is done in order to discover their unexpected possibilities through their careful organisation in space and time. In this sense, Burrows' movement research troubles the distinction between reality and illusion, between neutrality and readability, between 'typicality' and 'exceptionality' (Peltonen, 2001)—which is ultimately the microhistorical project of rethinking the micro-macro link by investigating 'clues' and 'altering the scale of observation' (Levi, 1991: 97).

The relationship between the micro and the macro, between the particular event and its wider significance, is attended to throughout Burrows' body of work—as I discussed in Chapter 2 in relation to the notion of the 'minor', referring to artistic languages and practices in which the collective and the political resonate through the personal. Burrows' dance shares with the microhistorical method an 'attention to specific or singular phenomena', which often implies 'starting an investigation from something that does not quite fit, something odd that needs to be explained' (Peltonen, 2001: 349). It also implies a commitment to the materiality of *memory*, which for microhistorians speaks of the 'existence of things in themselves' (Renato Serra in Ginzburg, 1993: 29).

This productive tension between the individual and the collective is specifically manifested in his more recent pieces, which interweave more openly the personal with the political. In particular, as already highlighted in Chapter 2, Burrows and Fargion's 2014 duet *Body Not Fit for Purpose* juxtaposes explicit references to political issues with mundane details and childhood memories: incommensurable, yet entangled, worlds; emblems of an inability to comprehend the strings and mirrors that connect one sphere to the other. Yet the piece is an attempt at doing so (as, I argue, are all others); it responds to a desire 'to make sense of the present and of my politics' (Burrows, 2015: 84). Through gestural sequences, musical phrases and, occasionally, song or speech introduced by laconic titles, private events are cited alongside, or in entanglement with, major international politics headlines, all along acknowledging that the dancing body is an inadequate vehicle to discuss important issues. The Arab-Israeli conflict gets a mention alongside the recycling rules for organic waste. Burrows' artist pages published on *Performance Research*, written in the third person, address the paradox of this duet: 'He is fully aware that his gestures are essentially unable to express / his anger about the neoliberal economy, / his fears for the planet and his inability to process the complexities of the Middle-East' (Burrows, 2015: 81).

For microhistorians such as Ginzburg and Carlo Levi, a 'peculiar event or phenomenon is taken as a sign of a larger, but hidden or unknown, structure' (Peltonen, 2001: 349). In developing this line of thinking, I also wish to consider where Burrows' practice might diverge from the micro-historical perspective, since his choreography's attention to the minutiae of movement is articulated on the plane of immanence, as a way of thinking/practising in which the historicity of choreography is manifested in the materiality of the dance itself and in the viewers' experience of it. While premised on a clear working method based on compositional principles, Burrows' choreography assumes the undermining of its underlying conceptual structure as an integral part of the creative process. Despite its strong reliance on a working method articulated around principles, it both upholds and defies the idea that a structure might be found or followed. For Burrows (2010a: 2), '[a] principle is not a rule, it's just a way to take care of some of the decisions, leaving you free to do what you do best, which is to be intuitive'. Ultimately, the principles the work is founded upon boil down to repetition, to archaeology: 'a daily practice – make something each day' (Burrows, 2015: 81).

On the process of making *Body Not Fit for Purpose*, Burrows (2015: 82) writes:

> It was odd to see how everything was altered depending on where you put it, so the mathematical sense of structure faded away and instead you had this impression that information was being teased out and placed in the right order, so you could read it. And what appeared readable one day seemed impenetrable the next, so it was only by repeated glimpses at odd moments that you could finally decide what spoke loudest.

In Burrows' own account of his choreographic process, there is the acknowledgement of glimpses of readability occurring through the creative labour; there is the possibility of signification, which is nevertheless always eluded, always undone. I would advance that every new work is an attempt at dealing with the unattainable goal—the 'unfinished business', as Burrows and Fargion so often call it when speaking about their practice—of making sense of the world through performance, through music and dance, through the body. So then perhaps, in Burrows' dance, the larger, unknown picture that the microhistorical model seeks to delineate does not point towards transcendence but rather towards the future or at least towards a particular future. And perhaps it is in this 'utopian' project that

Burrows' work is closest to the microhistorical method, since, as Osborne reminds us, 'history (like art) is inherently utopian. This is something that ties art to history. It is beyond the scope of all actually existing social subjects. It projects collectivity beyond all actually existing forms' (Osborne 2013: 194). It is in this utopia, I contend, that the po(i)etic force and the political potential of the work unfold.

In *Body Not Fit for Purpose*, political positioning is made explicit through references to big socio-economical issues, blurring the distinction between the micro and the macro. Similarly, the simplification of scenic elements is counterbalanced by abundant textual references to complex content in a way that confounds the two dimensions polarised by minimalism: less and more. In this respect, if Burrows' body of work shares a 'reductionist' approach with other European choreographic experiments, in which Lepecki (2004) reads the articulation of a critique of spectatorship, I argue that in Burrows' choreography, the questioning of normative codes does not lead to a dismissal of reference principles, but rather to a critical engagement with them and to their productive interruption. In the case of *Body Not Fit for Purpose*, the dramaturgy combines order and chaos: it follows a regular structure, which nevertheless embeds 'sudden change' within a repetitive sequence (Burrows, 2015: 81). 'Passing through a place of joyful immersion, then emptiness and the slow emergence of a song, grunted under the breath, holding the body in its rhythm' (Burrows, 2015: 82), it offers a critical restaging of the concerns of minimalism and frustrates the distinction between reduction and excess. I suggest that po(i)etic implications can arise from a reductive aesthetics and a 'microscopic' attention to the details of movement and that an affirmative response is articulated through the personal and idiosyncratic references woven in the dance.

To conceptualise the potentialities opened by this engagement with small, local things, I invoke Gianni Vattimo's theorisation of 'nihilism as emancipation',[17] which acknowledges that, in an increasingly multifaceted society, the awareness of the finitude, locality and temporality of our condition is central to our ability to experience freedom and overcome disorientation. A prominent voice in Italian political theory and best known as a philosopher of postmodernity and theorist of 'weak thought', Vattimo is not widely discussed in Anglophone debates. The foundations of his philosophy lie predominantly in Heidegger's hermeneutics and in Nietzsche's nihilism. Vattimo (2009: 20) conceives nihilism as 'the dissolution of all ultimate foundations', a condition for the attainment of emancipation on a collective level. Discussing Vattimo's concept of freedom, James Martin (2010: 334, 335) reflects on how Vattimo's idea of freedom does not equate to 'self-mastery' and does not imply unlimited subjective choice; rather, it goes hand in hand with 'a sense of contingency' and the acknowledgement of 'our own finitude'. Vattimo expresses it as follows: 'To live in this pluralistic world means to experience freedom as a continual oscillation between belonging and disorientation' (Vattimo cited in Martin, 2010: 335).

In this sense, the insistence on a peculiar, local, often vernacular choreographic and dramaturgical language in Burrows' oeuvre points towards the possibility of freedom and emancipation. In Vattimo's terms, 'disorientation' is counterbalanced in Burrows' work by clear 'assertions of belonging' (Martin, 2010: 335), through which his dances connect with the 'historicity' and 'contingency' of our own reality (Vattimo quoted in Martin, 2010: 334). Furthermore, the device of repetition, which so distinctly characterises Burrows' art (intended here as his choreography as well as his writing), becomes the dispositif through which the work's emancipatory, utopian, po(i)etic experience is actualised in its historical sense, as a means of connecting past, present and future. Intervening between disorientation and belonging, repetition (in dance as much as in language) traces a thread that connects the contingent moment with the memory of a past and, in doing so, envisions a future—the utopian, po(i)etic project of emancipation and freedom. Burrows writes about this, reflecting on the role that repetition plays in his creative practice. In an article that 'copies' another, earlier one (Burrows and Ritsema, 2003), repeating its structure, Burrows (2015: 82) observes:

> When we repeat our own history like this, we are trying to make sense of the past and also to hold the future steady. We do this although we know there is no sense to be made, and no steadiness to be borrowed, but we are overwhelmed by possibilities and this repetition is sometimes all we have to guide ourselves by.

In his dances, as in his writing, there is a sense of an oscillation between holding on and losing, *preserving* and *squandering*. Burrows (2015: 83, original emphasis) quotes Bruno Latour on the idea of the *repetition of renewal*,[18] which in confounding sameness and difference registers a generative gap: 'The *repetition of harping on the same old thing* is opposed by the *repetition of renewal*: the first seems faithful but isn't, the second seems unfaithful, yet it alone preserves the treasure that the other squanders while believing it's preserving it'. It is in the light of this condition of *same but not similar*[19] that I construe Burrows' dance as a practice that, in its encounter with the minutiae of the everyday and in its reuse of the past, is characterised by productive incompleteness; it performs a jump; it creates a hole, in which a utopian, po(i)etic—and political—possibility of imagining freedom and a future is materialised. It is in this incommensurability between preserving and squandering, between repeating and changing, between remembering and forgetting that the dis/appearance of meaning and structure in Burrows' dances—the gaps and holes in the dramaturgical texture of *The Stop Quartet*, the empty moments and inadequate gestures in *Body Not Fit for Purpose*, for instance—comes closer to fulfilling the promise of reality of the minimalist project.

I maintain that Burrows' work acknowledges the critical legacy of its formalist and conceptual premises, while also continuing to grapple with their underlying questions, searching for a solution that works for him, for today and for the art form he operates within. Burrows' choreography offers a historically situated rethinking of minimalism and of the formalist dance tradition. It also takes as its inevitable starting point the specificity of the artistic discipline he works with, which, even in the postconceptual 'expansion to infinity of the possible material forms of art' (Osborne, 2013: 48), still predominantly relies on its main medium: the human body. If the '*withdrawal* of artistic subjectivity' is what conceptual and minimalist processes were premised on, as resulting from 'the use of formal numerical rules (rather than poetic intuition)' (Osborne, 2013: 66, original emphasis), Burrows is critically and urgently aware of what it means to work out a path between or beyond these opposing forces and 'end up somehow stuck between the two': 'and yet it is perhaps in this place that the real work begins' (Burrows, 2014: 85).

> For this most immaterial and impermanent of art forms in an increasingly disposable global art market, no structure, score, improvisation, material, image, movement or idea can ever matter enough to argue. In this we begin and end with the image of a human being walking onstage to endure, resist and confront an audience, whose discomfort reveals something to us about our own uncertainty and bloody-mindedness in the world. And that is enough for me, whether or not the piece has a beginning or an end, and regardless of whether the middle is structured or not. (Burrows, 2014: 86)

It is in this contending with inadequacy, in this accepting incompleteness as a potentially generative condition, that I see the affirmative potential of Burrows' rethinking of the formalist tradition. The final section of this chapter looks more specifically at the interplay of remembering and forgetting that characterises Burrows' choreography, interrogating how this paradoxical, productive, po(i)etic historicity is actualised in the material and affective dimension of the dance.

CHOREOGRAPHY'S 'RETROACTIVE ONTOLOGY': REMAKING THE SAME PIECE

In his recent writing, Burrows reflects on the material and affective dimension of dance memories; the dancing body is described as an 'unstable' place where a negotiation between 'familiar movement' and detours to untravelled 'backroads' takes place (Burrows, 2017). He writes that the memory of a movement (from his own dancing or from somebody else's) is like a recognisable taste in his mouth and observes: 'when a familiar movement rears up in the fog [...] I swerve to avoid it' (Burrows, 2017). In a talk written for Tanzkongress (held in Düsseldorf in 2013) entitled 'Rebelling Against Limit',[20] he considers the role that the remains of the past play in both the reception of a work of dance and the embodied performance of it. He talks about how the 'echo of performance', 'the residual shape of other films, musical phrases, patterns of words, rhythms, sounds, half-forgotten dances and the detritus of bits and pieces of broken images and logic' influence our understanding of the piece we are watching: 'These traces of buried form sing, speak, dance, think, feel and act alongside every performance we watch, whether we want them there or not, manifesting themselves within our own physical memory to direct, re-order and anticipate at sensory-level the flow of what we are seeing' (Burrows, 2014: 81). Here Burrows (2014: 82) maps correspondences between formal concerns and bodily experiences, reflecting on how embodiment moves 'beyond' form and ultimately 'becomes [...] its own form':

> The body is also sometimes called a score, being that repository of memory and possibility at cellular level which holds within itself a map of where you've been and might yet go: the body as an archive of trace elements, configuring and re-configuring themselves on the border between the private and that which is communicated.

The distinction between score and perception, between the structural and the affective, is troubled by the consideration that, through the process of making and the process of receiving a work of dance, 'the organizational part gives way eventually to this sensory realm' (Burrows, 2014: 82). This is where Burrows (2014: 83) sees the 'transformative shift' triggered by dance—but also by music and poetry—'[b]y reconnecting familiar images or language in new and startling ways'. He considers how the process of making performance work entails negotiating between knowing and not knowing, navigating through 'gaps' between possible connections, experiencing uncertainty and loss of control in dealing with fragments and attending to layers, 'wrestling with [...] traces of meanings': a 'journey' which, on some level, is shared or mirrored by the spectators or 'witnesses' of the performance, who are called to 'kni[t] their sense of the unfolding piece' (Burrows, 2014: 84, 85). Burrows' language in this talk is vivid and involved: as he attempts to grapple with the paradoxical forces at play in making and viewing performance, he adopts a register that sets this text apart from his customarily concise prose. There is a sense of urgency in laying bare the emotional side of what is ultimately an unfathomable process, in recording the affective states the experience of making performance work travels through: the 'exhausted' patience, the 'frustration', the 'disorientation', the 'desire' for a resolution and the 'lack of faith' in it (Burrows, 2014: 85).[21] In this respect, the recalling of familiar images that Burrows' pieces enact is not a simple repetition of available material; instead, it is grounded on a reflection—both critical and affective—on their relevance in the historical present and in relation to the singular conditions of his (and Fargion's) practice.

While a vast part of this chapter has focused on *The Stop Quartet* and, in a less detailed manner, on *Body Not Fit for Purpose*, a wider look at Burrows' body of work highlights traces of minimalism in the layering of 'familiar images' that compose his dances.[22] For instance, making *The Quiet Dance* with Fargion, which is a piece premised on the idea of walking, Burrows was concerned about the viability of this starting point, as walking is a performative practice already used in minimalist dance[23]:

> we had always had a longing to make a piece which used walking. This always seemed impossible to do because that piece belongs to minimalism. But this time we talked about it a lot, we agonised about it and we decided that it was time that we had to risk that. Partly because we wanted to make another performance together where we both moved, and walking is something that

Matteo, as an untrained dancer, has; it's his as much as it's mine. Having said that, the odd thing is – we are now in the last two weeks of working on the performance and I got up very early this morning, I looked at the tape we have been recording in rehearsals and suddenly I was very struck by the fact that, in a way, it's not that you see walking. It's become something entirely of its own. […] In some ways, I think of this performance now as being an attempt to make the piece that lies just underneath all the other pieces we have ever made. And that's why we called it *The Quiet Dance*. (Burrows in Perazzo, 2005: 3)

If walking was for Burrows and Fargion a memory of minimalist dance, ultimately its remembering seems to result in its disappearance or rather in a generative reframing of its trace. Following Heller-Roazen's discussion of the ways in which languages can persist through their vanishing, I point to how 'the "remainder" first emerges, so to speak, in the process of remaining, and it remains, for this reason, utterly unlike that to which it bears witness' (Heller-Roazen, 2005: 126). The active recollection of the performative practice of walking in *The Quiet Dance* leads to the realisation of the malleable, changeable ontology of dance, which, as all culturally and historically specific idioms, is subject to inevitable mutation. If dance—like language—persists over time, whether or not it is practised/spoken, 'it does not remain itself. It may last, but only as another' (Heller-Roazen, 2005: 127). As I have suggested elsewhere,[24] the walking in *The Quiet Dance* comes to epitomise a journeying through life, which is as much an unfolding of personal events as it is a traversing of the historicity of the medium. Through the entanglement of remembering and/as forgetting that the language and labour of choreography entail, the formalist movement tradition *remains* in Burrows' dance as something other—as the catalyst that mobilises affective and intensive signification, thus undermining the exclusion of subjectivity from the artistic process predicated by minimalism. As Chapter 5 further argues drawing on Roberto Esposito's notion of the impersonal, subjectivity is articulated in this and other works by Burrows (and, so often, Fargion) by unsettling conventional understandings of how the personal may be constructed choreographically—which implies a reimagining of the boundaries of the subject through relationality and plurality.

Another attempt at 'remaking' minimalism is Burrows' first duet with Fargion, *Both Sitting Duet*, which, as already mentioned in Chapter 2, is a gestural transcription of Morton Feldman's 1982 piece *For John Cage*.[25]

Summarising the creative process, Burrows (2002: 28) points to the inter-play between appearance and disappearance, remembering and forgetting:

> we [...] decided to look for something that we could place between us as a starting point. [...] We looked at texts, movies, music and concepts. In the end we found nothing and we decided that we would [...] work for a week and see what happened. On the first day, Matteo walked in and he said, 'I've found the thing that we were looking for and it's so obvious that we couldn't see it.' He pulled out the score of a piece of music by Morton Feldman, [...] which Matteo and I had both been obsessed with about seven or eight years ago.

Repetition clearly informs the making of the duet, since transcribing a musical score into a choreography involves reproduction. Yet a transla-tion is never an exact copy of an original and always assumes an element of adaptation and unfolds through unplanned and often unintended changes. One of the unexpected effects of the translation of *For John Cage* into *Both Sitting Duet* is related to the mood and atmosphere of the work. While working on the choreography, Burrows and Fargion were surprised to see that what they had always considered as a 'hovering, rocking, quiet' piece of music was transforming through their gestural execution into a 'more jolly and folkdancey' work (Burrows cited in Hutera, 2003). Commenting on this unexpected shift, Fargion said: 'We were not following the mood, but using the score as a map' (Cripps, 2004). I suggest that the duet exem-plifies Burrows and Fargion's idea of composition as the labour of layering remembered and/as forgotten material.[26]

At some level, the piece is a self-referential dance, made of patterns of hand movements, composed according to musical principles. However, through the act itself of translation and in the choreomusical collaboration the piece develops, the work acknowledges difference and dialogue as cru-cial components of the creative process. Variations are introduced in the choreographic score to simplify or complicate gestural patterns. Changes are also made to the musical score, by altering Feldman's regular tempo and breaking its 'monolithic' uniformity (Fargion, 2005). In this sense, the work can be seen to belong to a category of translations that Wal-ter Benjamin describes in *The Task of The Translator* (written in 1921) as 'more than transmissions of subject matter': translations in which 'the life of the originals attains its latest, continually renewed, and most complete unfolding' (Benjamin, 1996: 255). By exploring the modalities and codes of dance in relation to those of music, the piece also becomes a reflection on the dynamics between two people, a dancer and a musician, on their friendship and ways of collaborating. In doing so, the work unsettles conventional strategies of signification and questions the distinction between meaning and absence of meaning.

Another, lesser-known, example of a 'translation' of a minimalist work is the duo's reinterpretation of Reich's *Clapping Music* via the version of it that Burrows and Fargion performed at the Greenwich Dance Agency in 2006 during a programme called 'The Small Dance'.[27] In this five-minute stage intervention, which has the economy of means of Burrows and Fargion's duets, the two artists face the audience from behind a microphone and a music stand holding a score and engage with the contrapuntal dynamics of Reich's clapping piece. In Reich's score, the two pairs of hands begin clapping in unison but, while one player performs an unchanging rhythmic pattern, the other regularly moves forward by one beat, until the unison is restored (Reich, 2002). In email he sent me, Burrows (2006a) commented on his and Fargion's interpretation of the work:

> we like it because we are interested in counterpoint, and particularly in the effect that the sharing of a counterpoint has on the performers in a live context. This means the way in which each performer has to give up something of themselves to the music which arrives between the two players, or dance in the case of dance. Having said that, it's important to say that the way in which *Clapping Music* operates isn't how Matteo and I do things. *Clapping Music* is quite conceptual, in that it's a single idea worked out as a pattern that begins and goes through a series of logical changes until it works itself out and returns to its beginning. What we try to do, however, is to work free of logical patternings and follow rather intuitive decisions. In this way, we're influenced more by Morton Feldman.

Burrows' work, as is illustrated by this piece as much as by his entire oeuvre, is preoccupied with the paradox of negotiating the tension between structure and intuition; as such, it exemplifies a crucial concern of contemporary art—intended, with Osborne (2013), as art conceived from the postconceptual condition of being constituted by concepts which find articulation through diverse material forms and across different instantiations. As 'translations' of past works of art (music or dance), these pieces disrupt the historical unity of the 'original' scores, shifting their borders and intervening in their 'afterlife'. Freed from the constraints of fixed historical boundaries, the minimalist works that Burrows revives are also exposed to the possibility of becoming methodologically and semantically malleable. In allowing intuition to play with the predetermined conceptual and compositional structure, they open to the unknown and to the affective experience—a po(i)etic intervention—occurring in the process of making, performing and receiving the piece.

A similar 'openness to new possibilities that are not yet understood' (Burt, 2017: 162) is detected by Burt in his analysis of *Cheap Lecture* (2009), Burrows and Fargion's translation of John Cage's *Lecture on Nothing* (1949). In Burrows' (2010b) own words, the piece is 'the product of a pleasurable negotiation with the given form', which replicates the 'micro-macrocosmic structure' of Cage's score, composed of smaller and larger units and their repetitions:

> *Cheap Lecture* follows this micro-macrocosmic structure, replacing Cage's words with new words and adding a layer of piano music, most of which is drawn from Schubert. The words and music are counterpointed throughout the performance by 139 projected words and phrases.

In Burt's (2017: 161, 162) discussion of the work, Burrows and Fargion's *Cheap Lecture* 'sets up a dialogue between Cage's philosophy and their own. […] They in effect secularise Cage's mysticism while testing his structural principles to breaking point'. In rethinking the process of translation as an interrogation of the cultural situatedness of the original from the standpoint of a differently determined present, *Cheap Lecture* is offered to the audience as a redoing of the past that, in recalling it, also foregrounds its distance. It is construed as a performance of *same but not similar*, which nevertheless, in highlighting relationality, overcomes the self-referentiality of the formalist tradition opening instead to plurality and co-presence.[28]

As I have argued elsewhere,[29] in Burrows' choreography signification occurs in the crevices generated by the strata of activity and the layers of material, in the rigorous formalisation of content and in the odd, at times absurd,[30] subjectivisation of the form. It is perhaps because of this urgent awareness of the complexity of the task, of the paradoxical tension between structure and intuition that presents itself with every new process of creation, that Burrows often talks about how his pieces are ultimately all the same work.[31] He made this remark, for instance, in an interview I conducted with him on the occasion of the revival of *The Stop Quartet* in 2008,[32] which followed the first trilogy of duets with Fargion:

I wanted to revisit *The Stop Quartet* because essentially it's the same piece as the three duets I made more recently with Matteo Fargion. It shares with them the same love of counterpoint, the same structural games, the same duration, the same joy of rhythm and pulse and the same ideas of openness in performance. (Burrows, 2008)

The piece was revived for two nights at Kaaitheater in Brussels (where I saw it) with the original cast of performers. For Burrows, it was an opportunity to rethink the 'formality' of his earlier, more 'conventional' dance pieces within the context of his later interest in more 'human' and 'intimate' ways of performing (Burrows, 2008).

Through the multiple instantiations of recurring concerns, Burrows' works articulate their 'distributive' and stratified character, demonstrating their 'retroactive ontology' (Osborne, 2013) as open-ended choreographies that exist through repeated occurrences and across varying formats. By virtue of their own relationality and malleability, Burrows' dances attain critical function and transformative potential in relation to their historical conditions: while traces of minimalism are found as fragments among the layers of the dances, the works exist as dialectical processes rather than fixed objects and, as such, defy closed categorisations. I see Burrows' choreography as an archaeological, microhistorical practice that simultaneously remembers and forgets the overlapping layers of its artistic past: historical traces are pulled out, examined and exposed alongside other choices, other decisions; familiar fragments alternate with new ways, working out continuities as well as gaps and inviting a questioning attitude from the spectators.

What stands out most distinctively are the layering and stratified nature of the works. The dances discussed in this chapter are representative of a practice which acknowledges that the past lingers into the present and potentially already prefigures a future. They conceive of signification as occurring through processes of recognition, association and displacement; they feed on dialogue and on experiences of coming together—with other artistic voices as much as with instances of the dance medium's experienced/witnessed past. This suggests that a reading of the traces left by minimalism in Burrows' work might be enhanced by ideas of history as archaeology, of self-referentiality as relationality and of presence as co-presence. The present of Burrows' dances is a paradoxical time, which is both a now and an again, a temporality inscribed with the past, which is qualified by its relationship and coexistence with what remains and what disappears.

NOTES

1. See, for instance, Dougill (1988), Percival (1995, 2003–2004) and Craine (1998).
2. On the ephemerality of performance, see Phelan (1993). On the notion of engaging performance as what remains, see especially Schneider (2011).
3. The idea of the afterlife of works of art and dance is construed in Osborne (2013) and Lepecki (2010), respectively, following Walter Benjamin's notion of the afterlife of objects as crucial to a materialistic understanding of history.
4. See the call for papers for the conference 'Minimalism: Location Aspect Moment' 14–15 October 2016, University of Southampton/Winchester School of Art (https://minimalism2016blog.wordpress.com).
5. For a historical account of the Judson Dance Theater and for a definition of the term 'analytic', which refers to the 1970s phase of American postmodern dance, following the 1960s 'breakaway' period, see Banes (1987).
6. Rainer states: 'Although the benefit to be derived from making a one-to-one relationship between aspects of so-called minimal sculpture and recent dancing is questionable, I have drawn up a chart that does exactly that' (Rainer, 1974: 63).
7. For an overview and analysis of Butcher's oeuvre, see Butcher and Melrose (2005).
8. Beside *The Stop Quartet*, Volans composed music for *Blue Yellow* (1995), a dance film by Adam Roberts commissioned and danced by Sylvie Guillem; *Walking/music* (1997) for William Forsythe's Ballett Frankfurt; and *Things I Don't Know* (1998), comprising a solo danced by Burrows and a duet danced by Dana Fouras and Ragnhild Olsen.
9. About a dozen newspaper reviews and approximately as many journal articles from the 1990s.
10. Forsythe's interest in Burrows' work also led to a direct collaboration with him, since 'Burrows made a variant of his masterly *The Stop Quartet* for Ballett Frankfurt', resulting in the 1997 piece *Walking/music* (Brown, 2003: 19). Burrows' own account (2006b) reports that the choreography for Ballett Frankfurt was commissioned by Forsythe after he saw his earlier piece *Very*. Burrows observed that he was not satisfied with the piece he created for Forsythe's ensemble and said that he considers it as 'a pale imitation of *The Stop Quartet*' (2006b), in that he tried to work on the same ideas that underpin the 1996 piece but without achieving the same organic interrelation between methodological principles and their practical application.

11. Roberts created films of most of Burrows' pieces from the 1990s to the early 2000s; the films were assembled in a collection released in DVD format, offering a retrospective of ten years of Burrows' work (Roberts, 2004). For a review of this audio-visual collection, see Perazzo (2006). Roberts' film of *The Stop Quartet* is also now accessible online (https://www.youtube.com/view_play_list?p=55DA3E23BEDC5F8E), via Burrows' own website (Burrows, n.d.). Another available document of *The Stop Quartet* is a recording of a live performance which took place at Laban, London, in 1996, held by the Laban Library and Archive (Burrows, 1996). While this video is a useful record of the performance, and possibly the only live recording of the piece publicly accessible, I have used Roberts' film as my main source, since its release in DVD format and online makes it more widely available.

12. Roberts' films 'complement qualities and characteristics of the live choreographies, interpreting them through the specificity of the filming medium' (Perazzo, 2006: 45).

13. By adopting the term 'postconceptual', I am stepping into the contentious territory of the naming of the wave of innovative dance work created in Europe since the 1990s. The term 'conceptual dance' associated with this composite scene has been object of debate in both artistic and critical settings. An example of this is the roundtable discussion entitled 'Not Conceptual' curated by Burrows, with the choreographers Jérôme Bel and Xavier Le Roy and the dramaturg and dance theorist Bojana Cvejić, as part of the 'Parallel Voices' season of public talks and events at Siobhan Davies Studios (London, 22 February 2007, http://www.siobhandavies.com/watch-listen/2007/10/03/test/). In the course of their conversation, the speakers remarked on the ambiguity of the term 'conceptual dance', with Cvejić describing it as a 'misnomer'. About the legacy of critical and analytical definitions of conceptual art, specifically in relation to Bel's choreographic work, see also Siegmund (2017). Nevertheless, it is important to note that Osborne uses the term 'postconceptual' as a critical category rather than as a tool for a periodic classification based on formal or stylistic features. With this term, he indicates the 'geo-politically reflective art of the historical present' (Osborne, 2013: 176). Moreover, in the specific domain of dance scholarship, the legacy of conceptual art on contemporary European choreography is acknowledged by Lepecki (2004) in his pioneering survey and theorisation of the work produced within this experimental scene.

14. Small sections of the analysis of *The Stop Quartet* offered in this chapter have been reworked from my earlier publication: see Perazzo Domm (2012).

15. See also Van Imshoot (2005).

16. 'The most basic ingredient was a step, and you could in effect call the piece "The Step Quartet", because [...] that's almost all the material, it's just a series of steps' (Burrows, 2006b).

17. See especially Vattimo (2003, 2009).

18. As elaborated in *Rejoicing: Or The Torments of Religious Speech* (Latour, 2013: 72, 73).
19. Here I pick up on Burrows' reference to Latour (2013: 73).
20. The talk was given as part of the 'Misery of Form' event (8 June 2013); see http://www.tanzkongress.de/tanzkongress2013/en/subjects/choreographic-methods.html#event-52-0. The text of the talk is published in Noémie Solomon's edited collection *Danse: An Anthology* (2014). The talk has also been performed as a lecture concert with Fargion.
21. More of this affective engagement transpires from an even more recent text, entitled 'Traces' and written for the catalogue of Siobhan Davies' *material/rearranged/to/be* (The Curve, Barbican, London, January 2017).

> Whenever I dance I'm confronted by who I used to want to be,
> and the future wish I had for myself returns as history
> and I wrestle with it.
> And it's from this place of negotiation with what never was
> that choreographic decisions get made.
> And the desire to strip dance back to a disinterested mode,
> is born partly out of this refusal to succumb
> to the overwhelming sense of lost and wished for self
> that floods us when we dance.
> And the mass of barely readable emotions.
> And the flickering references.
> And the mad sensitivity of skin.
> And the stumbling we call gravity.
> And the terrible self-consciousness.

>   (Burrows, 2017)

22. A further project, in which Burrows reworks minimalist traces is *52 Portraits*, devised with Fargion and the film-maker Hugo Glendinning, which echoes minimalism in the seriality of its structure. This was a digital project which ran for the 52 weeks of 2016 through the weekly online release of a video portrait of a dance or performance artist. For a discussion of this work, see Chapters 5 and 6.
23. For further discussion on *The Quiet Dance*, see Chapter 5. A conceptualisation of how Burrows rethinks and retraces the choreographic past in *The Quiet Dance* and in *Speaking Dance* can be found in Perazzo Domm (2010).
24. In an earlier article, I discuss how *The Quiet Dance* and other pieces by Burrows articulate subjectivity by deconstructing conventional binaries of form/content, personal/impersonal (Perazzo Domm, 2012).
25. Aspects of *Both Sitting Duet* are examined further in the following chapters: Chapter 4 reflects on how the piece rethinks rhythm and/as friendship,

and Chapter 5 offers further discussion of how it articulates subjectivity and plurality. For a detailed analysis of the work, see my earlier publication, Perazzo Domm (2008), which this chapter reworks and continues.

26. Other recognisable images which make up the archaeological strata of the piece are collective memories of pioneering works of contemporary dance (e.g. the idea of a gestural piece performed from a seated position found in De Keersmaeker's *Rosas Danst Rosas*) and fragments of Burrows' ballet past (via a section in which he performs ballet arm positions to Fargion's slow rhythmical clapping).

27. 'The Small Dance' was a programme of short and small dances hosted by the Greenwich Dance Agency, London, on 15 July 2006, as part of London's Big Dance festival. Burrows and Fargion performed *Clapping Music* on a few other occasions (including at Kaaitheater in Brussels in October 2006).

28. In Burt's reading, what is ultimately construed through this work is a performance of friendship that performs relationality as conceived 'from a position of difference' (Burt, 2017: 159).

29. See, for instance, Perazzo Domm (2012).

30. Burrows talks about 'absurdity' in the text 'Rebelling Against Limit', placing its occurrence in the process of composing familiar images in innovative ways, which requires the audience to navigate the continuities and the gaps between layers: 'The moments of too great a leap teeter on a knife edge between sudden understanding or liberation, and the snapping shut of that string of consequent thought, image or emotion we've been following' (Burrows, 2014: 85).

31. I will touch upon this point again in Chapter 5, when discussing how subjectivity is articulated in Burrows' pieces. I have also made reference to the repeated occurrence of themes and concerns in Burrows' body of work in an earlier article: see Perazzo Domm (2010).

32. The piece was performed at Kaaitheater in Brussels on 10 and 11 October 2008 (https://www.kaaitheater.be/en/agenda/the-stop-quartet). The interview I conducted with Burrows on revisiting the piece was used for the programme notes for the performance (and is also available here: http://www.jonathanburrows.info/#/text/?id=51&t=content).

References

[Anon] (1997) 'Dance', *The Independent*, 12 April.

Banes, Sally (1987) *Terpsichore in Sneakers: Post-modern Dance*, 2nd edn. Middletown: Wesleyan University Press.

Battcock, Gregory (ed.) (1968) *Minimal Art: A Critical Anthology*. New York: E. P. Dutton.

Benjamin, Walter (1996) 'The Task of the Translator', in Marcus Bullock and Michael W. Jennings (eds.) *Walter Benjamin: Selected Writings. Volume 1, 1913–1926*. Cambridge, MA: Belknap Press of Harvard University Press: 253–263.

Boxberger, Edith (1996) 'Liberating the Imagination: Jonathan Burrows in Conversation with Edith Boxberger', *Ballett International/Tanz Aktuell*, 12: 46–49.

Bräuninger, Renate (2014) 'Structure as Process: Anne Teresa de Keersmaeker's *Fase* (1982) and Steve Reich's Music', *Dance Chronicle*, 37 (1): 47–62.

Brindle, Reginald Smith (1987) *The New Music: The Avant-garde Since 1945*, 2nd edn. Oxford: Oxford University Press.

Brown, Ismene (1996a) 'Doing a Jig of Funny Walks', *Daily Telegraph*, 29 May.

Brown, Ismene (1996b) 'One Step Beyond', *Daily Telegraph*, 22 October: 20.

Brown, Ismene (1996c) 'Old and New Under One Umbrella', *Daily Telegraph*, 25 October.

Brown, Ismene (1997) 'Starlife: Jonathan Burrows, the Choreographer with a Different View of Beauty', *The Telegraph Magazine*, 24 May: 74.

Brown, Ismene (2003) 'The Vanishing Man of British Dance', *The Daily Telegraph*, 13 October: 19.

Burrows, Jonathan (1996) *The Stop Quartet*, video-recording of performance and post-performance talk, 1 May, London: Laban.

Burrows, Jonathan (2002) 'Playing the Game Harder', *Dance Theatre Journal*, 18 (4): 25–29.

Burrows, Jonathan (2006a) Unpublished email exchange with Daniela Perazzo Domm, 13 August.

Burrows, Jonathan (2006b) Unpublished conversation with Daniela Perazzo Domm, London, 7 September.

Burrows, Jonathan (2008) Unpublished conversation with Daniela Perazzo Domm, Brussels, 10 September.

Burrows, Jonathan (2010a) *A Choreographer's Handbook*. London and New York: Routledge.

Burrows, Jonathan (2010b) 'About the Score for *Cheap Lecture*'. http://www.jonathanburrows.info/#/score/?id=2&t=content. Accessed 10 April 2018.

Burrows, Jonathan (2014) 'Rebelling Against Limit', in Noémie Solomon (ed.) *Danse: An Anthology*. Dijon: Les Presses du Réel: 81–87.

Burrows, Jonathan (2015) 'Body Not Fit for Purpose', *Performance Research*, 20 (5): 81–86.

Burrows, Jonathan (2017) 'Traces'. http://www.jonathanburrows.info/#/text/?id=193&t=content. Accessed 10 April 2018.

Burrows, Jonathan (n.d.) *Jonathan Burrows*. http://www.jonathanburrows.info/. Accessed 20 December 2018.

Burrows, Jonathan and Etchells, Tim (2004) Unpublished public talk moderated by Adrian Heathfield, London, Riverside Studios, 3 November.

Burrows, Jonathan and Ritsema, Jan (2003) 'Weak Dance Strong Questions', *Performance Research*, 8 (2): 28–33.

Burt, Ramsay (2003) 'Memory, Repetition and Critical Intervention', *Performance Research*, 8 (2): 34–41.

Burt, Ramsay (2017) *Ungoverning Dance: Contemporary European Theatre Dance and the Commons*. Oxford: Oxford University Press.

Butcher, Rosemary and Melrose, Susan (eds.) (2005) *Rosemary Butcher: Choreography, Collisions and Collaborations*. London: Middlesex University Press.

Carroll, Noël and Banes, Sally (1982) 'Working and Dancing: A Response to Monroe Beardsley's "What Is Going on in a Dance?"', *Dance Research Journal*, 15 (1): 37–41.

Constanti, Sophie (1996a) 'Dance: Unspoken; the Place Theatre, London', *The Independent*, 15 March: 8.

Constanti, Sophie (1996b) 'Jonathan Burrows Group', *Dancing Times*, 86 (1030): 959.

Craine, Debra (1998) 'Hell Is the Twentieth Century: Dance Umbrella', *The Times*, 28 October: 34.

Cripps, Charlotte (2004) 'Sitting Out the Dance: Are You Ready for a Duo Who Won't Move from Their Chairs for Your Entertainment?', *The Independent*, 4 November.

Crisp, Clement (1996) 'Dance Reinvented', *Financial Times*, 10 June: 15.

Deleuze, Gilles and Guattari, Félix (1986) *Kafka: Toward a Minor Literature*. Translated by Dana Polan. Minneapolis: University of Minnesota Press.

Dorris, George (1997–1998) 'Dancing in the Isles: George Dorris Looks at How Some British Contemporary Dance Fared in New York', *Dance Now*, 6 (4): 46–49.

Dougill, David (1988) 'How to Play the Pyjama Game: Hymns by Jonathan Burrows', *Sunday Times*, 26 June.

Dunning, Jennifer (1997) 'Testing the Limits of Boredom, Intelligently', *The New York Times*, 3 November: E3.

Fargion, Matteo (2005) Unpublished conversation with Daniela Perazzo Domm, London, 14 September.

Foster, Hal (1996) *The Return of the Real: The Avant-garde at the End of the Century*. Cambridge: The Massachusetts Institute of Technology.

Foucault, Michel (1972) *The Archaeology of Knowledge*. Translated by A. M. Sheridan Smith. New York: Pantheon.

Fried, Michael (1968) 'Art and Objecthood', in Gregory Battcock (ed.) *Minimal Art: A Critical Anthology*. New York: E. P. Dutton: 116–147.

Gablik, Suzi (1994) 'Minimalism', in Nikos Stangos (ed.) *Concepts of Modern Art: From Fauvism to Postmodernism*, 2nd edn. London: Thames & Hudson: 244–255.

Giannachi, Gabriella, Kaye, Nick and Shanks, Michael (eds.) (2012) *Archaeologies of Presence*. London and New York: Routledge.

Ginzburg, Carlo (1993) 'Microhistory: Two or Three Things That I Know About It', *Critical Inquiry*, 20 (1): 10–35.

Ginzburg, Carlo (2007) 'Minutiae, Close-ups, Microanalysis', *Critical Inquiry*, 34(1): 174–189.

Grüny, Christian (2017) 'Where Now? Who Now? When Now?', *Warehouse*. http://warehouse.industries/en/entry/where-now-who-now-when-now/. Accessed 20 July 2017.

Heller-Roazen, Daniel (2005) *Echolalias: On the Forgetting of Language*. New York: Zone Books.

Hutera, Donald (2003) 'Both Talking: Interview with Jonathan Burrows and Matteo Fargion', *Dance Umbrella News*, Autumn.

Jones, Chris (1998) 'Rosemary Butcher', in Taryn Benbow-Pfalzgraf (ed.) *International Dictionary of Modern Dance*. Detroit, New York and London: St. James Press: 85–86.

Jordan, Stephanie (1992) *Striding Out: Aspects of Contemporary and New Dance in Britain*. London: Dance Books.

Kaye, Nick (1994) *Postmodernism and Performance*. Basingstoke and London: Macmillan.

Latour, Bruno (2013) *Rejoicing: Or the Torments of Religious Speech*. Translated by Julie Rose. Cambridge: Polity Press.

Lepecki, André (2004) 'Concept and Presence: The Contemporary European Dance Scene', in Alexandra Carter (ed.) *Rethinking Dance History: A Reader*. London and New York: Routledge: 170–181.

Lepecki, André (2010) 'The Body as Archive: Will to Re-enact and the Afterlives of Dances', *Dance Research Journal*, 42 (2): 28–48.

Levi, Carlo (1991) 'On Microhistory', in Peter Burke (ed.) *New Perspectives on Historical Writing*. Cambridge: Polity Press: 93–113.

Mackrell, Judith (1996) 'Dance, Jonathan Burrows: Riverside/Touring', *The Guardian*, 30 October: 14.

Mackrell, Judith (1996–1997) 'Pattern and Passion', *Dance Now*, 5 (4): 54–59.

Martin, James (2010) 'A Radical Freedom? Gianni Vattimo's "Emancipatory Nihilism"', *Contemporary Political Theory*, 9 (3): 325–344.

Meisner, Nadine (1996) 'Closing in on Ballet? Nadine Meisner and Jonathan Burrows Quibble over Styles and Influences', *Dance Theatre Journal*, 13 (2): 3–5.

Meisner, Nadine (1997) 'Wrestlers in Golden Trainers: Jonathan Burrows', *The Times*, 18 April: 34.

Mertens, Wim (1983) *American Minimal Music: La Monte Young, Terry Riley, Steve Reich, Philip Glass*. London: Kahn & Averill.

Osborne, Peter (2013) *Anywhere or Not at All: Philosophy of Contemporary Art*. London and New York: Verso.

Peltonen, Matti (2001) 'Clues, Margins and Monads: The Micro-Macro Link in Historical Research', *History and Theory*, 40 (3): 347–359.

Perazzo, Daniela (2005) 'The Sitting Duo Now Walks, or the Piece That Lies Quietly Underneath: Daniela Perazzo Interviews Jonathan Burrows,' *Dance Theatre Journal*, 21 (2): 2–7.

Perazzo, Daniela (2006) 'Review. Jonathan Burrows Group: Dance Films by Adam Roberts', *Dance Theatre Journal*, 21 (3): 45–47.

Perazzo Domm, Daniela (2008) 'Jonathan Burrows and Matteo Fargion's *Both Sitting Duet* (2002): A Discursive Choreomusical Collaboration,' in Janet Lansdale (ed.) *Decentring Dancing Texts*. Basingstoke: Palgrave Macmillan: 125–142.

Perazzo Domm, Daniela (2010) 'Traces of History: Jonathan Burrows' Rethinking of the Choreographic Past', *Contemporary Theatre Review*, 20 (3): 267–282.

Perazzo Domm, Daniela (2012) 'The "Struggle" of the Subject: Productive Ambiguity in Jonathan Burrows' Choreography,' *Choreographic Practices*, 3: 99–117.

Percival, John (1995) 'Beginners Welcome to a Ballet Masterclass: Dance', *The Times*, 22 December: 27.

Percival, John (2003–2004) 'Jonathan Burrows/Matthew Hawkins', *Dance Now*, 12 (4): 74–75.

Phelan, Peggy (1993) *Unmarked: The Politics of Performance*. London: Routledge.

Rainer, Yvonne (1974) *Yvonne Rainer: Work 1961–73*. Halifax: The Press of the Nova Scotia College of Art and Design.

Reich, Steve (2002) *Writings on Music, 1965–2000*. Oxford: Oxford University Press.

Roberts, Adam (2004) *Jonathan Burrows Group: Dance Films by Adam Roberts*, choreography by Jonathan Burrows, London: Jonathan Burrows Group.

Schneider, Rebecca (2011) *Performance Remains: Art and War in Times of Theatrical Reenactment*. London and New York: Routledge.

Siegmund, Gerald (2017) *Jérôme Bel: Dance, Theatre and the Subject*. London: Palgrave Macmillan.

Solomon, Noémie (ed.) (2014) *Danse: An Anthology*. Dijon: Les Presses du Réel.

Van Imshoot, Myriam (2005) 'Jonathan Burrows on Scores: An Annotated Interview'. http://olga0.oralsite.be/oralsite/pages/Jonathan_Burrows_on_Scores/. Accessed 22 March 2018.

Vattimo, Gianni (2003) *Nihilism and Emancipation: Ethics, Politics and Law*. Edited by Santiago Zabala, translated by William McCuaig. New York: Columbia University Press.

Vattimo, Gianni (2009) 'Nihilism as Emancipation', *Cosmos and History: The Journal of Natural and Social Philosophy*, 5 (1): 20–43.

CHAPTER 4

Rhythm as Friendship: Movement, Music and Matteo

Throughout Jonathan Burrows' oeuvre, examples abound of pieces that foreground rhythm as the pivotal element around which his po(i)etic rethinking of choreographic conventions is organised. In early works, such as *Hymns* and *Stoics* (discussed in Chapter 2), for instance, sequences of pedestrian gestures arranged paratactically are juxtaposed to (often familiar) musical tunes—Anglican hymns in the former and an eclectic mix including a country song and a waltz in the latter. These compositional choices reinforce or interrupt the regularity of the musical soundscape and generate an intensive, often paradoxical, register that troubles accepted understandings of genres and codes. Later on, through the collaboration with Matteo Fargion, in the 'equal partnership' they established from *Both Sitting Duet* onwards, rhythm becomes the common ground from which the dancer and the musician interrogate the possibilities of interaction between the two art forms (Fig. 4.1).[1] In this and in the subsequent works they have since created together, dance and music engage in what, in Jacques Derrida's words, can be defined as a 'field of infinite substitutions' (Derrida, 1978: 289). Through this interplay, a key feature of Burrows' poetic(s) (of) dance, as I conceptualise it in this book, is rhythm.

In a talk on rhythm delivered at Mousonturm in Frankfurt am Main, Germany, on 19 May 2016, and repeated at the 'Body ^ Space ^ Object ^ Memory ^ Identity' symposium at the Centre for Dance Research, Coventry

© The Author(s) 2019   119
D. Perazzo Domm, *Jonathan Burrows*,
New World Choreographies,
https://doi.org/10.1007/978-3-030-27680-5_4

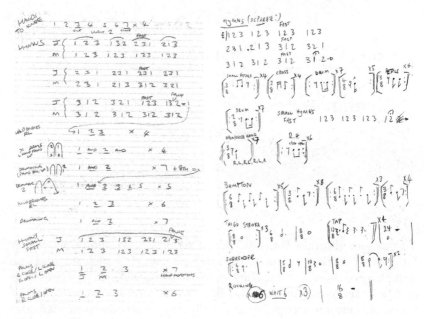

Fig. 4.1 *Both Sitting Duet*, parallel scores (2002) (© Jonathan Burrows and Matteo Fargion)

University, on 20 May 2016,[2] Burrows (2016) attempts to put into words the crucial, yet elusive role that rhythm plays in the process of creation:

> Making a performance
> is about how to get from one thing to the next thing,
> in a convincing manner.

> And then to keep doing that
> for a while,
> until a continuity happens,
> which we might call rhythm.

> And then to wait for that continuity
> to give you permission to deviate.

> And at the same time to know
> when to throw out the changes

that took you North instead of South,
or South instead of North.

Until what you're left with feels like nothing
and is everything.

And at the same time to ignore that
and do whatever it is you wanted to do,
and see what it looks like.

Because what feels convincing
is probably just an old rhythm
that already got approval.

And old rhythms are ok too,
especially if you think they're new.

And finding a new rhythm
is a matter of luck,
and work,
and being stupid enough to keep on trying.

Thus rhythm is about ordering and spacing, repeating and deviating; it is as much about searching for new patterns as about relying on what is already there; it shapes a composition but does not hold the key to its signification. In this talk, Burrows (2016) invokes Derrida: 'I read something from Derrida / about rhythm haunting our tradition / without ever reaching the centre. / Which suggests rhythm as something that moderates from the edge, / but in itself has no particular meaning. / And this mediating rhythm is everywhere and ubiquitous / to the point of invisibility'.

On one level, the focus of Burrows' speech is naming the unnameable, explaining the unexplainable—as conveyed in these observations about the process of creating work: 'we'd moved the music several times before / and it was never right, / and then it was right, / and I thought what is this "right"? / […] I didn't know what had happened' (Burrows, 2016). On another level, rhythm is identified as that which conjoins, as an 'experience of shared time':

I avoided work this morning
by playing English folk tunes.

I've always done it
and it's a kind of art,
and also no art
and I won't mention it again.

I do it because I like to sit,
maybe twenty of us,
trying to play music,
suffering moments of euphoria
when the right tune follows the right tune at the right speed,
keeping the pace down low.

And after three hours
the feeling gets stronger.

And we don't talk much.

In this chapter, I interrogate the potentialities opened by Burrows' under-standing of rhythm and its dramaturgies. On the one hand, I examine how rhythm operates compositionally in specific examples of choreogra-phy. On the other hand, reflecting on how conceptualisations of rhythm intersect with theorisations of subjectivity and relationality, I examine how rhythm informs the ways in which partnership is articulated in Burrows and Fargion's shared artistic practice. In particular, drawing on Derrida's writ-ings on rhythm and on friendship, on Gilles Deleuze and Félix Guattari's conceptualisation of rhythm and refrain and on Franco Berardi's idea of conjunction as 'becoming-other', I argue that rhythm serves as more than a compositional tool in Burrows and Fargion's dances. I conceptualise its function as poetic and poietic, in so far as rhythm produces affective com-munication and enacts a specific understanding of relationality. I contend that this, in turn, practises a specific modality of thinking about politics to the extent that it foregrounds a relationship with the other based on what Berardi calls 'conjunction'—as opposed to the 'machinic functionali-ty' of 'connection'—which implies and figures friendship and love (Berardi, 2012: 124).

In the following paragraphs, I attend to the ways in which rhythm oper-ates in Burrows and Fargion's pieces and interrogate its poetic, poietic and political articulations. In particular, I discuss *Speaking Dance* (2006), *Cheap Lecture* (2009), *The Cow Piece* (2009) and *Body Not Fit for Purpose* (2014),[3] specifically focusing on how their rhythmical arrangements qualify them as 'choreographies of friendship'—thus prefiguring my discussion of duets, plurality and collaboration in Chapters 5 and 6. The conceptualisation of friendship that follows furthers a line of thinking developed in writings on Burrows by Valerie Briginshaw (2005 and 2009) and, especially, Ramsay Burt (2017). While the theoretical premises they invoke are germane to my argument, I specifically locate Burrows and Fargion's understanding of partnership, conjunction and friendship in the way in which rhythm operates in their performances. Ultimately, I argue that such understanding of rhythm supports the interplay between singularity and plurality, between self and other, which I identify as distinctive of their choreographies—and of their poetics.

SPACING AND REPETITION: ON POETRY AND PARTNERSHIP

Chapter 2 discusses, among other works, two duets which are emblematic of the idea of relationality enacted in Burrows' performances. *Hymns* with Simon Rice and *Both Sitting Duet*, the first duet with Fargion, embody a reflection on the dynamics between two people, their friendship and ways of collaborating. In *Hymns*, the intersection of the personal and the collective affords the piece a transformative quality: the piece explores intimacy and subjectivity by conjuring memories and personal references, while at the same time engaging with normative canons and shared traditions in ways that subvert accepted associations, through humour and parody. In *Both Sitting Duet*, the performance of rhythmical sequences of hand gestures rethinks the relationship between two art forms, dance and music, by foregrounding Burrows and Fargion's personal friendship. As Burrows once said to me in an interview: 'I think with *Both Sitting Duet*, although it deals with a lot of abstract patterns of hand movements and so forth, the real subject is that Matteo and I have known each other and have been best friends for fifteen years. That's the story. It's the only story a dance can tell well' (Burrows, 2005).

As I have written elsewhere (Perazzo Domm, 2008), a first substantial contribution on *Both Sitting Duet* was published in 2005 by Briginshaw,[4] who analyses its structural dynamics in the light of Deleuze's concept of repetition and its intrinsic potential for change. Briginshaw explores the resonances between the 'transgressive character of Deleuze's notion of repetition, which does not repeat the same, but reveals singularities', and the minute variations of the duet's movement patterns, which expose the repetitions to uncertainty, making them unpredictable and therefore 'productive rather than reductive' (Briginshaw, 2005: 16, 19). This element of surprise accounts for the openness of the work, which, as Briginshaw argues, breaks the notions of replica, origin and representation, suggesting new ways of conceiving the relationship between dance and music and thus acquiring a radical, transformative potential. Drawing on Deleuze's notions of individuation and difference, self and other, Briginshaw investigates how the subversive potential of the piece lies also in the relationship between the two performers, and calls attention to their intense interaction, evident intimacy and subtle complicity, which several critics have linked to their long-standing friendship and numerous years of artistic collaboration (Brown, 2003; Frater, 2004; Parry, 2004). Their relaxed attitude and the unselfconscious looks and gestures they exchange throughout the piece reveal the ease with which they work together, sharing each other's art and inhabiting each other's space.

This new mode of relating to each other is embodied in the duet by the musical notion of counterpoint, which informs many combinations of patterns of gestures in the movement sequences, and by the interpretation of it that the two performers have discovered in working on the piece. As Burrows has explained, while his understanding of counterpoint had always implied 'a tension between the parts', Fargion introduced the new perspective that 'counterpoint assumes love between the parts' (Burrows, 2002: 28). Difference is at play in the piece also in the Derridean sense of a deferral of completion that undermines the logic of centrality and hierarchy, by suggesting a new way of collaborating that is neither one of dependence nor of independence of one from the other, but is built around the space between the two. This reading suggests ideas of complementariness and desire, of striving to fill each other's voids while never fully completing the other, which seem to be the principles upon which the choreography is constructed.

Derrida's notion of *différance* as difference and deferral of meaning finds a related concept in his idea of rhythm, as it is theorised in 'The Double Session' (Derrida, 1981b) and in 'Desistance' (Derrida, 1998): here Derrida articulates how differentiation and deferral are also at play in rhythm. On the one hand, rhythm is constituted by 'repetition, spacing, caesura'; on the other hand, rhythm precedes the subject, which is 'constituted by' rhythm: 'There is no subject without the signature of this rhythm, in us and before us, before any image, any discourse, before music itself' (Derrida, 1998: 31). What seems significant, in relation to the conceptualisation of rhythm I construct in this chapter, is the role that Derrida attributes to spacing in discussing the constitutive elements of rhythm. Talking about the 'blanks', the 'whites' that punctuate writing, the spacing 'that unites and differentiates' the 'semantic valences', Derrida writes about the 'non-sense or non-theme of the spacing that relates the different meanings to each other [...] and in the process prevents them from ever meeting up with each other' (Derrida, 1981b: 252–253). Rhythm is explained as the need for spacing between thoughts and always implicates an alterity: 'One must learn the necessity of a scansion that comes to fold and unfold a thought. This is nothing other than the necessity of a rhythm—rhythm itself' (Derrida, 1998: 3).

While the rhythmical structure of Burrows' choreographies might more obviously justify the association of his dance with poetry, I argue that rhythm—with its repetitions and spacing—also informs Burrows' modalities of working together with other artists. Of the many collaborations he has established during his career, the one with the composer Fargion is the longest standing and most transformative. Originally from Italy, Fargion studied composition with Kevin Volans in South Africa and with Howard Skempton in London. Beside his thirty-year collaboration with Burrows, with whom he has shared the conception and creation of all their pieces since the early 2000s, Fargion has also worked extensively with other dance artists: he has composed music for UK-based choreographers Siobhan Davies (*Art of Touch*, 1995; *Bank*, 1997; *In Plain Clothes*, 2006), Russell Maliphant and Stephanie Schober, among others. More recently, he has written music for theatre (including for Thomas Ostermeier at the Berlin Schaubühne) and for the Norwegian artist Mette Edvardsen (*oslo*, 2017). Fargion also teaches composition workshops for dancers, including at Anne Teresa de Keersmaeker's Performing Arts Research and Training Studios in Brussels.[5]

Fargion's artistic research investigates how 'structure and form [...] can support or transform very personal material' in the creative process, specifically through the use of repetition: 'I do one thing once, or one thing a lot and by repetition it begins to tell you something... the right things repeated the right amount of times though, not just repetition for its own sake' (Fargion, 2008). In his work with Burrows, he has been drawn to how the visualisation of rhythm through dance necessarily entails a simplification of the music material in order for the choreographed movement to reach a clarity of purpose. In an interview with me (Fargion, 2005), he discussed how this process requires both an adherence to the rules and an ability to bend the rules and work intuitively, through 'a hand-crafted kind of work'. This is achieved through negotiation, between a desire (typically Fargion's) to keep going with the same material and the urge (typically Burrows') to introduce change, meeting 'somewhere in the middle' (Fargion, 2005).

Burrows and Fargion's artistic collaboration is indistinguishable from their personal friendship. It implies both a trust in the other person and an openness to not-knowing, to inhabiting the in-between. As Derrida (1997: 220) writes, the possibility of friendship rests on 'non-assurance', on the 'risk of misunderstanding'—a 'disproportion' that is 'the condition of sharing' (Derrida, 1997: 220). In *Politics of Friendship*, Derrida attends to the triangulation between friendship, poetry and politics:

> This is the obscure friendship of rhyme: alliance, harmony, assonance, chime, the insane linking [...] of a couple. Sense is born in a pair, once, randomly and predestined.

> [... A] friendship should always be poetic. Before being philosophical, friendship concerns the gift of the poem. But sharing the invention of the event and that of the other with the signature of a language, friendship engages translation in the untranslatable. Consequently, in the political chance and risk of the poem. Would there not always be a politics of the rhyme? (Derrida, 1997: 166)

The work that Burrows and Fargion have created together has become emblematic of a kind of research that rethinks the relationship between dance and music and has inaugurated innovative ways through which the two art forms can communicate, interrupt and reframe one another. Their partnership sets up correspondences which do not resolve their respective alterity: it strives for assonance while acknowledging, and emphasising, its inaccessibility; it works with an idea of coming together founded on an irreducible disproportion. In the remainder of this chapter, which examines some of Burrows' duets with Fargion, I discuss how they implicate a po(i)etic and political positionality both through their rhythmical arrangements and through the forms of friendship they enact.

DISPROPORTION AND DISSYMMETRY IN *SPEAKING DANCE* (2006)

Speaking Dance is Burrows and Fargion's third duet and opens with the (by now familiar) entrance of the two performers in plain clothes and their short walk from backstage—understated and matter-of-fact, where relaxed and nervous body language blend into each other. They then sit down on two chairs in front of the audience, in a manner that has become recognisable since *Both Sitting Duet*. As I watch its premiere at The Place Theatre, London, in October 2006 (as part of the Dance Umbrella festival), for a moment this opening leads me to assume that, after the walking diversion of *The Quiet Dance*,[6] Jonathan and Matteo might have gone back to the 'static' position of a musical duo. The first surprise is that this time the ping-pong game is not of hand gestures but of words, although the title already suggested this. The opening sequence is a rhythmical repetition of 'left', 'right', 'left', 'right' and develops around chains of signifiers that could almost function as a demonstration of the Saussurean principle of the syntagmatic relations of phonemes ('left', 'lift'; 'stop', 'step'; 'come on', 'come up')—which, however, already points to a Derridean difference/deferral, to the undecidability, the uncertainty, the in-between of signification. As the spoken sequence progresses, the words become more evocative, but continue to navigate an open horizon of sense: 'running', 'falling', 'standing', 'waiting', 'thinking', 'silence', 'voices', and then even 'small dance', 'stupid dance', 'tired dance', 'fragile dance', 'weak dance',[7] 'doubting dance'.[8] Pointing in all sorts of directions, these terms seem to tell us about the non-mutuality, the not-knowing that Burrows and Fargion's collaboration across dance and music is founded on.

The title itself points to both the relationality and the incommensurability between 'speaking' and 'dancing' and the beginning of the duet articulates the lack of assurance implied in the attempt to speak a dance as a way of making it visible. As Burrows (2010a) explains in notes published on his website, 'the opening of *Speaking Dance* is a rapid counterpoint of loosely connected words, written around the idea of describing a dance that you can hear but never see'. Small gestures, such as clapping and the rubbing of hands against each other, accompany the vocal performance, made of spoken words and oral exclamations. After the first ten minutes of this cut-and-thrust exercise, the work takes a different direction, catching unaware those in the audience who, on the grounds of the two previous duets, expected the piece to be built around repetitions and variations of the opening pattern from beginning to end. Instead, Burrows stands up and performs a dance swinging his arms and twisting his upper body, while Fargion sits quietly or sings Italian folk songs accompanying his voice with clapping at a faster rhythm.

In working on the piece, Burrows and Fargion struggled with 'rebellious' material that did not seem to fit into any overarching structure (Burrows, 2006). After strenuously resisting breaking their loyalty to their own working principles, they finally surrendered to this intrusion and decided to allow the composition to be diverted and transported by a variety of impulses. This could explain critics' descriptions of the piece as 'more episodic' than the previous two (Simpson, 2006–2007: 82). As Burrows explains,

> Matteo and I agreed that we really didn't have the stamina or the patience to make a third piece which held to one thing, as *Both Sitting Duet* and *The Quiet Dance* do [...]. So then we thought, what if we allowed ourselves much more freedom to have ideas and work on them, and make a lot of material, in music, in dance, in words and all the combinations, and just work fast and not question too much what we are doing [...]? Matteo was very doubting because this is not how he works; he wanted a *raison d'être* to begin with, he wanted a principle; but I said, 'I don't think we have a choice. We have to let ourselves work and, at this point, we have to trust ourselves to some extent'. (Burrows, 2006)

What holds the disparate vocal and gestural material together is the clarity of the rhythmical patterns, with words and movements following regular beats and occasionally even sequences counted out loud in sets of eight: 'cross, two, three, four, five, six, seven, eight'; 'jump, two, three, four, five, six, seven, eight'. As in *Both Sitting Duet*, the performers openly refer to their scores on notebooks they hold on their laps, or in their hands. Nevertheless, *Speaking Dance* departs from the previous two collaborative works and, after their reduction to silence, vocal lines and ambience sounds, returns to music in the form of recorded tunes (ostensibly played back from a small stereo positioned on the floor next to the performers) and of notes and melodies played loudly by the duo on mouth organs.

A main tune, based on a chorale from Johann Sebastian Bach's *St. Matthew Passion* (1727), links together the different musical and vocal scores of the piece.[9] It is used in different forms, including for a score entitled *Love*, with lyrics made of the repetition of the word 'love', which had previously been written and sung by Fargion on the occasion of Burrows' wedding. The *Love* score is used in *Speaking Dance* in different versions: it is sung by Fargion and Burrows together or by Fargion on his own, while Burrows, standing up, executes arm patterns mostly borrowed from sequences of *Both Sitting Duet* with hands moving, turning and sliding over laps and knees. The same tune also features in the piece with different lyrics: for instance, in a version for brass band and drums with the duo singing sequences of verbs like 'shove, punch, poke, [...] shake, cut, squeeze, stretch, jump'[10] in an energetic, galvanising manner, which sounds almost like the instructions shouted by a trainer during a workout class at the gym. The tune also accompanies other sections in different arrangements, including a slowed-down version on the organ to which Burrows frantically performs a pattern of hand gestures and Fargion shouts a sequence of words in a frenzy.

The piece travels from the world of words to those of dance and music, with a common denominator connecting them all, rhythm. Audience expectations are challenged again and again—for instance, when, quite late in the piece, Fargion stands up for the first time while Burrows remains seated. The situation seems to signal that the roles are about to be inverted and that the musician is preparing to dance, while the dancer will provide the rhythmical base. But Fargion remains still in his standing posture, while Burrows recites with urgency a long text containing the phrase 'only in his dreams did he know how to fly', which is a direct quotation from a section of Rudolf Laban's *Mastery of Movement* describing examples of movement scenes.[11] Fargion's immobility is in stark contrast with the expressive images of reaching, lifting and soaring evoked by the words read out by Burrows in a loud, high, overacted tone: 'tracing the strangest patterns on the ground [...] he felt excited [...] he reached out to touch the ends of the world [...] he turned to the spot where he was standing, clinging to it, for this was where he would make his dwelling [...]. The lifting and sinking came in endless repetition'. Applause and laughter marked this moment on the night of the premiere at The Place, in recognition of the 'insane linking', the 'infinite disproportion' (Derrida, 1997: 166, 220) of the elements (terms, images, references, performers) the piece juxtaposes, of its attempt to translate the untranslatable, to work with dissymmetry and risk misunderstanding.

Further sequences engage with this lack of reciprocity, producing humour and laughter in response to the improbability of the pairings the dramaturgy proposes. One such sequence is a scene that many early reviewers of the performance commented on (Burt, 2006; Simpson, 2006–2007; Williams, 2006) for its funny character of slapstick comedy. A pattern of three hand gestures is accompanied by the words 'chicken', 'yes', 'come', written on pieces of papers which Burrows and Fargion produce from their pockets, meticulously unfold and show to the audience. Although it has been assumed that the gestures were devised as illustrations of the words (Burt, 2006; Williams, 2006), the hand movements are in fact quotations from *Both Sitting Duet*, where they are executed with no reference to chickens and calling.[12] Words were subsequently attached to the gestures, thus exposing the humorous incompatibility between verbal language and movement—the disproportion between 'speaking' and 'dancing'.

This lack of symmetry between sound and movement, as between music/musician and dance/dancer, is also the condition for their assonance, for their friendship: the inevitable not-knowing of the other makes a po(i)etic non-coincidence possible and becomes political due to the risk that choosing the possibility of failure implies. The collaboration between Burrows and Fargion is founded on non-assurance, on disproportion, in the Derridean sense I discussed above. It embraces the non-coincidence between sign and sense that characterises poetic signification and the unknowability of the other that makes friendship possible.

NOT-KNOWING AND NON-RECIPROCITY IN *CHEAP LECTURE* (2009) AND THE *COW PIECE* (2009)

After the initial trilogy of duets (comprising *Both Sitting Duet*, *The Quiet Dance* and *Speaking Dance*), Burrows and Fargion created *Cheap Lecture* and *The Cow Piece*, two thirty-minute pieces commissioned in 2009 by the Cultuurcentrum Maasmechelen and Dans in Limburg (Belgium). Both works, which are usually performed one after the other without intermission, adopt the principles of John Cage's *Lecture on Nothing*, a talk on composition in which the micro-structure of the piece's units is mirrored by its macro-structure, according to a concept that Cage followed for his music scores.[13] The resulting compositions, while arranged around series of repetitions, are conspicuously punctuated by accents and pauses which occur in odd and counter-intuitive moments. In these works, the intricate rhythmical structure offers the duo a tight form with which they can navigate the relationship between their respective individualities. The performers let go of something of themselves, which in turn allows for sharing to take place. As in Derrida, in these duets rhythm precedes the subject: one's own incompleteness is foregrounded and an open or empty promise is made to the other—a sort of holding back that makes sharing possible. Discussing Derrida's concept of spacing, as articulated in 'Positions: Interview with Jean-Louis Houdebine and Guy Scarpetta' (Derrida, 1981a), Louise Burchill (2011: 39) writes that

> The term [spacing] designates, first, an interval or 'in-between' that would be the index of an irreducible exteriority, rendering it thereby impossible for an identity to be closed up within its proper interiority, but it is also meant to be the index of a 'productive', 'genetic' movement that indicates an irreducible alterity.

Concurrently, alterity is accounted for in rhythm also through repetition. The cadence of accents signals both a consonance and a lack of identity, opening a generative space within the semantic process that acknowledges the other—poetically and politically. As Clare Connors (2011: 141) points out in her analysis of rhyme that works with ideas of 'bodily' and 'thinking' rhythm from Derrida's writings, '[p]oetically, rhythm gives rhyme, gives the measure by which accents will coincide. And conversely rhyme—rhyme as phonic coincidence without perfect identity—opens up the space in which rhythm can mark its beats' (Connors, 2011: 143).

As Derrida (1997) suggests, rhyme and friendship are alike: they both imply a relation that offers a 'breathing space', that allows for the untranslatable, the unthinkable to occur in the 'gaps between and within' the relata—the words, the friends (Connors, 2011: 144). 'What the rhyme between friendship and rhyme suggests [...] is a politics before identity or individualism' (Connors, 2011: 146). This qualifies both relationships as forms of cross-pollination, of auto-germination, insofar as they both defy expectations of coincidence. Rhyme 'substitutes and exchanges nothing. It links, echoes, mocks, confirms, sounds out' (Connor, 2011: 145). As Agamben (1999: 64) writes, '[a]ll poetic institutions participate in this non-coincidence, this schism of sound and sense — rhyme no less than caesura. For what is rhyme if not a disjunction between a semiotic event (the repetition of a sound) and a semantic event, a disjunction that brings the mind to expect a meaningful analogy, where it can only find homophony?' Working with Derrida's notions of rhythm and friendship, I argue that the spacings, the silences between sounds or movements that intersperse these two pieces, producing interruptions in unexpected places, play a crucial role in constructing the performers' individual singularities and their relationship.

I saw both works as a double bill at Kaaistudios, Brussels, in 2009. *Cheap Lecture* is a spoken piece in which Burrows and Fargion stand in front of the audience, behind microphones, and read their talks rhythmically, observing precisely calculated pauses, varying their speed of elocution and marking the end of each page of the script by letting it float down to the floor. Writing about the rhythmical structure of the work, Burrows (2010b) explains that the resulting performance is 'the product of a pleasurable negotiation with the given form, which causes us to speak fast or slow in the wrong places and place emphasis on the wrong syllables'. A projection on the wall behind them shows selected words and phrases from the texts they are reading; the timing of the slides is precisely calculated—as Fargion says in the lecture, 'the time of the changing of the projected words is in counterpoint to the flow of our speaking; the speed of the projected words is in counterpoint to the flow of our speaking—marking boundaries of thoughts as they pass'. The talk is accompanied by piano music inspired by Franz Schubert; it is first played back from a recording and, later in the piece, performed live on the piano by Fargion. The music also informs the talk's rhythmical structure, functioning—in Fargion's words from the talk itself—as 'a wall of rhythm against which our thoughts can lean' (Fig. 4.2).

The lecture has several humorous moments, achieved by taking the audience in and out of its main subject: the making, the event and the experience of performance. It reflects on the creative process, defying normative ideas about choreographing and presenting dance. Burrows and Fargion talk about the effects of working with ease or with effort, about composing by following rules or making choices, about borrowing material (the phrase 'everything is stolen' is repeated more than once), about approaching a work 'empty handed' as a generative condition of not-knowing: 'We don't know what we are doing and we are doing it'. They make reference to the audience, to the perception of time when watching a piece, to the circularity of the relationship between performers and spectators: the former 'give the audience clues as to how they might sit', while the latter grant the performers 'permission to relax and do best what we've come to do'.

While there is playfulness in the way in which Burrows and Fargion perform their talk, the piece is built around the po(i)etic principles it discusses and performs, which emphasise the centrality of rhythm in performance, intended as both a semantic and a collaborative event. In the talk, Fargion mentions how the 'silences' that punctuate the piece enable it to achieve

Fig. 4.2   Jonathan Burrows and Matteo Fargion in *Cheap Lecture* (2009) (Photograph by Herman Sorgeloos)

'complexity', so that, as Burrows says, 'some sense will slowly be made': 'meaning is what accumulates in collaboration between what happens in the gaps between words and the gaps between thoughts'. In a similar way, the relationship between the two performers is a negotiation of space and emphasis, according to the musical principle of counterpoint: as Fargion says, 'counterpoint assumes a love between the parts. I must be exactly myself and at the same time I must give up myself [...] to the person next to me'. I suggest that the interplay between simplicity and complexity that characterises the precisely arranged rhythmical structure is mirrored in the interplay between individuality and plurality upon which the friendship of the duo is built. This is achieved through the 'negotiation and contamination of singularity and concept, exception and rule' (Derrida, 1997: 220).

Similarly constructed around the encounter between these extremes is the choreography of *The Cow Piece*, in which an array of material—including gestural, spoken and musical—is presented by Burrows and Fargion, each standing behind a small table upon which six plastic toy cows are

arranged. The work is a rapid succession of scenes in which the two performers speak, read out texts, count, whistle, sing folk songs, play a variety
of instruments (including a mandolin and an harmonium for Fargion, an
accordion for Burrows and a mouth organ for both), gesture with their
hands and arms, and move the cows on the tables as if in a children's
game—making them shuffle, lie down, hop, jump off the table, die. The
unpredictability of the arrangement and the sheer nonsensical nature of the
performed actions make this the duo's most overtly comical piece. Burrows and Fargion perform their respective parts nearly independently of
each other (at times also reading or singing different texts simultaneously,
creating a cacophony of voices). Only occasionally, they come together to
play a folk tune, performed vigorously by Burrows on the accordion and
by Fargion on the mandolin.

In the piece's opening, Fargion makes the cows speak, declaring in Italian their respective actions as he moves them: *ballo* ('I dance'), he lifts a
cow; *canto* ('I sing'), he lifts another; *vado* ('I go'), he moves one forward;
muoio ('I die'), he turns one on its side; *dormo* ('I sleep'), he turns another
on its side; *sbaglio* ('I make a mistake'), he slaps one; *scappo* ('I run away'),
he makes one hop forward. While most of the movements seem to represent
the meanings of the cows' statements, some actions are paired randomly—
for example, with *penso* ('I think'), Fargion slaps the cow, just as de does
with 'I make a mistake', and lifts and shuffles can be used for a number of
different actions/conditions, from 'I dance' to 'I speak' (Fig. 4.3). Mean-
while, Burrows is engaged in a similar activity (he also says the actions in
Italian), but is less vocal, so the audience's attention is more likely to be
on Fargion. As the piece progresses, both performers move in and out of
their engagement with the plastic toys. Overall, while Fargion seems more
consistently intent on handling the cows (he calls them by name, he arbi-
trates their disputes, he hangs them putting a noose around their necks),
Burrows transitions across a variety of actions, which involve a more open
spatiality and a wider range of dynamics: he bows and thanks the audience,
bending his torso stiffly, almost mannequin-like; he repeatedly performs a
sort of mysterious ritual by the table, which involves sliding his hands and
resting his forehead on it, or he steps back from the table waving his arms
and turning swiftly on the spot; he even attempts the old magic trick of
the tablecloth, which he tries to pull from underneath the cows, failing and
falling to the floor with the cows, in a comical scene.

Burt (2017: 157) describes *Cheap Lecture* and *The Cow Piece* as 'human-
scale pieces', performed with 'democratic virtuosity', meaning that 'most

Fig. 4.3 Matteo Fargion in *The Cow Piece* (2009) (Photograph by Flavio Romualdo Garofano)

of the individual actions […] are within the capabilities of most people'. More specifically, he discusses these works as performances of friendship, arguing that they exemplify the radical passivity that is central to an ethical relationship between self and other. Rather than being revealed through a display of intimacy—in what Burt sees as a move towards a more impersonal relationship than the overt friendliness of the first three duets—Jonathan and Matteo's friendship is articulated through a negotiation of their respective 'position of difference', which implies the 'loss of self' as the condition for their openness to the other (Burt, 2017: 159). Through an analysis of the pieces' structures in relation to Cage's *Lecture on Nothing*, Burt (2017: 162) argues that Burrows and Fargion's works 'secularise Cage's mysticism' and articulate a 'pragmatic openness to new possibilities' which reveals the ethico-aesthetic potential of their generously passive approach.

Burt's observations on the human-scale and secularity of these two works by Burrows and Fargion prompt me to engage further with Derrida's thought, upon which my analysis of the correspondences between poetic rhythm and friendship is based. Significantly, for Derrida, a human dimension is the condition for friendship, a relationship which cannot be entertained with God: 'Friendship [...] can only be human', inasmuch as 'thought *of the other*' can only involve a human other, rather than a divine entity (Derrida, 1997: 224). In turn, the need for the other, the desire to establish relations, is in itself the condition for thinking:

> Following the same logic, there is thought, there is thinking being – if, at least, thought must be the thought of the other – only in friendship. [...] I think, therefore I need the other (in order to think); I think, therefore the possibility of friendship is lodged in the movement of my thought in so far as it demands, calls for, desires the other. (Derrida, 1997: 224)

Yet, this is only one possible understanding of friendship. In his exploration of the notion and of its political import, Derrida shows us how contradictory and unstable such a category is. In *Politics of Friendship*, he invokes divergent philosophical discourses to interrogate a provocative motto, a paradoxical apostrophe attributed to Aristotle, which provides the starting point for each of the chapters of the book and the different theoretical perspectives they are built upon: 'O my friends, there is no friend'. It seems significant that a similar near-chiasmic structure is adopted in *Cheap Lecture* through the statement 'we don't know what we are doing and we are doing it'—which is in itself a translation of Cage's 'I have nothing to say and I am saying it' in *Lecture on Nothing* (1961: 109). In constructing his analysis around a remark that performs a reversal upon itself, Derrida (1997: 221) accounts for the many 'ruptures', 'mutations' and 'zigzags' that intersect the notion of friendship, debunking any linear history or understanding of the idea. He also advances a discourse on friendship as rupture and reversal itself—as a non-reciprocity that implies heterogeneity and a 'zigzagging' relationship with the other. A friendship that is also a way of negotiating difference, the other face of antagonism: in the case of Burrows and Fargion, their differences spill into the ways in which they elicit different kinds of humour—Fargion's quirkiness and Burrows' wry wit. A friendship that upsets harmonious views of balanced mutuality and face-to-face interaction and becomes political through its near-impossibility, its continuous undoing of itself.

Jonathan and Matteo do not perform face-to-face; from *Both Sitting Duet* onwards, they have reconfigured the mutual frontality and interdependence of the dance duet, thus upsetting conventional representations of friendship. When they engage in their hilariously or puzzlingly absurd actions and scores (with little interaction with each other) in *The Cow Piece*, when they read their respective texts in odd rhythms in *Cheap Lecture*— not knowing what they are doing, but nevertheless doing it—they show us a friendship built on not-knowing and non-reciprocity. In the occasional moments in which they do come together to play a folk tune or read a text in unison, they reveal another possible configuration, another possible rhythm of their friendship, where enacting the contradiction is part of the game. Their friendship constructs a politics that moves beyond known paradigms of interaction, rethinking the relationship between self and other by zigzagging in and out of obvious rhythmical and relational patterns.

Burt (2017) identifies a level of impersonality in Burrows and Fargion's performance of friendship in these two 2009 works. Burrows (2010d) himself sees this as a change from the 'transparent, friendly relationship' of the first three duets, insofar as the communication between him and Fargion becomes less direct (e.g. it is mediated by the slide projections in *Cheap Lecture*)—as he says in an interview with Ixiar Rozas. In another interview for Motion Bank, a research project on choreographic practice by the Forsythe Company,[14] Burrows and Fargion (2011) explain that they created the choreography for *The Cow Piece* independently of each other, as two simultaneous solos. In dialogue with these positions, which emphasise non-mutuality, I suggest that Burrows' choreographic work articulates subjectivity and relationality by foregrounding the 'impersonal' as a way to undo accepted paradigms of singularity and plurality (as I more specifically discuss in Chapter 5). In the present chapter, the concern with rhythm, which I highlight as crucial to Burrows' rethinking of choreographic conventions, offers a perspective from which to engage with *Cheap Lecture* and *The Cow Piece* as two instances of Burrows and Fargion's zigzagging through possible compositional structures and friendship patterns—through reversals and restages[15] that demand a different way of historicising the work, not in terms of linear developments and certain turns, but rather as series of unplanned interruptions and paradoxical possibilities.

Rhythm and Chaos in *Body Not Fit for Purpose* (2014)

Another such reversal is at work in Burrows and Fargion's *Body Not Fit For Purpose*, the duet made in 2014. As I discuss in Chapters 2 and 3,[16] the work is a succession of short sequences of hand movements, spoken words or singing performed to music played by Fargion on the mandolin and occasionally by Burrows on the mouth organ. This is another piece which follows a tight rhythmical arrangement, namely the structure of La Folia, one of the oldest European melodies, which is used to compose the gestural sequences performed by Burrows (with one instance in which Fargion joins in). Burrows (2015: 82) writes about how the structure works in an article based on his and Fargion's notebooks and observations, published in an issue of *Performance Research* on repetition:

> This is the structure of La Folia.
> ABA CDC AB
> This is the structure of La Folia.
>
> Although simple, it was popular amongst classical composers because of the thing it does with expectation.
> After an opening rush the A repeats. We recognise it and feel good, and we think we know what's happening. Then on through C, D and C again before slipping back to the start, only to stop, suddenly and surprisingly, in B, which leaves us wanting more. And in the middle of this, the D (this D) plays once only, and remains memorable.
> Although simple, it was popular amongst classical composers because of the thing it does with expectation.
>
> This is the structure of La Folia.
> ABA CDC AB

Reversal is at play in two ways in the duet, both of which entail a rupture, a mutation. It informs the sequences' near-chiastic structure, which reflects itself in a symmetrical manner from the centre but with a twist at the end, where the pattern is abruptly interrupted. It is also implied in the gesture itself of remaking an old rhythm, which is both followed to the letter and radically modified by overlapping heterogeneous acoustic and gestural material in the composition (Fig. 4.4).

What is significant in this duet is its engagement with a traditional rhythmical pattern that informed a number of European social dances from the late sixteenth century onwards (Hudson, 1973). This choice of musical referent speaks of an interest in what Burrows calls 'old-fashioned' procedures (Burrows cited in Perazzo, 2005: 4) and popular traditions—including the social dance forms he trained in and still practices (as I discuss in Chapter 2), but also the folk rhythm and songs that are employed in many of the works.[17] These forms entail a ritualistic aspect that involves a negotiation of one's singularity both with the plurality of the group and with the rigour of the structure that governs it. In this sense, rhythm becomes the

Fig. 4.4 Jonathan Burrows and Matteo Fargion in *Body Not Fit for Purpose* (2014) (Photograph by Ben Parks)

pattern that makes possible the relationship between tradition and invention, between self and other. In order to engage with how rhythm, as 'the relation of a subjective flow of signs (musical, poetic, gestural signs) with the environment' (Berardi, 2012: 131), operates as a relational paradigm, I invoke Berardi's conceptualisation of how repetitive structures and refrains shift signification towards a poetic, affective register. Drawing on the Deleuzoguattarian concept of *ritournelle*, and specifically on Guattari's (1995 and 2011) theorisation of the refrain as a catalyst for social cohesion, Berardi discusses the role that rhythm can play in a society characterised by a crisis of social solidarity, such as the one we experience in late capitalism. According to Berardi, rhythm—assumed as the special configuration that can bridge between singular occurrences and 'universal chaos'—becomes the 'essential feature' that enables us to make sense of the world (Berardi, 2012: 131).

In *A Thousand Plateaus*, Deleuze and Guattari (1987: 344) write about the *ritournelle* as a 'territorial assemblage. Bird song: the bird sings to marks its territory'. The refrain makes us feel at home by bringing comfort and a sense of stability against chaos:

> A child hums to summon the strength for the schoolwork she has to hand in. A housewife sings to herself, or listens to the radio, as she marshals the antichaos forces of her work. [...] A mistake in speed, rhythm, or harmony would be catastrophic because it would bring back the forces of chaos [...].
> (Deleuze and Guattari, 1987: 343)

Yet rhythm has more in common with chaos than we might think: they both exist in 'the in-between'—between milieus,[18] every one of which is 'coded, a code being defined by periodic repetition; but each code is in a perpetual state of transcoding or transduction. [...] Chaos is not the opposite of rhythm, but the milieu of all milieus' (Deleuze and Guattari, 1987: 345). In this sense, rhythm does not imply homogeneity, but rather the 'coordination between heterogeneous space-times': unlike metre, which is 'dogmatic', rhythm is 'critical' and 'changes direction' (Deleuze and Guattari, 1987: 345, 346).

Rhythm, as 'the milieus' answer to chaos', is also implicated in processes of territorialisation (Deleuze and Guattari, 1987: 345). For Deleuze and Guattari, a territory emerges when the qualities of rhythm acquire a 'mark', a 'signature'—when rhythm becomes 'expressive' (Deleuze and Guattari, 1987: 347). Hence, territoriality is not simply determined by spatio-temporal conditions, but is identified by expressive components. Because rhythm is linked to territoriality, it can also be employed to produce deterritorialisation. This, as discussed in Chapter 2, is a distinctive characteristic of minor practices, which, by employing major codes from a minoritarian position, deterritorialise dominant modalities, making them strange and engaging their affective rather than signifying potential. In this respect, Burrows' and Fargion's focus on rhythm plays an important part in the minorisation of the language of dance that this book identifies as underpinning their poetics. If in Chapter 2 I draw attention specifically to how the work deterritorialises dominant dance vocabularies and conventions, in this chapter I foreground rhythm as a medium of both territorialisation and deterritorialisation—that is, as implicated in marking a territory or in deviating from a territory's signature forms of expression. Deleuze and Guattari (1987: 331) write about music as 'a creative, active operation which consists in deterritorializing the refrain': music 'uproots the refrain from its territoriality'. Similarly, I argue, Burrows and Fargion's dance-music collaboration deterritorialises known rhythms pushing choreography beyond accepted correspondences between sign and sense and towards an intensive register.

Reflecting on how signification functions in *Body Not Fit for Purpose*, Burrows (2015: 82) writes:

> Repeating each sequence until it sinks into something that needs no thought, that can be pulled out of nowhere, that no longer seems like a burden to be remembered. Passing through a place of joyful immersion, then emptiness and the slow emergence of a song, grunted under the breath, holding the body in its rhythm.

The structure of La Folia guides rhythm between steadiness and change, allowing the work to inhabit a space between milieus: between gesture and word, between movement and music, between tradition and invention, between the familiar and the unfamiliar—calling for a transversal approach to signification that invites an affective response from the audience.

> When we follow the structure of La Folia our actions repeat, and what is seen or heard again reassures us and then disappears, worn out by familiarity. This act of disappearance reveals moments of sudden change, which carry a loaded charge as though something important happened. [...] When I repeat a gesture it marks its trace also as rhythm, which itself appears to carry meaning. This appearance of musical meaning is an accident of emphasis – it must be

important because I did it again. This accidental emphasis coincides with the spectator's own physical responses, their self-consciousness and heartbeat. They become the subject. (Burrows, 2015: 82, 83)

By following the rhythmical structure of La Folia, the piece zigzags in and out of territoriality, oscillating between stabilising and uprooting sense and meaning. As one reviewer of a performance of *Body Not Fit for Purpose* at the Lilian Baylis Studio (Sadler's Wells, London) comments, '[s]trongly resembling sign language, the gestures seem to have definite meanings, yet we can't actually read their content, an obvious comment on what the programme calls "the uselessness of dancing to express anything of any real concern"' (Weibye, 2015). This non-coincidence enables a meeting between heterogeneous paradigms of understanding, troubling frames of signification based on semantic compatibility. Importantly, by drawing on a musical scheme employed in popular dances of the Baroque period, the work also gestures to a social space-time long forgotten by our post-industrial present—a present that, according to Berardi (2012: 123, 124), has undergone an 'anthropological shift' that can be summarised as a 'shift from conjunction to connection as the paradigm of exchange between conscious organisms'.

As Berardi argues, our digitalised and mediatised society has moved towards a mode of interaction that revolves around functionality and relies on the standardisation of relationships: Berardi (2012: 124) calls such modality, in which 'each element remains distinct and interacts only functionally', 'connection'. This is in contrast to a relational modality that engages heterogeneous elements in a transformative encounter. Berardi terms the latter 'conjunction': 'Singularities change when they conjoin, they become something other than what they were before their conjunction' (Berardi, 2012: 124). Conjunction entails exchanges which break with codified semantic models and require the involvement of our senses to deal with the irregularities and changeability of the interaction. Berardi associates this modality with a condition of social solidarity that is no longer experienced in post-industrial societies, but that could be rediscovered through rhythmic and poetic practices that enable us to navigate between heterogeneous milieus and re-territorialise. For Berardi (2012: 124), conjunction, like love, is a 'becoming-other'—a generative fusion from which new possibilities emerge. Significantly, friendship is conceptualised in antithesis to functionality also by Derrida (1997: 197), who suggests that '[f]riendship is irreducible and heterogeneous to the tool

[…], to instrumentalization or—if one can widen and modernize things in this way—to all technical dimensions'.

Through the final twist in the structure of La Folia, with its abrupt interruption, *Body Not Fit for Purpose* introduces an element of irregularity—'an accident of emphasis' in Burrows' words—that awakens our senses and forces them to adjust and respond to the perceived change. At the same time, it also reassures us by employing 'an old rhythm that already got approval' (Burrows, 2016), thus pointing to a poetic and generative (poietic) space between rhythm and chaos, between tradition and innovation, in which making sense means accepting the intrinsic contradictions of signification and engaging one's senses. By drawing inspiration for its rhythmical arrangements from 'old-fashioned' musical sources (the melodic themes of *Body Not Fit for Purpose*, as well as the traditional Italian songs of *Speaking Dance* and the references to folk and popular traditions that can be found throughout Burrows' oeuvre), Burrows' choreography also gestures towards a model of social cohesion that, although lost, could be reclaimed through rhythm and poetry—through their ability to inhabit the in-between: the im/personal space between singularity and environment and the poetic non-coincidence between sign and sense. Ultimately, this points again towards friendship, as a relational modality that engages the political space between self and other.

In this sense, I argue that Burrows and Fargion's collaborative/rhythmical projects are both poetic and poietic, insofar as they operate through the non-coincidence between sign and sense. In the possibility of misunderstanding, they produce an excess and overflow of sense. I suggest that in its engagement with alterity and uncertainty, their work also becomes political: it offers an example of resistance to the status quo and to dominant modalities of knowing and doing. In the words of Derrida, their 'friendship engages translation in the untranslatable […], in the political chance and risk of the poem' (Derrida, 1997: 166).

Notes

1. The gestural dance the duo execute from a seated position is created through a dialogue with a pre-existing musical score, which 'is converted to movement by transposing each acoustic and rhythmic combination into a particular physical pattern' (Perazzo Domm, 2008: 127–128). As I observe in Chapter 3, the piece's compositional structure is arrived at through a process

of layering of material, informed by the interplay of remembering and for-getting of the past—both artistic and personal. Specifically, the music piece the choreography originates from, Morton Feldman's 1982 *For John Cage* for violin and piano, *disappears* in its customary acoustic dimension, whilst *remaining* in the movement dynamics of the dance:

> The relationship between music and dance in *Both Sitting Duet* is con-structed around their shared fluid condition of presence and absence, whereby the disappearance of the music makes way for the appear-ance of the dance, which in turns allows the rhythmic and acoustic qualities of the musical text to return in a different form. In a per-formative embodiment of the Derridean notion that 'nothing [...] is ever simply present or absent' (Derrida, 1981a: 24), the interplay of the music and the dance can be said to generate a 'movement of play' in which the language of choreography becomes the 'field of infinite substitutions' (Derrida, 1978: 289). The centrality of the one and the subordination of the other are questioned, reversed and reinterpreted in the light of their mutual 'supplementarity'. (Perazzo Domm, 2008: 128)

2. I attended the second of these events. The text of the talk is avail-able on Burrows' website: http://www.jonathanburrows.info/#/text/?id=188&t=content.
3. On *Body Not Fit for Purpose*, see also Chapters 2 and 3.
4. Later reworked in Briginshaw (2009).
5. For details on Fargion's artistic career, see also Burrows (n.d.).
6. This piece is briefly discussed in Chapter 3 as an example of a reworking of minimalism and, in more detail, in Chapter 5. For a conceptualisation of how the piece rethinks dance's relationship with its own history, see Perazzo Domm (2010).
7. Possibly a reference to Burrows' piece with Jan Ritsema *Weak Dance Strong Questions*, about which see Chapter 1.
8. As Marion Jones (2006) commented, 'what was particularly lovely was hear-ing how even banal words build meanings; how some were like fragments of thought while watching a performance'.
9. I am grateful to Matteo Fargion for sharing with me this and the following information about the musical score of the piece through a series of informal conversations.
10. These verbs are quoted from Laban's *Mastery of Movement*, where they are given as examples of basic bodily actions and 'derivatives' (Laban, 1971: 77).
11. See Laban (1971: 56), examples 1, 4, 5, 6. In an interview, Burrows explained: 'we didn't know it was Laban; we just found a piece of paper

stored away in a vast file of ideas months and months before, and we thought I had written it. I knew I hadn't, but it did sound like me, somehow; but that was more because it was the kind of thing that I like. Then I looked through my bookcase, I saw the spine of a Laban book and I remembered it was from there. So I pulled it out and I found the extract. It seemed very nice that, in a piece which would be about trying to visualise a dance that you can't see, even though we do it in some way not how Laban would have intended it, at the end of the day you come back to Laban! I liked that' (Burrows, 2006). For a more detailed discussion of how the Laban references are used in the piece, see Perazzo Domm (2010).

12. As Burrows (2010a) explains, 'the words "Chicken, Yes, Come" [...] coincide with the gestures "ring, thumb, flick". This material is a translation of a section of the earlier piece *Both Sitting Duet*, called "sign language"'.

13. I also discussed this in Chapter 3 in relation to how *Cheap Lecture* reuses the minimalist past. See also Burrows (2010b and 2010c).

14. The Motion Bank project, which run for four years (2010–2013), is documented on a website (http://motionbank.org/) containing choreographic scores, videos of performances and interviews and other resources provided by and produced in collaboration with the participating artists: Burrows and Fargion, Deborah Hay and Bebe Mille and Thomas Hauer.

15. Returns and reversals are modalities of engagement with the archaeology of dance, as I discuss in Chapter 3.

16. In Chapters 2 and 3, I focus on how *Body Not Fit for Purpose* deterritorialises dominant choreographic canons and engages with political content.

17. From the early *Hymns* to the traditional Italian songs, Fargion sings in *Speaking Dance* (e.g. *Il ballo del fazzoletto*, *Là nella valle* (an Alpine song), *O cara mamma* (a popular song about the hardship of working in the rice fields in northern Italy).

18. In *A Thousand Plateaus*, Brian Massumi suggests that 'milieu' should be understood in relation to all three meanings of the French term: 'surroundings', 'medium' and 'middle' (Deleuze and Guattari, 1987: xvii).

REFERENCES

Agamben, Giorgio (1999) *The End of the Poem: Studies in Poetics*. Translated by Daniel Heller-Roazen. Stanford, CA: Stanford University Press.

Berardi, Franco 'Bifo' (2012) *The Uprising: On Poetry and Finance*. Los Angeles: Semiotext(e).

Briginshaw, Valerie A. (2005) 'Difference and Repetition in *Both Sitting Duet*', *Topoi*, 24 (1): 15–28.

Briginshaw, Valerie A. (2009) 'Affective Differences and Repetitions in *Both Sitting Duet*', in Valerie A. Briginshaw and Ramsay Burt (eds.) *Writing Dancing Together*. Basingstoke: Palgrave: 183–203.

Brown, Ismene (2003) 'The Vanishing Man of British Dance', *The Daily Telegraph*, 13 October.

Burchill, Louise (2011) 'In-Between "Spacing" and the "Chôra" in Derrida: A Pre-originary Medium?', in Henk Oosterling and Ewa Plonowska Ziarek (eds.), *Intermedialities: Philosophy, Arts, Politics*. Lanham, MD: Lexington Books: 39–50.

Burrows, Jonathan (2002) 'Playing the Game Harder', *Dance Theatre Journal*, 18 (4): 25–29.

Burrows, Jonathan (2005) Unpublished conversation with Daniela Perazzo Domm, London, 26 May.

Burrows, Jonathan (2006) Unpublished conversation with Daniela Perazzo Domm, London, 9 November.

Burrows, Jonathan (2010a) 'About the Scores for *Speaking Dance*'. http://www.jonathanburrows.info/#/score/?id=3&t=content. Accessed 10 August 2018.

Burrows, Jonathan (2010b) 'About the Score for *Cheap Lecture*'. http://www.jonathanburrows.info/#/score/?id=2&t=content. Accessed 10 August 2018.

Burrows, Jonathan (2010c) 'About the Scores for *The Cow Piece*'. http://www.jonathanburrows.info/#/score/?id=1&t=content. Accessed 10 August 2018.

Burrows, Jonathan (2010d) 'Interview on Voice, Language and Body, with Ixiar Rozas'. http://www.jonathanburrows.info/#/text/?id=45&t=content. Accessed 10 August 2018.

Burrows, Jonathan (2015) 'Body Not Fit for Purpose', *Performance Research*, 20 (5): 81–86.

Burrows, Jonathan (2016) 'Talk on Rhythm: Written for Bojana Kunst as Part of an Event at Mousonturm, Frankfurt, 19 May 2016'. http://www.jonathanburrows.info/#/text/?id=188&t=content. Accessed 20 June 2018.

Burrows, Jonathan (n.d.) *Jonathan Burrows*. http://www.jonathanburrows.info/. Accessed 20 December 2018.

Burrows, Jonathan and Fargion, Matteo (2011) 'J+M in Brussels 2011—*The Cow Piece*'. http://scores.motionbank.org/jbmf/#/set/patterns-and-pulse. Accessed 10 August 2018.

Burt, Ramsay (2006) 'Jonathan Burrows and Matteo Fargion, "Speaking Dance", The Place Theatre, Wednesday 18th October 2006', *Critical Dance*, 21 October. http://www.ballet-dance.com/forum/viewtopic.php?p=183116&highlight=#183. Accessed 3 November 2006.

Burt, Ramsay (2017) *Ungoverning Dance: Contemporary European Theatre Dance and the Commons*. Oxford: Oxford University Press.

Cage, John (1961) 'Lecture on Nothing', in *Silence: Lectures and Writings by John Cage*. Middletown, CT: Wesleyan University Press: 109–126.

Connors, Clare (2011) "Derrida and the Friendship of Rhyme", *The Oxford Literary Review*, 33 (2): 139–149.

Deleuze, Gilles and Guattari, Félix (1987) *A Thousand Plateaus: Capitalism and Schizophrenia*. Translated by Brian Massumi. Minneapolis: University of Minnesota Press.

Derrida, Jaques (1978) *Writing and Difference*. Translated by Alan Bass. London and Henley: Routledge & Kegan Paul.

Derrida, Jacques (1981a) *Positions*. Translated by Alan Bass. Chicago: The University of Chicago Press.

Derrida, Jacques (1981b) 'The Double Session', in *Dissemination*. Translated by Barbara Johnson. London: The Athlone Press: 173–286.

Derrida, Jacques (1997) *Politics of Friendship*. Translated by George Collins. London and New York: Verso.

Derrida, Jacques (1998) 'Introduction: Desistance', in Philippe Lacoue-Labarthe, *Typography: Mimesis, Philosophy, Politics*. Edited by Christopher Fynsk. Stanford: Stanford University Press: 1–42.

Fargion, Matteo (2005) Unpublished conversation with Daniela Perazzo Domm, London, 14 September.

Fargion, Matteo (2008) 'Transcript of Conversation Between Siobhan Davies and Matteo Fargion'. https://www.siobhandavies.com/whats-on/talks-events/matteo-fargion-conversation/. Accessed 20 January 2019.

Frater, Sarah (2004) 'Brothers in Arms Are Making Waves', *Evening Standard*, 12 November: 43.

Guattari, Félix (1995) *Chaosmosis: An Ethico-Aesthetic Paradigm*. Translated by Paul Bains and Julian Pefanis. Sydney: Power Publications.

Guattari, Félix (2011) *The Machinic Unconscious: Essays in Schizoanalysis*. Translated by Paul Bains and Julian Pefanis. Los Angeles: Semiotext(e).

Hudson, Richard (1973) 'The Folia Melodies', *Acta Musicologica*, 45 (1): 98–119.

Jones, Marion (2006) 'Jonathan Burrows and Matteo Fargion: Speaking Dance, the Place', *londondance.com*, 23 October. http://www.londondance.com/reviews_details.asp?C=Jonathan+Burrows+%26+Matteo+Fargion&P=Speaking+Dance&V=The+Place. Accessed 27 October 2006.

Laban, Rudolf (1971) *The Mastery of Movement*, 3rd edn. Revised and enlarged by Lisa Ullmann. London: Macdonald & Evans.

Parry, Jann (2004) 'Dance: There's No Need to Be so Modest', *The Observer*, 14 November.

Perazzo, Daniela (2005) 'The Sitting Duo Now Walks, or the Piece That Lies Quietly Underneath: Daniela Perazzo Interviews Jonathan Burrows', *Dance Theatre Journal*, 21 (2): 2–7.

Perazzo Domm, Daniela (2008) 'Jonathan Burrows and Matteo Fargion's *Both Sitting Duet* (2002): A Discursive Choreomusical Collaboration', in Janet Lansdale (ed.) *Decentring Dancing Texts*. Basingstoke: Palgrave Macmillan: 125–142.

Perazzo Domm, Daniela (2010) 'Traces of History: Jonathan Burrows' Rethinking of the Choreographic Past', *Contemporary Theatre Review*, 20 (3): 267–282.

Simpson, Jane (2006–2007) 'Speaking of Dance', *Dance Now*, 15 (4): 82.

Weibye, Hanna (2015) 'One Flute Note/Body Not Fit for Purpose, Lilian Baylis Studio, Sadler's Wells: Another Clever, Comic Double Bill from Jonathan Burrows and Matteo Fargion', *The Arts Desk*, 3 February. https://www.theartsdesk.com/dance/one-flute-notebody-not-fit-purpose-lilian-baylis-studio-sadlers-wells. Accessed 10 August 2018.

Williams, Ann (2006) 'Jonathan Burrows and Matteo Fargion: "Speaking Dance"', *Ballet.co Magazine*, 19 October. http://www.ballet.co.uk/magazines/yr_06/nov06/aw_rev_jonathan_burrows_and_matteo_fargion_1006.htm. Accessed 14 November 2006.

CHAPTER 5

Duets and (Self-)portraits: Choreographing the Im/personal

Jonathan Burrows' choreography embodies a compelling response to the ambivalent conceptualisations of the subject formulated by contemporary literary and philosophical discourse.[1] Post-structuralist positions challenge the autonomy and individuality of the author and postmodern theory affirms the vanishing of the subject in a society overwhelmed by technology, where it loses its distinction from the object and becomes a 'function of the world of objectivity' (Vattimo, 1991: 46). Yet, the crisis of the subject does not always imply its complete disappearance, but rather its problematisation: it is thought of as a discontinuous entity inhabiting a fluid condition of 'presence-absence', 'a subject which can no longer be thought of as a strong subject' (Vattimo, 1991: 47). The Italian philosopher of 'weak thought' Gianni Vattimo (1991) talks of 'Being as event', drawing on Martin Heidegger's questioning of metaphysical conceptions of presence and of humanistic theories of the subject. Similarly, the Deleuzoguattarian idea of 'becoming' highlights the heterogeneous and relational aspects of processes. In *A Thousand Plateaus*, Gilles Deleuze and Félix Guattari (1987) articulate ideas of multiplicity and ambiguity, arguing for transitory and interconnected processes of becoming. This is a generative idea of subjectivity, conceptualised also through Deleuze's (1994) theorisation of difference as the productive and constitutive dimension of existence.

© The Author(s) 2019
D. Perazzo Domm, *Jonathan Burrows*,
New World Choreographies,
https://doi.org/10.1007/978-3-030-27680-5_5

Compositional and performative characteristics of Burrows' dances, such as his meticulous consideration of the formal elements of the choreography and his deadpan performance, mean that his work is often perceived by reviewers and audiences as displaying a degree of detachment and depersonalisation, as rejecting narrative and expressive modes and denying subjectivity. Historically, critical responses to Burrows' choreography have labelled his work as 'abstract'[2]—a definition which implies a disengagement with the question of the subject and of its modes of articulation through dance. Diverging from these interpretations, this book argues that the forms of performance presence embodied in Burrows' pieces, rather than signalling the disappearance of the subject, engage with subjectivity in transversal ways, acknowledging its elusiveness and emphasising its constitutive plurality. In Chapter 2, I have discussed how the deterritorialisation of the language of dance is actualised in Burrows' works also through the interplay of the personal and the collective. In Chapter 4, I have focused on how rhythm shapes his dues with Matteo Fargion around non-reciprocity and disproportion, undoing conventional relational paradigms. In this chapter, I reflect on how, in Burrows' dances, rethinking relationality and dialogue is critical for the articulation and perception of subjectivity. This, far from being a pre-defined entity that the choreographer wishes to portray through his work, can be understood as an 'event' that emerges from the paradoxes and interruptions between choreography and embodiment and between performing and watching, as well as in partnered dancing and collaborative creations. I argue that Burrows' choreography articulates a mode of subjectivity that foregrounds the ambiguity of the person by deconstructing its conventional connotations and embracing its 'impersonal' dimension.

To investigate this openness and rethinking (through practice) of the space occupied by the subject, I invoke Roberto Esposito's notion of the 'third person' as a compelling reconceptualisation of the category of the person which invites a reformulation of its boundaries and points towards a different understanding of its signifying potential. Examining different theorisations of the notion of the person across bio-ethical, theological and legal discourses, Esposito (2012) reflects on the exclusionary logic that invariably underpins the concept of personhood: a person is, first and foremost, that which is not a thing. Supposedly, this demarcation safeguards the value of human life and guarantees human rights. Esposito's innovative theoretical enquiry foregrounds how the category of the person, due to its 'performative role', 'a role productive of real effects', has resulted in a series of 'procedures of exclusion' which have widened the gap between human being and citizen, between soul and body and between different forms of life (Esposito, 2012: 9). Esposito's invitation is thus to reflect on the paradoxical category of the impersonal, conceived as that which enables 'a radical opening to relationality' with other living phenomena, envisioning the possibility of 'mov[ing] across thresholds' and 'think[ing] politically outside of traditional forms' (Campbell, 2010: 142, 143).

> Of course the impersonal lies outside the horizon of the person, but not in a place that is unrelated to it: the impersonal is situated, rather, at the confines of the personal; on the lines of resistance, to be exact, which cut through its territory, thus preventing, or at least opposing, the functioning of its exclusionary dispositif. (Esposito, 2012: 14)

Calling upon Émile Benveniste's linguistic study of personal pronouns as a founding text, Esposito identifies the third person as 'the only true plural' (Esposito, 2012: 108), insofar as it 'completely evades the dialogical regime of interlocution' as it is understood in more traditional conceptualisations of personhood—that is, as an exchange that rehearses fixed modes of interaction (Esposito, 2012: 15). While Esposito's focus is theoretical and addresses the ways in which various twentieth-century philosophical positions (from Simone Weil to Emmanuel Levinas, Maurice Blanchot, Michel Foucault and Deleuze) have conceptualised the elusive notion of the impersonal, he also acknowledges the role that the arts have played in rethinking the personal subject and in pointing towards new regimes of meaning.

In the following paragraphs, I examine examples from Burrows' body of work, from *Hands* (1995), an early piece for the camera, to the more recent *52 Portraits* online video project (2016), while also referencing the contribution he has made to choreographic discourse across practice and theory. I argue that the impersonal and plural modalities that Burrows' voice embodies generate aesthetic, performative and discursive interruptions, which open the possibility of new signifying registers. Moreover, I suggest that, by reconfiguring the relationship between body and thought, this rethinking of plurality acquires ethico political significance: by breaking with traditional understandings of what Esposito (2012: 9) calls the 'dispositif' of the person, 'based on the assumed, continuously recurring separation between person as an artificial entity and the human as a natural being', Burrows' work challenges the exclusionary logic upon which the notion of the person is based and envisions a new idea of the person as an open, multiple and collective category—a 'figure that has yet to be fathomed', which is 'both singular and plural', subjective and material (Esposito, 2012: 151).

SINGULARITY AND PLURALITY: *A CHOREOGRAPHER'S HANDBOOK* (2010)

In framing Burrows' poetics (as I indicate in Chapter 1) I aim to populate the 'point of intersection, the fluid interstice' that is a dance poetics and investigate how 'different polarities', experiences and 'exchanges are negotiated' (Louppe, 2010: 7). As an active player in experimental dance circles, Burrows often engages with choreographic research across practice and theory in academic contexts, including through his current role as Senior Research Fellow at the Centre for Dance Research, Coventry University. To interrogate the ways in which the subjective voice is reframed in Burrows' works, I engage with different kinds of 'writings'—not only as they are performed through his choreo*graphies,* but also as they are articulated through his numerous interviews (published and unpublished), workshops, curatorial projects, peer-reviewed articles,[3] essays,[4] public talks and symposium keynotes.[5] Moreover, Burrows is author of a well-known choreography handbook (Burrows, 2010), which offers movement artists and students a series of reflections on choreographic principles and creative problems. In relation to these writings, I propose to reflect on the productively ambiguous relationship between what Ramsay Burt (2017: 158) defines as the 'even-handed and fair' approach of *A Choreographer's Handbook,* which 'validates many different ways of making dance' and Burrows' own idiosyncratic creative and aesthetic choices, which over the years have resulted in a recognisable style. I venture that the interplay between plurality (of suggested approaches) and singularity (of practised ways of working) points to a generative paradox in which 'the non-person [is] inscribed in the person' (Esposito, 2012: 151): this treading on the margins of the personal, dipping in and out of its boundaries, becomes a way of acknowledging its complexity and changeability, rejecting exclusionary principles and enabling alternative ways of articulating subjectivity and signification.

Published in 2010, Burrows' handbook draws on years of experience of leading choreography workshops in a range of dance training settings. This widely read companion to choreography, which to date has been translated into four languages,[6] presents key ideas, procedures and reflections concerning dance-making in an accessible way, through stories, anecdotes, tasks and questions. It makes reference to specific memories and annotations collected through collaborative processes and teaching and mentoring projects, which highlight the challenges and paradoxes of the art of making dances. In presenting the reader (most likely a movement artist in training or looking to develop their practice) with a series of prompts, exercises and principles, Burrows' handbook does not set out to instruct on how to choreograph, but rather acknowledges the role that an artist's 'own peculiarities' play in the development of their own artistic voice (Burrows, 2010: xii). The same peculiarity is a defining trait of Burrows' own choreographic work, which in Britain has often been described as 'eccentric' (Parry, 1996), beyond categorisation and 'cryptic' (Brown, 2015)—definitions which have arguably contributed to his marginalisation within (if not exclusion from) critical accounts of British and European experimental choreography.[7]

As Burt (2017) points out, *A Choreographer's Handbook* accommodates multiple ways of approaching a particular choreographic problem, empowering the reader to acknowledge their own priorities and starting points, to make choices that work for them. 'Do whatever you need to do. […] It depends what kind of person you are and what kind of piece you're making. The difference between these ways of working is not as wide as is sometimes imagined. It's just a choice: how do you want to work?' (Burrows, 2010: 2, 3). If suggestions are offered, they are usually phrased as 'this is just one way of […]': 'if it doesn't work, drop it' (Burrows, 2010: 4). Nevertheless, this does not equate to an 'anything goes' approach. There is a strong sense that an artist working on choreographic material would know when something works: 'You could do anything, but it has to be the right anything' (Burrows, 2010: 81). Intuition plays a key role, as does the coherence of the artist's creative process: 'You are you, and you can only make what you can make' (Burrows, 2010: 2). Yet, what this 'you' is remains elusive; it is the responsibility of an artist to identify their course, navigating the uncertain path between setting and breaking rules, between knowing and not knowing. As writer and dramaturg Jeroen Peeters (2010) points out in his review of the book, '[t]o find out how Burrows himself actually works, one has to read between the lines of *A Choreographer's Handbook*. He uses material that comes easily, prefers to develop composition in a linear way, borrows many principles from composers of contemporary music but also likes dub reggae'.

Burrows' dances are constructed as methodically composed scores performed in a rigorous manner, where spontaneity and ease are reserved to the way in which scenic presence (both individual and relational) is articulated on stage. As already discussed in Chapter 1, the only piece in Burrows' body of work that does not use set material is *Weak Dance Strong Questions*, the duet Burrows created with Jan Ritsema in 2001, which is based on improvisation. Paradoxically, among all of Burrows' choreographies, this is perhaps the work that has been most extensively discussed in performance scholarship. Exploring the political potential of choreographic ideas, Emilyn Claid (2010) briefly references this piece in an essay focusing on the practice of embodying stillness, which the British artist-scholar has investigated through her own choreographic research. Intended as an exploration of the confluences between theory and practice, Claid's writing offers insights into the connections between thinking and moving, which *Weak Dance Strong Questions* exemplifies. More recently, performance theorists have drawn on the philosophy of Deleuze to propose an understanding of Burrows' dance as a mode of thinking through performance. In *Theatres of Immanence*, Laura Cull Ó Maoilearca briefly mentions Burrows' collaboration with Ritsema suggesting it entertains a dialogue with the 'materialist, processual thought' of Deleuze (Cull, 2013: 2). Bojana Cvejić's Deleuzian reading of *Weak Dance Strong Questions* (which I also discuss in Chapter 1) illuminates the ways in which this dance negotiates its relationships with space, dance partner and bodily habituations through the questioning of the practice of presence and togetherness and through the problematisation of the relationship 'between sensibility and thought, dancing and thinking' (Cvejić, 2015: 159). Cvejić demonstrates how Burrows and Ritsema's duet problematises the equivalence between improvised movement and spontaneous self-expression through a series of principles, formulated as problems, which allow movement to be questioned 'by movement itself' (Cvejić, 2015: 128).

Yet, as I argue elsewhere, and as I discuss in Chapters 3 and 4, most of Burrows' choreographic works beside *Weak Dance Strong Questions*

develop within the boundaries of a fixed score, composed through a painstaking process involving the shaping and adjusting, measuring and balancing of the material. However, openings are given in performance by the way in which Burrows accepts his own being there, and that of his dance partners, to happen and unfold in an informal and unformalized way. His dances do not presuppose a stage persona, in the same way that they do not pre-devise their own narrative. (Perazzo Domm, 2012: 101).

This chapter builds on these ideas, positing that Burrows' dances articulate subjectivity by embracing what Esposito calls an 'impersonal' register of meaning.

DECONSTRUCTION OF THE PERSONAL SUBJECT IN *HANDS* (1995)

Burrows has observed that it is often the limitation posed by a choreographic score that allows freedom to emerge (Burrows, Le Roy, and Ruckert, 2004): it enables the spontaneity and the artistic intimacy he shares with his dance partners to emerge in performance—especially with Simon Rice in *Hymns* (1988), with Henry Montes in *The Stop Quartet* (1996) and with Fargion in the number of duets they have created and performed together since 2002. He traces the ideal mode of performance presence and attitude he aims to achieve in a work back to the delicate familiarity that was captured through his stage relationship with Rice in *Hymns*:

> When I look at the tape of *Both Sitting Duet*, when I look at the tape of *The Quiet Dance* and when I look at the first twenty-five minutes of *The Stop Quartet*, which is the duet with Henry Montes, it's all the same piece. It's all the same as that first little, delicate fragment of *Hymns*. (Burrows, 2005)

However, such a slippery quality is liable to be lost as unintentionally as it can be found:

> In a way, the thing about that first tape of *Hymns* is that it remains important because there was something about it which seemed to be a seed of something that felt right for me. And my hunch is that, in many ways, a lot of the pieces that I've made since then are attempts to put right the thing that went wrong when that little delicate fragment of a duet turned into a bit of a cute, ironic routine. The other things I've made since have been attempts to understand what it was – and what it still is – that I like about that first fragment, and what was lost, why it was lost. On the one hand, that really frustrates me and, on the other hand, I guess that's what keeps me going now, because I don't feel like I've quite finished with that. I find it very difficult to remain so naïve for so long and to be such a slow developer, it's very frustrating.

But, on the other hand, it gives me something to push against, I suppose. (Burrows, 2005)

In this respect, it is revealing that Burrows has nearly always been interpreter as well as creator of his own choreographies, with the exception of a few early works, of some performances of the *Stoics Quartet* (1991), of the piece *Our* (1994) and of choreographic commissions.[8]

Significantly, while Burrows has performed in most of his pieces, he has rarely created solo works, with the exception of early choreographic attempts made during his Royal Ballet training and of the work for the camera *Hands* (1995), produced for the BBC and the Arts Council of England and broadcast on BBC2 as part of the 1995 'Dance for the Camera' series (Perazzo, 2006). In this short video piece, however, the intricate relationship with Fargion's score for string quartet and the extensive limitations imposed by the camera framing, under the direction of Adam Roberts, appear to be crucial factors in the definition of Burrows' scenic presence. The choreography of *Hands* is based on patterns of basic hand gestures executed in counterpoint between the right and the left hand at a purposefully set tempo. The four-minute black-and-white film frames almost exclusively Burrows' hand movements as they unfold on his lap: delicate gestures of fingers tapping or sliding on the top of his thighs, a hand closing into a fist, then gently opening—the fingers never fully stretched—to reveal a palm for what it is; a thumb folding and pressing onto the fleshy spot at the base of the little finger; or a thumb joining the tip of the middle finger, or of the ring finger, then leading the hand into a sliding or looping motion; wrists twisting, inwards and outwards, alternating; a hand grabbing the other and dragging it closer or shaking it, firmly but softly. Precise yet silky movements, expertly executed by hands that could be trusted to measure, mould, make—smoothly, easily.

The hand movements, confined by the boundaries of the film frame, 'allow the choreography to open itself up and incorporate the unseen by drawing the attention not to Burrows himself (whose face and body, apart from his hands and lap, are not included in the frame), but to the dialogue of his dancing with the music and with the world that is left out by the camera' (Perazzo Domm, 2012: 104). At the beginning, we are introduced, diagonally, to a space that looks like a craftsman's workshop; as the camera pans in on Burrows' figure, we get a glimpse of his torso, up to his chin, and then we are immediately taken down to his apron-covered lap. The fixed-frame close-up reveals that the hand gestures are already in progress—sparse, to begin with, and then more frequent. After every phrase, they move back to their resting position, folded on his thighs—rejoining, even if momentarily, the condition of stillness of their background: like a bas-relief, in which the narrative is organised around scenes transitioning into each other. Moreover, the tones of grey of the black-and-white film limit the sensory stimulations, so that our focus is entirely on the hands moving and on their relationship with the music.

This small hand-dance—'a beautiful miniature', as Duerden (2001: 553) called it—is devised around the simplicity of its movements and the clarity of their relationship with the musical accompaniment. I suggest that it articulates the performing subject through the unfolding of an 'impersonal event' (Esposito, 2012: 142): it embodies a subject, which, in a Deleuzian sense, materialises on 'the plane of immanence, meaning a sphere of life that is entirely coextensive with itself' (Esposito, 2012: 143). It is remarkable that, as one of the very few solos created by Burrows, this is not a piece that expresses an identifiable singular voice, spoken from the position of the 'I'. Arguably, the work adopts an impersonal mode of enunciation, in the sense conceptualised by Esposito[9]: 'rather than a single voice [...], we have the set of things said, the differences and connections, the articulations and digressions' (Esposito, 2012: 135).

While the camera framing fragments the performing body in a way that may suggest the objectification and denial of the subject, I maintain that the detailed and prolonged viewing of the gestural behaviour of the dancer, made possible by the fixed position and clear focus of the film, produces 'the conditions for an unusual and intensified intimacy between spectator and performer, whose subjectivities are both called into play' (Perazzo Domm, 2012: 104). Yet the subject that is summoned by limiting our view to specific parts of the body (hands, forearms, thighs), rather than allowing us access to the whole figure of the dancer,[10] is an impersonal subject—a subject that reclaims the unity of the living being by challenging the reification of the body and questioning the principle that qualifies personhood on the basis of degrees of life (Esposito, 2012). Burrows' headless figure in *Hands* actualises a deconstruction of the personal subject, pointing towards an impersonal person, a third person, 'because it refers to something or someone that cannot be circumscribed within a specific subject—in the sense that it can relate to everyone and no one' (Esposito, 2012: 15). The piece also rethinks relationality by establishing a transversal communication with the audience: we are denied a frontal meeting with the subject and are offered instead an altered encounter with 'an exteriority that calls into question and overturns its prevailing meaning' (Esposito, 2012: 14).

DUETS BEYOND INTERLOCUTION: *BOTH SITTING DUET* (2002) AND *THE QUIET DANCE* (2005)

In investigating how Burrows' choreography articulates subjectivity by reimagining relationality and plurality, a crucial consideration is that most of his works are duets, in which he performs alongside a partner. For over fifteen years now, Burrows' most regular artistic partner has been the composer Fargion, who, since *Both Sitting Duet*, the germinal work they created together in 2002, has performed with him in ten duets.[11] In Burrows' *A Choreographer's Handbook*, choosing a dance partner comes under the 'material' of a dance: 'The performer I choose to work with is the first and most important material of a dance piece. Everything that happens is bound by that choice. Who did I choose and what can they do?' (Burrows, 2010: 5). It also comes under 'collaboration': 'Collaboration is about choosing the right people to work with, and then trusting them. You don't, however, have to agree about everything. Collaboration is sometimes about finding the right way to disagree' (Burrows, 2010: 58).

How is relationality embodied in the space between two performers? And how can the dialectic of the duo overcome the fixity of roles of a two-way exchange? As already outlined in the previous chapters (especially 2 and 4), in *Both Sitting Duet*, Burrows and Fargion sit side by side in front of the audience and perform sequences of hand movements devised by transposing the notes of Morton Feldman's piece for violin and piano *For John Cage* into gestures that the two performers execute in varying relational and dynamic patterns, playing with (and stretching our understanding of) unison and counterpoint, repetition and variation. In an earlier publication examining this duet (Perazzo Domm, 2008), I offered a reading of the work as a dialogue which enacts a conversation between dance and music, between a dancer and a musician, between an existing musical score and its gestural execution, between the performed choreography and the traces and contexts its movements may evoke for the spectators. The terms 'dialogue', 'conversation' and the metaphor of two people 'talking' frequently recur in reviews of the work, which celebrate Burrows and Fargion's innovative approach to collaboration (Fig. 5.1).[12]

What I wish to draw attention to here is the way in which this conversation is set-up, which, I argue, does not replicate the modalities of

Fig. 5.1 Jonathan Burrows and Matteo Fargion in *Both Sitting Duet* (2017) (Photograph by Luca Ghedini courtesy of Xing)

an exchange between two fixed interlocutors. In a dialogical exchange, as Esposito points out drawing on Benveniste's analysis of personal pronouns, 'the *I* always addresses a *you*, just as a *you* always presupposes an *I* that designates it as such [and] only takes on meaning from the *I* that interpellates it' (Esposito, 2012: 15, original emphasis). The two involved in a dialogue are defined by each other; their roles, even if reversible, are confined to either one or the other of two closed options; they are also bound to the here and now of the dialogical exchange and cannot escape the contemporaneity and fixed temporality of their condition as speakers. Rejecting the idea of 'a relationship based on exchange between a "subjective person", indicated by the *I*, and a "non-subjective person", represented by the *you*', Esposito's 'third person' opens the possibility of a 'non-person', thus troubling the traditional semantics of personal identity and reframing the notion of plurality (Esposito, 2012: 106, original emphasis).

It seems to me that the situation produced by *Both Sitting Duet* exceeds the boundaries of the dialogic form in terms of the horizons of meaning it points towards; I suggest that Burrows' and Fargion's performed presence defies conventional understandings of personal connotations and is situated 'at the confines of the personal' (Esposito, 2012: 14), reaching outwards, towards a plurality that encompasses more than the duo. The relationship they establish does not feed on the mirroring between two interlocutors, on the echoing of their respective voices; rather, it points to what might be found beyond the boundaries of each of the individuals, to the unknown, to the possibility of multiple voices interjecting and enriching the conversation. Writing about collaboration in *A Choreographer's Handbook*, Burrows (2010: 58–59) observes:

> In the gap between what you each agree with, and what you disagree with, is a place where you might discover something new. It will most likely be something you recognise when you see it, but didn't know that you knew. This is the reason to collaborate. From the writer Adrian Heathfield: 'It's not as if, in a collaboration, you're moving towards what that other person has said, you're moving towards what they haven't said.'

This openness to plurality is reflected in the basic set-up and performative mode of *Both Sitting Duet*: Burrows and Fargion are not turned towards each other, alternating in performing the role of the subject; instead, they face the audience and concomitantly perform their gestural scores in a matter-of-fact way, without recurring to stage personas.[13] Rather than occupying the positions of 'I' and 'you' and performing closed subjects which take it in turn to 'defin[e] a field of relevance' (Esposito, 2012: 105), they are, in Esposito's terms, two 'third persons', who are ultimately two impersonal persons, two non-persons. To explain this paradoxical thought, Esposito quotes Benveniste's observations on the third person (as a pronominal and verbal form):

> 'Because it does not imply any person, it can take any subject whatsoever or no subject, and this subject, expressed or not, is never posited as a "person".' Benveniste's argument is that the third person is not limited to weakening or modifying the distinguishing traits of the other two persons; rather, it reverses them into their opposite by pushing them into a space outside their own formulation. (Esposito, 2012: 107)

I suggest that the articulation of the personal through the impersonal is not simply a feature of individual examples from Burrows and Fargion's collaborative body of work, but qualifies their creative production as a whole. In the piece that followed their first duet, *The Quiet Dance*, created in 2005, the format of the duet/dialogue is again opened up through a third-person modality, which evades the closed sphere of interaction between two singularities and extends into an indeterminate field of signification which feeds on the interplay between singular and plural, between thinking and moving, between inside and outside. In a similar fashion to *Both Sitting Duet*, the beginning of *The Quiet Dance* sees the two performers walk onto the stage beside each other. Burrows and Fargion, in everyday clothes, stand diagonally to the audience and begin repetitive sequences of flat-footed steps, taken stiffly and with overt, yet seemingly unmotivated determination. When they walk, their arms swing by their sides, then bend sharply, while they trace a descending trajectory, progressively crouching down and bowing forward as they move: as they stride across the stage in careful patterns, an odd vignette develops in front of us, juxtaposed to a soundtrack of sparse birdsong. They take it in turn to walk along diagonal paths, away from each other and then back, the steps of the one accompanied by a sound made by the other—again and again. There is no apparent reason for their movements and their gaze and attention wander, as if distracted by other sounds, other thoughts. Equally, the vocalisations they produce, a long 'aaahhh' cry or a 'sshhh' sound, are not accompanied by emotion or intention.

The blatant simplicity of the actions, the incongruity of the relationship between sounds and movements and the playful use of repetitions and variations through well-timed interruptions make this opening scene appear curiously comical and provoke laughter. Yet the cry we hear (Fargion's and then Burrows' 'aaahhh') 'still invokes a notion of falling, dread or non-specific fear' (Etchells, 2007) and what we see are two middle-aged men shrinking through repeated series of steps, which may suggest they are enacting their (humorous? tragic?) journeys through life. In two earlier publications (which I draw upon here), I have highlighted the dialogical composition of this work, which weaves traces of the past into the present (Perazzo Domm, 2010) and combines nods to a subjective stance towards the world with creative methods that privilege detachment and impersonality (Perazzo Domm, 2012). My first encounter with the work has shaped my analysis:

When I saw *The Quiet Dance* for the first time at its premiere in Munich in August 2005, what I read was the life of two people, their journeys, their experiences and intersections, and the different moods and phases of their relationship. Burrows and Fargion 'walk' separately and together, towards each other and away from each other; they interact on an equal level or they alternate in guiding and pushing one another. Now they play like children, now they pause and think. When Burrows repeatedly looks up to the ceiling and then suddenly lies down on his back with a succinct series of almost robotic actions, an image of dying springs to mind. Repeatedly, at different moments during the piece, they perform quick and contorted arm patterns in counterpoint, which echo gestures of prayer and the sign of the cross. Towards the end of the piece, as they walk with their torsos bent forwards and touch the floor with the back of their right hands, with cadenced movements of the arm in various directions, I wondered whether such gestures, suggestive of spreading seeds, were a metaphor for sowing life. At periodic intervals, they meet in the centre, softly clap their hands once and crouch down facing each other, thus marking the end of a phase of activity and signalling a pause. During several sections of the performance they produce vocalizations with ascending and descending notes, which are tightly interwoven with the movement patterns, and appear to mirror the ups and downs of their journey. After seemingly incessant repetitions of winding trajectories and brisk diagonal crossings of the stage, they come to a halt and let their hands do the wandering instead: moving back and forth and around in circles, their hand trails seem to condense these moving journeys, which in turn summarise their life adventures and encounters. (Perazzo Domm, 2012: 111–112)

It seems to me that what this piece constructs is an im/personal narrative which is both deeply rooted in its performing subjects and radically estranged from them. Pursuing Esposito's thinking on the impersonal, I suggest that the work expresses itself in the third person, 'the "non-person" [which] always refers to [...] a someone who is not recognizable as *this* specific person, either because it does not refer to anyone at all or because it can be extended to everyone' (Esposito, 2012: 107, original emphasis). The horizon of meaning the piece points to is not confined by the boundaries of the dialogue between an *I* and a *you* as it unfolds in a specific present situation; rather, its field of reference and of relevance eludes the present and is expanded to encompass what is outside—it stretches into the unknown and the unsaid: as Heathfield (in the quote I refer to above) puts it, it moves towards what the other person has not said. In a conversation I had with Burrows while he was still working on the piece with Fargion, we discussed this entanglement between inside and outside, between singularity and plurality, in relation to the images that the work concentrates on. When I asked him about how personal these images were, he replied:

I think we have been trying – although the piece has a certain intimacy, as all the pieces that I make have – that it shouldn't exclude other people. So something that's too personal doesn't open a door for an audience to come in. I suppose I would say that we were trying to look at something personal enough that it would still have a door open for somebody else watching from the outside. (Perazzo, 2005: 4)

Throughout the performance, Burrows and Fargion occupy a position that blurs the distinction between inside and outside. As they execute their steps and gestures, they are both doing and watching, moving and thinking: they are both present and absent. As Tim Etchells (2007) points out in an article about Burrows and Fargion's first trilogy of duets, these 'switches of their attention' are 'somehow the heart of the work':

They are doing things (movements, sequences, actions) and as they do so, they seem to be thinking about them. If this sounds unworthy of mention I have to remember how much dance isn't like that; how often there's no sense of this separation between action and do-er, no sense of a person present to be thinking, no sense of thinking at all. Here though the thinking, or the possibility of it, is with us from the start, from the moment they walk on and glance to us watching. As things proceed sometimes Jonathan and Matteo seem puzzled or perplexed by what they do and at other times they're apparently amused, but whichever or whatever their attitude is we're always aware of them as thinking subjects just behind and inside the action.

This leads Etchells to observe that 'they are very here and very now': a sense of presence which, counter-intuitively, he sees in opposition to the condition of 'immersion', of being 'absent' or deeply absorbed in the work that characterises more traditional dance performances (Etchells, 2007). Yet, Etchells also detects a certain kind of 'absence' in the work, one that comes with 'no mystery, no great otherness': 'They look absent only in the way that a man working in a builder's merchants might retreat briefly to his own mental space when you ask him how many three foot lengths you can get from so many metres of timber' (Etchells, 2007). I would argue that this shifting between 'immersion' and being 'here and now' signals a blurring of the distinction between presence and absence and articulates an impersonal performative modality. By attending to what Joe Kelleher (2008) describes as 'the stopping, the looking, the noticing, the thinking while the thing goes on', Burrows and Fargion's performance of *The Quiet*

Dance unfolds 'between the lines', taking place in a 'provisional' space between on and 'off the score'.

This in-betweenness, this indeterminacy can be traced to the constitutive plurality of the third person: because it is not limited by the expression of the subjective qualities of a specific person, the signifying scope of the third person extends to a plurality of identities, so that it is at the same time singular and plural. I venture that this working across thresholds of performative modalities, this moving and thinking outside conventional ways of dancing, pushes dance to its 'outer confines', 'opening it up and turning it inside out like a glove' (Esposito, 2012: 146). It makes the language of dance stutter—as Esposito observes drawing on Deleuze's notion of the minorisation of a major language: 'the language is made to sway, twitch, and crack until it explodes into a new linguistic identity' (Esposito, 2012: 146). This brings me back to the argument that underlies this book as a whole, which pursues a Deleuzian reading of language (Deleuze's thinking on the literature of Marcel Proust and Franz Kafka, among other writers) to conceptualise how Burrows' choreography 'opens up a kind of foreign language within [the] language [of dance], [...] a becoming-other of language', a humorous, paradoxical and elusive practice of resistance 'that escapes the dominant system' and exposes an affective register of signification (Deleuze, 1998: 5).

According to Esposito, Deleuze articulates 'the most compelling' philosophy of the third person (Esposito, 2012: 142). Through his notions of the event, of the assemblage, of the rhizome, of the body without organs and of the becoming, Deleuze deconstructs the category of the person and points to a conception of the subject as an 'impersonal event' (Esposito, 2012: 142) and of life as 'a multiplicity of presents; in a word, as immanence' (Cull, 2013: 3). In *Essays Critical and Clinical*, Deleuze examines how these concepts are at work in the sphere of language and literature and how the impersonal is articulated through writing. Here, he suggests that '[t]o write is not to recount one's memories and travels, one's loves and griefs, one's dreams and fantasies' (Deleuze, 1998: 2), as this would mean to 'infantilise' literature, to use it as a 'psychoanalytical' tool. Instead, he maintains that literature

> exists only when it discovers beneath apparent persons the power of an impersonal – which is not a generality but a singularity at the highest point [...]. It

is not the first two persons that function as the condition for literary enunciation: literature begins only when a third person is born in us that strips us
of the power to say 'I'. (Deleuze, 1998: 3)

Burrows and Fargion's duets elude the logic of the first and second person
(whether singular or plural) and widen their scope to encompass more than
their own 'memories and travels'. Their performance mode is located outside the opposition between intentness and estrangement, deconstructing
dominant approaches to performance and paradigms of meaning, towards
a creative, performative practice of the impersonal. This opens the possibility of an unexpected, inventive and intensive communication with the
audience, which moves beyond the horizon of conventional understanding
and, as I argue in the next section, acquires significance as a political act.

IMPERSONAL SINGULARITIES IN *52 PORTRAITS* (2016)

In the *52 Portraits* online project, Burrows and Fargion, in collaboration
with the film-maker Hugo Glendinning, explicitly adopt the third-person
form to make a series of video portraits of dance figures, which include
internationally renowned choreographers, emerging artists, dance industry
professionals and researchers. On 4 January of 2016, the first video of
this digital project was released online, and every following Monday until
the end of the year a new portrait was made available on the *52 Portraits*
website (and via a free email subscription). The portraits are short gestural
pieces, of the duration of one to four minutes, accompanied by Fargion's
and/or his daughter Francesca's off-screen singing; the lyrics, written by
Burrows, are based on brief interviews with the featured performers, whose
autobiographical stories and memories of dancing are quoted verbatim.
The project includes forty-five solos, six duets and one quartet (the final
portrait, performed by the artistic team), all shot by Glendinning with a
nearly fixed camera. Each dance is individual to the artist who devises and
performs it, but follows a recognisable format, thus linking each piece to
the other ones in the series, as well as to the distinctive compositional
principles and choreographic framing employed by Burrows and Fargion
in their own duets and in other choreographic projects. In all the videos,
the artists sit at or move around a table and chair(s) in a manner that is
reminiscent of the set-up of Burrows and Fargion's works (many of which
are seated performances or make use of a table): these simple props are the
only identifiable items in an otherwise neutral black-box setting (Fig. 5.2).

Fig. 5.2   *52 Portraits* (2016), from top left: Marquez & Zangs, Dan Daw, Hetain Patel, William Forsythe, Andros Zins-Browne, Crystal Pite, Jonzi D, Alexandrina and David Hemsley, Wendy Houston, Kloe Dean, Namron, Flora Wellesley Wesley, Zenaida Yanowsky, Botis Seva, Mette Ingvartsen, Siobhan Davies (Photograph by Hugo Glendinning)

In this project, Burrows and Fargion's already interdisciplinary collaboration across dance and music extends to the medium of film. The two artists had worked with film and film-makers before: notable examples are the short film *Hands* directed by Roberts, which is examined earlier in this chapter, as well as the 1995 film danced by Sylvie Guillem, *Blue Yellow* (directed by Roberts, with music by Kevin Volans).[14] More recently, in 2012–2013, they contributed to William Forsythe's Motion Bank website project (The Forsythe Company, n.d.), which documents seven of their duets through video recordings of performances, research sessions, rehearsals and interviews on their creative process and images from their score books. *52 Portraits* continues this exploration of film and digital technologies, while also suggesting a specific kind of enquiry, which engages with how the different elements of the work (dance, music, lyrics, film) combine and interact to create a portrait of the featured person—often interfering with each other and disrupting recognisable narratives. The project has been described (with a phrase credited to Fargion) as 'an epic

love song to an art form'—the art form of dance (Smith, 2016), a definition which acknowledges the work's serial, durational form and narrative
character, traceable to an oral source. In the context of my enquiry into
how Burrows' choreography troubles conventional conceptions of the category of the person, what is significant about this project is that it engages,
almost directly, with the question of the relationship between singularity
and plurality: it does so by moving to and fro between the nexus of the
first and second person and the position of the third person, rethinking the
formats of interlocution and impersonality.

On my laptop screen, I watch the portrait of the hip-hop artist Botis
Seva, founder and artistic director of Far From the Norm, released on 18
April 2016. Sat at a table (which figures as the continuation of my laptop,
as Burrows intended it, while also, according to Glendinning, offering a
'surrogate stage'),[15] Seva has his head bent forward, his hands joined at the
fingertips, as if in contemplation, or gathering concentration in preparation
for what is to come. 'Botis grew up in Battersea, but he moved around a
lot with his mum; he moved around a lot with his mum': Fargion's singing
is soft and level and mirrors the steady, almost soothing beat of the music.
Seva's joined hands twist and travel sideways, locked in the stretch and
tension of their respective push, until they escape their reciprocal hold and
engage in freer loopings and convoluted movements, involving angular
wrists and elbows, with forearms gliding swiftly across the table. Fargion
sings: 'He started with hip-hop at school, because they used to do talent
shows – every year; and he just got into dancing; he just got into dancing'.
As the movements grow in size, Seva's figure grows taller and his arms
become like wings, pushing forward and then dragging sharply back, sliding
along the surface of the table, his hands cusped—until he suddenly pauses
to look at his empty hands, his head bowing forward once again. 'He says,
when he dances, it's the fact he doesn't have to think; he can just do what
he wants with it, and not be stopped or judged; and not be stopped or
judged; and not be stopped or judged'.

Hetty Blades (2017) examines the *52 Portraits* series in an article that
analyses the intersection of different authorial perspectives in screendance
works. Here, Blades pursues a line of thinking developed by Tamara Tomić-
Vajagić (2014: 82) in her discussion of the potential of dance performances
to produce 'ambivalent self-presentations' that 'blend [...] first- and third-
person perspectives', thus frustrating the distinction between portrait and
self-portrait. Tomić-Vajagić reflects on examples of dance performance

in which the performer's first-person account interferes with the chore-ographer's third-person perspective, generating ambiguous 'self/portrait effects'. Blades point out that, in *52 Portraits*, a 'blending of perspectives' occurs in the relationship between the lyrics and the artists' autobiograph-ical accounts, as well as between the words and the movements (Blades, 2017: 97). Drawing on Tomić-Vajagić, Blades suggests that, by occupying a '"liminal" space between perspectives', the work produces an ambivalent 'self/portrait effect' (Blades, 2017: 97).

Building on this notion of ambiguity, I interrogate the generative poten-tialities that emerge from inhabiting liminal spaces and moving across thresholds. In particular, I reflect on how ambivalence and indetermina-tion are constitutive of the impersonal, of the shift between the first and the third person which enables enunciation to step outside of the sub-ject/object opposition. This shift does not result in the total erasure of the 'I' in favour of an individuated third person: it implies a rethinking of these personal categories, which enables singularity to be inscribed in an inde-terminate impersonal form 'bursting with unexpected potential' (Esposito, 2012: 147). In this respect, I consider the ways in which Burrows, Fargion and Glendinning's project might be seen to rethink notions of subjectivity and collectivity, sparking a reflection on the positioning of 'minor' lan-guages and voices as sites of deterritorialisation and resistance in current artistic practice and discourse.[16] Interrogating the kinds of subjects that are engaged and portrayed in this series of works, the types of communi-ties that are possibilised, I ask: What is the relationship between the gestural portraits and the songs? What kinds of autobiographies emerge from these videos?

The process of making of *52 Portraits* involved the blending of differ-ent authorial voices, as is directly reflected in the composition of the lyrics for the accompanying songs. The first stages of the collaboration between the creative team and the featured artists revolved around dialogue: in a roundtable discussion as part of a public event about the project I curated in 2016,[17] Burrows recounted that, for each piece, he would contact the artist(s) with an email in which the ideas and practicalities of the project were explained and suggestions offered around how they might prepare their contribution. On the day of the video shooting, Burrows would ask the performer(s) a few questions, writing their answers down and selecting phrases to compose lyrics for Fargion's music. The aspects covered in these interviews were generally always the same (with some exceptions, when additional questions might be asked): What was the first room you ever danced in? What does it feel like when you dance? Is there an injury or an illness that you survived or endured? They were all very personal questions—almost 'too cheesy', as Burrows admitted—which led to some 'very moving' answers.[18] While the replies given by the featured artists were quoted from to the letter, the you/I interlocution that characterised their conversation with Burrows (both by email and live) was then transposed into a text written in the third person—as in the example above: 'Botis grew up in…', 'he says…'. Although the interview precedes the recording of the dance, the audio with the music and singing is added to the filmic images at a later stage; during the video shooting, the performers move to no soundtrack.

For Deleuze, it is the third person that makes literary enunciation possible: a life is materialised. Yet, this is not the same as 'projecting an ego': 'Of course, literary characters are perfectly individuated, and are neither vague nor general; but all their individual traits elevate them to a vision that carries them off in an indefinite, like a becoming that is too powerful for them' (Deleuze, 1998: 3). In *52 Portraits*, through the compositional framework of the films and the different layers of the process of making, the dialectic between first and second person, between a subjective and a non-subjective stance (Esposito, 2012), is eluded and, in the dance film, a figure is materialised which feeds on but exists outside this tension. I understand this figure as Esposito's third-person, which ultimately points to Deleuze's idea of immanence: an instance of life which is not defined by something that transcends it; an impersonal event in which 'the actor [is one] with what is acted upon' (Esposito, 2012: 143). Not a negation of the singularity of the subject, but rather a way of traversing the person and occupying a space which is neither inside nor outside.

In an interview about the project (Dunn, 2017: 23), Burrows discusses the paradoxical positioning of the video portraits between revealing personal traits and resisting autobiographical narratives:

no matter how abstract or distanced it seems, there is always a sense of the person revealed. Having said that though, the job of the dancer or performer is usually to resist the autobiographical impulse at all costs, because to embrace it is to reduce other rich and contradictory elements, like more abstract or formal things, and then you risk losing some of the peculiarities and uncertainties which make performance resonate.

I qualify the works as 'im/personal' portraits, which occur as events located at the intersection between singularity and plurality, presence and absence—or, as Heathfield put it reflecting on the project in the context of the above-mentioned roundtable, between the documentary and the abstract, as the films expose/conceal the different subjects through the spoken texts and the choreographic fabric.[19] Heathfield draws a parallel with *Body Not Fit for Purpose*, in which textual references to specific (political or experiential) content engage in a paradoxical relationship with 'abstract' hand movements (see also Chapters 2 and 4). In *52 Portraits*, there is a productive tension between the content conveyed by the lyrics and the danced movements. As the texts are composed from accounts given by the performers, the narrative of the portraits also unfolds as a relationship between memory and embodiment. In turn, this highlights the disjunction between the experience of dancing and the act of watching dance, between inside and outside: the interview texts are about what the dancers are feeling, which is in tension with the outside position of the viewer.

Heathfield sees in this irresolvable gap between interiority and exteriority a real space for play and generative production of ideas. Significantly, for Heathfield, this also points to the political force of the work and of Burrows' oeuvre as a whole, which consists in reviving abstraction as a political tool. Heathfield speaks of a 'politics of abstraction', which emerges from this movement: 'between something that is known and something that is withdrawn or opaque'.[20] In the next chapter, I build on this analysis of the dramaturgy of *52 Portraits* and on the understanding of the impersonal dimension of Burrows' choreography to conceptualise the ways in which his art, in particular through his interdisciplinary partnership with Fargion, reframes and rethinks ideas of collaboration and community; in doing so, I foreground the political potential of their practice and poetics.

NOTES

1. As I have written elsewhere: see Perazzo Domm (2012). This chapter is a development of some of the ideas I begin to discuss in my earlier article.
2. See, for instance, Duerden (1999) and Jones (1998).
3. See, for instance, Burrows and Ritsema (2003) and Burrows (2015).
4. See, for instance, Burrows (2014).
5. These include his keynote addresses for the DanceHE conference 'Resilience: Articulating "Knowledges" Through Dance in the 21st Century', The Montfort University, Leicester, 9 April 2015, and for the 'Post Dance' conference, Stockholm, 14–16 October 2015 (published as Burrows, 2018).

See also Burrows' website for a list of his talks, including scripts (Burrows, n.d.).

6. The handbook has so far been translated into German (Tanz Magazine, 2010), Slovenian (Maska, 2011), French (Contredanse, 2017) and Bulgarian (Metheor, 2017).

7. A broader discussion of Burrows' marginalisation in critical dance studies literature is offered in Chapter 1.

8. Among the most notable are: *Blue Yellow* for Sylvie Guillem (1995); *Walking/music* for Ballett Frankfurt (1997); *The Elders Project*, a Sadler's Wells Theatre commission (2014); *Eleanor And Flora Music* for Eleanor Sikorski and Flora Wellesley Wesley (known as Nora), in collaboration with Fargion (2015).

9. Esposito here draws on Foucault's theory of statements as articulated in the *Archaeology of Knowledge*.

10. Another piece which, through the medium of the camera, 'plays [...] with the appearance/disappearance of the dance and of the dancer's body' is *Blue Yellow*, a choreography commissioned for and danced by Sylvie Guillem as part of her 1995 'Evidentia' series for BBC2 (Perazzo, 2006: 46).

11. To date, Burrows' duets with Fargion are *Both Sitting Duet* (2002), *The Quiet Dance* (2005), *Speaking Dance* (2006), *Cheap Lecture* (2009), *The Cow Piece* (2009), *Counting To One Hundred* (2011), *One Flute Note* (2012), *Show and Tell* (2013), *Rebelling Against Limit* (2013) and *Body Not Fit for Purpose* (2014).

12. See, for instance, Hutera (2003) and Dunning (2004).

13. Drawing on Weil, Esposito explains the impersonal as the 'sacred' part of human beings, 'that which is not covered by their mask' (Esposito, 2012: 16).

14. Roberts (2004) also directed the first audio-visual collection of Burrows' pieces. About this collection of films, see also Perazzo (2006).

15. Glendinning, '*52 Portraits*: A conversation', talk at Kingston University London, 1 July 2016.

16. For a discussion of Burrows' work alongside the Deleuzoguattarian notion of 'minor' practices, see especially Chapter 2.

17. On 1 July 2016, when the series of portraits was half-way through its course, I organised a public event at Kingston University London to contextualise the project and hear from Burrows, Fargion and Glendinning about their creative process. Taking part in the conversation were also Sarah Whatley and Heathfield, alongside two of the artists featuring in the series, Kloe Dean and Antonio de la Fe.

18. Burrows, '*52 Portraits*: A conversation', talk at Kingston University London, 1 July 2016.

19. Heathfield, '*52 Portraits*: A conversation', talk at Kingston University London, 1 July 2016.

20. Heathfield, '*52 Portraits*: A conversation', talk at Kingston University London, 1 July 2016.

References

Blades, Hetty (2017) 'Screendance Self/Portraits', *The International Journal of Screendance*, 8: 93–103. Available at: http://screendancejournal.org/issue/view/193#.WTqfLTb06t8. Accessed 9 June 2017.

Brown, Ismene (2015) 'The Associates at Sadler's Wells Reviewed: Another Acutely Inventive Work from Crystal Pite. Plus: Are Jonathan Burrows and Matteo Fargion Losing Their Satirical Touch?', *The Spectator*, 14 February. https://www.spectator.co.uk/2015/02/the-associates-sadlers-wells-review-another-acutely-inventive-work-from-crystal-pite/. Accessed 9 June 2017.

Burrows, Jonathan (2005) Unpublished conversation with Daniela Perazzo Domm, London, 26 November.

Burrows, Jonathan (2010) *A Choreographer's Handbook*. London and New York: Routledge.

Burrows, Jonathan (2014) 'Rebelling Against Limit', in Noémie Solomon (ed.) *Danse: An Anthology*. Dijon: Les Presses du Réel: 81–87.

Burrows, Jonathan (2015) 'Body Not Fit for Purpose', *Performance Research*, 20 (5): 81–86.

Burrows, Jonathan (2018) 'Jonathan Burrows' Postdance Conference Keynote Address, Stockholm 2015', in Jo Butterworth and Liesbeth Wildschut (eds.) *Contemporary Choreography: A Critical Reader*, 2nd edn. London and New York: Routledge: 165–174.

Burrows, Jonathan (n.d.) *Jonathan Burrows*. http://www.jonathanburrows.info/. Accessed 20 December 2018.

Burrows, Jonathan and Ritsema, Jan (2003) 'Weak Dance Strong Questions', *Performance Research*, 8 (2): 28–33.

Burrows, Jonathan, Le Roy, Xavier and Ruckert, Felix (2004) 'Meeting of Minds', *Dance Theatre Journal*, 20 (3): 9–13.

Burt, Ramsay (2017) *Ungoverning Dance: Contemporary European Theatre Dance and the Commons*. Oxford: Oxford University Press.

Campbell, Timothy (2010) '"Foucault Was Not a Person": Idolatry and the Impersonal in Roberto Esposito's Third Person', *CR: The New Centennial Review*, 10 (2): 135–150.

Claid, Emilyn (2010) 'Still Curious', in Alexandra Carter and Janet O'Shea (eds.) *The Routledge Dance Studies Reader*, 2nd edn. London and New York: Routledge: 133–143.

Cull, Laura (2013) *Theatres of Immanence: Deleuze and the Ethics of Performance*. Basingstoke: Palgrave Macmillan.

Cvejić, Bojana (2015) *Choreographing Problems: Expressive Concepts in Contemporary Dance and Performance*. Basingstoke: Palgrave Macmillan.

Deleuze, Gilles (1994) *Difference and Repetition*. Translated by Paul Patton. London: Athlone Press.

Deleuze, Gilles (1998) *Essays Critical and Clinical*. Translated by Daniel W. Smith and Michael A. Greco. London and New York: Verso.

Deleuze, Gilles and Guattari, Félix (1987) *A Thousand Plateaus: Capitalism and Schizophrenia*. Translated by Brian Massumi. Minneapolis: University of Minnesota Press.

Duerden, Rachel Chamberlain (1999) 'Jonathan Burrows', in Martha Bremser (ed.) *Fifty Contemporary Choreographers: A Reference Guide*. London: Routledge: 47–51.

Duerden, Rachel (2001) 'Jonathan Burrows: Exploring the Frontiers', *Dancing Times*, 91 (1086): 551–557.

Dunning, Jennifer (2004) 'A Conversation Composed of Gestures', *The New York Times*, 19 March.

Dunn, Lawrence (2017) 'Jonathan Burrows + Matteo Fargion: On Making Portraits. Interview with Lawrence Dunn', *Cerenem Journal*, 6: 21–35. https://issuu.com/cerenem/docs/cj6-31jul_final. Accessed 10 January 2019.

Esposito, Roberto (2012) *Third Person: Politics of Life and Philosophy of the Impersonal*. Translated by Zakiya Hanafi. Cambridge: Polity Press.

Etchells, Tim (2007) 'Article by Tim Etchells on the First Trilogy of Duets'. http://www.jonathanburrows.info/#note1. Accessed 27 February 2018.

Hutera, Donald (2003) 'Both Talking: Interview with Jonathan Burrows and Matteo Fargion', *Dance Umbrella News*, Autumn.

Jones, Chris (1998) 'Jonathan Burrows', in Taryn Benbow-Pfalzgraf (ed.) *International Dictionary of Modern Dance*. Detroit, New York and London: St. James Press: 83–84.

Kelleher, Joe (2008) 'On Self-Remembering Theatres' [First published as: 'Sui Teatri Autorimembranti', in Viviana Gravano, Enrico Pitozzi and Annalisa Sacchi (eds.) *B.Motion: Spazio di Riflessione Fuori e Dentro le Arti Performative*. Milan: Costa & Nolan]. http://www.jonathanburrows.info/#/text/?id=105&t=content. Accessed 27 February 2018.

Louppe, Laurence (2010) *Poetics of Contemporary Dance*. Translated by Sally Gardner. Alton: Dance Books.

Parry, Jann (1996) 'Dance on the Edge', *Dance Now*, 5 (4): 67–75.

Peeters, Jeroen (2010) 'Resistance, Ignorance, Curiosity, Stupidity: On Jonathan Burrows' *A Choreographer's Handbook*', *Corpus*, 4 November.

Perazzo, Daniela (2005) 'The Sitting Duo Now Walks, or the Piece the Lies Quietly Underneath: Daniela Perazzo Interviews Jonathan Burrows', *Dance Theatre Journal*, 21 (2): 2–7.

Perazzo, Daniela (2006) 'Review. Jonathan Burrows Group: Dance Films by Adam Roberts', *Dance Theatre Journal*, 21 (3): 45–47.

Perazzo Domm, Daniela (2008) 'Jonathan Burrows and Matteo Fargion's *Both Sitting Duet* (2002): A Discursive Choreomusical Collaboration', in Janet Lansdale (ed.) *Decentring Dancing Texts*. Basingstoke: Palgrave Macmillan: 125–142.

Perazzo Domm, Daniela (2010) 'Traces of History: Jonathan Burrows' Rethinking of the Choreographic Past', *Contemporary Theatre Review*, 20 (3): 267–282.

Perazzo Domm, Daniela (2012) 'The "Struggle" of the Subject: Productive Ambiguity in Jonathan Burrows' Choreography', *Choreographic Practices*, 3: 99–117.

Roberts, Adam (2004) *Jonathan Burrows Group: Dance Films by Adam Roberts*, choreography by Jonathan Burrows. London: Jonathan Burrows Group.

Smith, Carmel (2016) 'Interview: 52 Portraits', *londondance.com*, 8 January. http://londondance.com/articles/interviews/an-epic-love-song-to-an-art-form-52-portraits/. Accessed 27 February 2018.

The Forsythe Company (n.d.) 'Seven Duets, Jonathan Burrows and Matteo Fargion'. http://scores.motionbank.org/jbmf/#/set/sets. Accessed 27 February 2018.

Tomić-Vajagić, Tamara (2014) 'The Self/Portrait Effects and Dance Performance: Rineke Dijkstra's *The Krazyhouse* and William Forsythe's *the Second Detail*', *Performance Research*, 19 (5): 82–92.

Vattimo, Gianni (1991) *The End of Modernity: Nihilism and Hermeneutics in Postmodern Culture*, revised edn. Translated by Jon R. Snyder. Baltimore: The John Hopkins University Press.

CHAPTER 6

Choreographies of Plurality: Rethinking Collaboration and Collectivity

A minor literature, Gilles Deleuze and Félix Guattari (1986: 17) write, has 'collective value' and is conceived as 'something other than a literature of masters'. Thinking through the notion of the 'minor' in relation to artistic practice, Simon O'Sullivan (2005) observes that the emphasis is on the 'collective production of work': 'In this way, we can see the artistic production of statements as a kind of precursor of a community (and often a nation) still in formation'. Framing Jonathan Burrows' choreography as a 'minor dance', this book has so far examined how it deterritorialises dominant canons and has postulated the practice's political potential. This chapter looks more specifically at the collective dimension of the work, furthering the argument that, if in contemporary art, as Peter Osborne (2013: 34) maintains, 'collectivity is produced by the interconnectedness of practices', a minor artistic practice such as the one created by Burrows with the composer Matteo Fargion, which is founded on the conjunction and 'friendship' between different disciplines, possibilises a sense of commonality while also envisioning new modes and understandings of collaborative work.

Building on my discussion, which is central to Chapters 4 and 5, of how Burrows' choreography unfolds through partnerships intended as transformative encounters and materialises through im/personal modes of address,

© The Author(s) 2019
D. Perazzo Domm, *Jonathan Burrows*,
New World Choreographies,
https://doi.org/10.1007/978-3-030-27680-5_6

I further interrogate how the performance work he has created with Fargion and other collaborators is articulated as both singular and plural artistic enunciation which gives voice to a possible community. I return, in the first instance, to the *52 Portraits* series to examine how it is located at the threshold between individuation and community, including in a compositional and dramaturgical sense. I then move on to examine Burrows and Fargion's 2017 work *Any Table Any Room*, a project which is recreated at each occurrence in collaboration with four local dance artists who are invited to take part in a three-day rehearsal period ahead of the performance dates. In both instances, I reflect on how the works engage with notions and practices of collaboration and on how they address—expose and trouble—accepted understandings of community. As part of this discussion, I also consider other collaborative and collective projects Burrows has devised, such as the cross-disciplinary 'salon' events in non-theatre spaces (*Return of the Salon*, 2015–2017)[1] and the recent *Music For Lectures* project (2018).

In this sense, this chapter continues to extend its enquiry beyond Burrows' performance work, considering more broadly the contribution he has made to the field and discourse of experimental dance. Specifically, following on from the previous chapter's engagement with Burrows' writings (for publication, lectures or talks), I am interested in examining how Burrows' textual outputs are preoccupied with understandings and practices of collaboration. In tandem with his work for the stage, his talks and essays are invested in conveying a sense of plurality of voices and of a community made possible by modes of collaborative artistic practice which transcend geographic and disciplinary boundaries. The *52 Portraits* series includes international dancers and choreographers who work with different ideas of dance and different styles, alongside dance scholars and performance artists; *Any Table Any Room* is recreated anew with four local artists every time it is performed; *Music For Lectures* combines a talk by an invited artist with music performed live by Burrows, Fargion and his daughter Francesca Fargion. Similarly, Burrows' writings invoke a multiplicity of contributors from a range of artistic and cultural fields, who are engaged in shared thinking/practice. I suggest that the community projected by this extended artistic practice is of a 'speculative' nature, as Osborne puts it. It represents 'speculative collectives' which reflect the 'radical re-spatialization of social relations' of the historical present towards 'new forms of transnational interconnection' (Osborne, 2013: 195)—and, I would add, new modes of working across fields of practice.

Paradoxically, expanded understandings and instantiations of artistic practice, in terms of both their transdisciplinarity and their transterritoriality, draw attention to the problems and contradictions of categories such as collectivity and collaboration, raising questions about their ability to account for a plurality of heterogeneous positions, and often 'registering their partiality and incompleteness' (Osborne, 2013: 195). In this respect, Bojana Cvejić (2004) has written about the notion of collectivity, asking to what extent it 'only conjure[s] images of collective political action in a strong ideological vein abolished after 1989? Is collectivism necessarily understood—and therefore, dismissed—as the tool for emancipatory politics by an obsolete model of the theatre and performance practices in the 60s?' In this sense, Cvejić problematises the term in relation to its political import, considering how, by invoking an idea of working together without central leadership, collectivity speaks both of failed historical attempts and of a modality which is dismissed by the neoliberalist focus on individual enterprise. She thus advocates for a rethinking of collectivism and commonality that rejects unison and homogeneity and acknowledges the political importance of heterogeneity, while also distinguishing between individualism as the preferred dimension of capitalism and singularity as a modality of critique and experimentation.[2]

In Burrows' textual outputs, conversations with fellow artists are often mentioned as implicated in the creative process, as productive encounters that punctuate and shape the journey of making work—danced or written. Sometimes these interconnecting voices are weaved into Burrows' talks and writings in the form of references to intellectual or artistic work from the public domain: André Lepecki's observations on the expressive nature of modern dance and Tim Etchells' words on absurdity are summoned in a text about working with structure and limitations (Burrows, 2014); a talk on rhythm (Burrows, 2016) references Jacques Derrida on rhythm as haunting, literary theorist Terry Eagleton on deviating from codes, philosopher Alva Noë on art and boredom, historian William McNeill on the joy of military marching, Islamic inventor, poet and musician Abbas Ibn Firnas on metronomes, composer Karlheinz Stockhausen on change and the beginning of a new moment, and singer and activist Ani DiFranco on 'working at the edge of our abilities'. Other times, the references are to private exchanges with colleagues or friends, whose words or practices have intersected with Burrows' thinking/doing: among the scholars and makers who are credited for their 'conversations, advice and shared writings' are Charlie Ashwell, Hetty Blades, Ramsay Burt, Katye Coe, Juan Dominguez,

Susanne Foellmer, Deborah Hay, Paul Hughes, Jamila Johnson-Small, Bojana Kunst, Emma Meehan, Joe Moran, Chrysa Parkinson, Jan Ritsema, Botis Seva, whose thoughts are acknowledged in Burrows' (2018a) talk on politics; or Mette Edvardsen, Bojana Cvejić, Jeroen Peeters, Simon Ellis, Efrosini Protopapa, Stefan Jovanović, who are mentioned in a talk on practice—'And by the way it doesn't matter if you know these [people] or not, it only matters that we go on speaking each other's names or else we'll all disappear' (Burrows, 2018b). A narrative is thus constructed that presents creative work as always premised on a heterogeneous effort to think through the questions the work addresses or the problems it stumbles upon: 'Because if there was ever an art form that advances collectively it's one that starts from the body' (Burrows, 2018a: 258).

To frame this practice and the critical narrative that emerges from Burrows' texts, which constructs it as a cumulative and shared activity, I consider the notions of community and collaboration from the point of view of the plurality, and necessary alterity, they strive to encompass. The processes and politics of collaboration have been given significant consideration in art and performance scholarship over the last decade or so. Most notably, Claire Bishop (2006: 178) has drawn attention to a 'recent surge of artistic interest in collectivity, collaboration, and direct engagement with specific social constituencies'. Offering a critical view of socially engaged art in her famous 2006 essay 'The Social Turn: Collaboration and Its Discontents', Bishop comments on how the rise of collaborative artistic practices has been accompanied by an 'ethical turn' in art criticism: a shift in attention towards working processes, by which 'aesthetic judgements have been overtaken by ethical criteria' (2006: 180).

Providing a more positive assessment of collaborative approaches in performance studies, Noyale Colin and Stefanie Sachsenmaier's edited collection *Collaboration in Performance Practice* (2016) explores modes of working together developed by artists in response to the sociopolitical conditions of our contemporary world, rethinking terms such as collectivity, authorship, democracy, responsibility, agency and recalibrating the focus to account for the practitioners' point of view. Colin and Sachsenmaier's (2016: 13) discussion of collaboration focuses on 'cross-disciplinary performance practices', which are realised through the working together of 'expert practitioners from [...] different disciplines' and in which '[e]ach collaborator's work advances to its own logic, yet in response to the evolvement of the others' input'. The book's editors ask questions which are pertinent to my investigation of Burrows' interdisciplinary collaborations with

Fargion and other artists: '[h]ow might we understand the "other" who is collaborator in the same event, yet also an "other" in terms of disciplinary expertise?' (Colin and Sachsenmaier, 2016: 13). Their argument draws on Martin Heidegger's concept of the 'others' as those with whom we share the world, to discuss the 'practice of "co-laborating" in cross-disciplinary collaborative performance-making' as one in which each collaborator

> is engaged in what is specific to her or his disciplinary experience and expectations, yet, equally works inventively in collaboration according to a collective intention at the level of the set-up. This sensibility towards the 'other' [...] allows for developments of practice that would not otherwise have occurred – a vital characteristic of inventive practice. (Colin and Sachsenmaier, 2016: 14)

Building on—but also departing from—this line of thinking, I wish to unpick Colin and Sachsenmaier's point that, in collaborative practices, individual identities are both guarded and broadened. To do so, I continue to work within the Deleuzoguattarian conceptual framework that informs Franco Berardi's (2012) idea of conjunction as a 'becoming-other', as I discuss in Chapter 4: a relationship with the other premised on friendship and love, which entails an exchange that transforms the individual not through 'compliance and adaptation' but rather through 'empathic comprehension' (Berardi, 2015: 18). This is a mode of coming together 'that can generate meaning without following a pre-ordained design, and without obeying any inner law or finality': it is an 'uncertain and unresolved oscillation', a 'weaseling [one's] way about' (Berardi, 2015: 20–22).

Theorising the relationship between experimental artistic practice and neoliberal capitalism, performance theorist and dramaturg Bojana Kunst (2015: 81) writes that '[o]ver the last decade, collaboration has become a key issue in the vocabulary of dancers, choreographers and other performing artists'. Reflecting, with the post-Marxist philosopher Paolo Virno (2004),[3] on the ways in which contemporary modes of production rely on general human competences (such as linguistic and communicative faculties) rather than on specialised skills, Kunst (2015: 78) observes that 'collaboration, communication and connection belong in the most fetishized fields of the present day', insofar as they embody the ideals of flexibility, mobility and linguistic ability that have become crucial in contemporary labour. 'Collaboration locates people in the present (time); it is only through collaboration, on the constantly changing map of places, that people can actually become visible in the present' (Kunst, 2015: 78). Hence, collaboration has become ubiquitous in today's economy and culture.

As creative production, since the 1990s, has become increasingly organised around discrete projects, professionals from different fields of artistic, critical and academic practice have more and more frequently opted to come together 'in view of a productive cooperation' (Laermans, 2012: 94). Social theorist Rudi Laermans (2012: 94) observes that, while collaboration has re-emerged as a predominant artistic modality, seemingly rehearsing the 'communitarian ethos' of the 1960s experimental practices, it has nevertheless relinquished its 'romantic' vision and turned to 'contingent' preoccupations: 'the utopian longing for a united "we" marked by a harmonious togetherness that informed 1960s dance avant-gardism' has been supplanted by 'the more impartial work ethic of "doing a project with others"'. While collaboration is now an indispensable ingredient of artistic processes, its critical potential as a modality that decentres the idea of authorship and dissolves the boundaries between artistic disciplines and professional roles is being diluted. As Kunst (2015: 77) argues, '[t]oday, it is so difficult to think of about collaboration as a transformative process because there is a certain excess of collaboration in our daily lives'.

Working with conceptualisations of modes of togetherness, in the next paragraphs, I examine Burrows' collaborative work as a way of thinking/practising with and through notions of community. Specifically, pursuing my engagement with Roberto Esposito's understanding of alterity and plurality (see also Chapter 5), I address and trouble ideas surrounding the relationship between community and dissensus, generosity and mastery. I argue that the practices of collaboration that Burrows and Fargion engage with are premised on the paradoxical confusion between 'giving' and 'stealing', where both are instances of an understanding of community as a duty towards the other. I also consider how their cross-disciplinary projects frustrate accepted understandings of expert professional practice and propose a reassessment of disciplinary commitment that debunks the notion of mastery.

GIVING AND STEALING: *52 PORTRAITS* AND A DISCOVERED COMMUNITY

As I begin to discuss in Chapter 5, the *52 Portraits* series, created by Burrows and Fargion with the film-maker Hugo Glendinning in 2016, features filmic sketches of a range of different dance artists, whose specificities are both highlighted and contained by the use of a recognisable format (a video filmed with a fixed camera, a black backdrop, a table, words sung syllabically to an accompanying music track), which gestures towards the idiosyncratic performance set-up that Burrows and Fargion have adopted in many of their duets. As a project that addresses the nexus between singularity and plurality, 52 Portraits also engages with questions of community and its politics. In this section, I discuss how the seriality of the work, based on the selection of an artist, or artistic team, for each Monday of 2016 for inclusion in the project (made available online through weekly releases of videos), extends the notion of self-portraiture beyond the featured individuals and possibilises an artistic community through the virtual durational catalogue it stages. The portraits, produced by London's Sadler's Wells, can be accessed freely via the project's website (Burrows, Fargion, and Glendinning, 2016) and are mainly intended for private fruition on personal mobile or desktop devices—although the series was also screened in its entirety in January 2017 in London and Bologna (Italy) and in a handful of other European locations in 2018.

Possibly due to its online format and circulation, 52 Portraits has received little critical attention in the press, although The Guardian calls it 'a lovely project—simple in format, rich in potential' (Mackrell, 2016) and The New York Times praises how the videos manage 'to articulate all that goes into becoming and being a dancer [...] on a refreshingly human scale, without oversimplifying' (Burke, 2016). The reflections I offer in the following paragraphs focus on how the work, by engaging in a selection of a specific number of representatives of the current international dance landscape, contends with the idea and format of the canon. I discuss how the series is both implicated in and resistant to mechanisms and politics of inclusion and exclusion, exposing and troubling accepted understandings of consensus and community.

On 1 July 2016, half-way through the fifty-two weeks of the project, I organised a public event about Burrows, Fargion, and Glendinning's 52 Portraits at Kingston University London, in which the artistic team discussed the creative process in conversation with Sarah Whatley, Adrian Heathfield and two of the dancers featured in the series, Kloc Dean and Antonio de la Fe. During the roundtable discussion, Heathfield remarked on the significance of the temporal tension the work is founded on: between the 'flash temporality' of the short films and the 'extended duration' of the work as a whole.[4] Hence, the project can be seen to exist between frameworks and temporalities: as short, individual portraits but also as a series, with a durational dimension. As Heathfield observed, while portraiture as a genre is supposed to disclose something about the subject's self,[5] the video dances happen very quickly—too quickly for us to be able to retain them in memory. Hence, as an event, the work is intrinsically indeterminate, insofar as the relationships between the individual portraits and with the project as a whole shift as a result of the large number of connections enabled by the breadth of the series.

In an interview 'on portraiture' with composer Lawrence Dunn (2017: 22), Burrows discusses the project in terms of its relationship to time and memory in the context of how dance is usually distributed and consumed online:

> I had been thinking for a long time about other ways dance might occupy the internet, other than music videos and short clips of spectacular dancing that you might see on Facebook. And the model for me was the year I spent on and off following Tim Etchell's [*sic*] daily political playbill series called *Vacuum Days*, which ran for the entirety of 2011. Matteo and I had a two year experience of working with exploratory digital software, motion capture and so forth, as part of William Forsythe's *Motionbank* project in Frankfurt, so we had some idea of that place where art meets the digital, but what I liked about Tim's project was that it wasn't about things looking digital but rather about the obvious ways we all use software. So we decided to make a project which would take the short form of Facebook postings, but give it this accumulating quality, so it might transcend the usual instant and forgettable nature of dance clips on social media.

The work as a series had a different pace during its dilated production period, punctuated by the Monday morning releases of the new videos and the week-long waits in-between. For Heathfield, what is discovered in the duration is 'a kind of community, which we can only understand through a cumulative temporality'; he sees the project as pressing forward the question: 'what kind of accommodation is this of dance and of the community of dancers?' In this sense, the project acquires a sociological dimension: 'there is a dynamic to the work which is that it takes a particular snapshot of a community of people and stitches new relations and new affinities between and through their work'.[6] At the roundtable, Whatley wondered to what extent the artists were aware of being part of a collective action and also drew attention to the question of what happens to the collection when it becomes 'the 52'.[7] As a completed series that is openly accessible online as a list of 52 links to video dances that any viewer can pick and choose from, the project begins to inhabit another dimension in which the selection of artists, now completed and final, risks being read as a canon, albeit a new one, offered as an alternative to the dominant canon of the dance tradition.[8]

In the interview I mentioned above (Dunn, 2017: 34), Burrows contextualises the rationale behind the selection of the fifty-two entries:

> The only principle for curating the project was that it must be people whose work we love. But as the project has developed so it has become clear that it can never give room for everyone who should be there, and so we are looking at ways to make clear at the end that the list of 52 is in no way comprehensive and that it could go on. And we have already been asked would we do it again in another context, and our preferred model would be that the idea is put into the commons and anyone who wanted to make or subvert or do whatever they want with their own portraiture, would be welcome. And the list of 52 is in a sense deliberately random, shifting from known to quite unknown people, through obvious choices but with occasionally surprising choices. And the important thing for me is that everyone is equal under the roof of the project, so when I was asked could someone show just the portraits of older performers as part of another event, I said no, because to single out the older performers would be to make a judgement on their age, and for me there is a politics in the fact of ignoring all the usual hierarchies which stereotype or marginalise artists for whatever reason.

In the context of the roundtable discussion, Fargion explained that the idea for the format of the short video dances of the series came from an earlier choreographic work, *The Elders Project* (2014), for which him and Burrows were commissioned by London's Sadler's Wells to work with nine former professional dancers from London Contemporary Dance Theatre, The Royal Ballet, Second Stride and the Siobhan Davies Dance Company to create a piece that drew on their bodily memories and personal stories of dancing. The outcome performance, presented in London in September 2014 and in Hendon (Greater London) the following month, featured sequences of movements accompanied by Fargion's singing, with lyrics composed from the dancers' own accounts of their experiences of dance (Elixir Project blog, 2018). The music had been used here as a 'vessel' for the performers' autobiographical accounts, and this approach to combining movement and lyrics felt like 'unfinished business', which the artists wanted to explore further.[9] As noted by Judith Mackrell (2016), the continuity between the two works resides also in their participant bases, as '[t]wo of the original subjects, Betsy Gregory and Namron, return to the project; the others range from the 29-year-old dance-maker Alexandrina Hemsley to the 91-year-old choreographer Robert Cohan, and from performance artist Hetain Patel to Royal Ballet principal Zenaida Yanowsky'. As such, the portraits account for a wide range of ages, performance experiences and approaches to movement:

> The range of body language across these portraits is as fascinating as you'd expect given the spread of their subjects. Jonzi D, the UK's spokesman for hip-hop and the noisy, affable host of Breakin' Convention, compresses a startling dark rage into his short repeated dance sequence. In one of the very few duets in the series Hemsley dances with her 76-year-old dad, and their busy, affectionate hand jives tell us so much about their easy, accommodating relationship with each other. (Mackrell, 2016)

Burrows commented, in the roundtable discussion, that a question was posed of 'how to allow for different directions and still make a coherent larger project', explaining that the work wants to resist categorisations of what constitutes a good or a bad approach to dance.[10] For Glendinning, the series can be considered as both one piece and many pieces. For Whatley, while each work reflects the history of the individual artists, it also reveals something of Burrows and Fargion's history, which 'moves forward replicating itself in different ways, in its form and in what it asks if itself'.[11] In answer to a question from the audience about the choices behind the order of the portraits, Burrows commented humorously that they had had to do some reorganisation to address a problem with a 'glut of middle-aged people', but also explained that they had been 'careful not to make it a nice balanced mixture of people. We are all too canny to that now; we know what that looks and feels like and it's meaningless. It's kind of gesture politics'.[12]

Antonio de la Fe, one of the subjects of the portraits, commented that the way in which the collaboration was framed highlighted the 'artistic licence' of each individual performer, also through the contract issued to the participants by Sadler's Wells, which commissioned each artist to make a piece of work which would then be weaved into a series by the artistic team.[13] This debate brings to the foreground the political dimension of collaboration in a number of ways: firstly, it exposes the ideological thrust of communitarian practices understood as harmonious coexistence of differences; secondly, it takes issue with the notion of consensus-based collaboration, pointing to the question of dissensus, intended with Rancière (2011: 2) as 'a conflict about who speaks and who does not speak'; finally, it unmasks the potential emptiness of practices of inclusion, their symbolic and tokenistic value—what Sara Ahmed (2012: 119) calls the 'nonperformative' character of commitments to diversity that 'do not bring into effect that which they name'.

Burrows frames the creative process further in terms of the mutuality it is premised on; in the above-mentioned interview on the way in which the project interprets portraiture, he says: 'these 52 meetings with different artists are anyway feeding and disrupting and interrogating what Matteo and I do and think and assume and doubt and wish for, so the exchange is mutual, and that's the point of doing it' (Dunn 2017: 24). Similar questions surrounding the collective dimension of artistic practice, the complicated relationship between giving and taking and the politics of consensus in collaboration are touched upon in Burrows' recent talk on politics:

> we're aware how the ways we work together are different and potential, and although we avoid the overused exhaustion of the word collective we're doing it anyway.
>
> Because the thing we have hasn't much value which makes us generous, so we give it away freely which is foolish and useful.
>
> And we help the others and we leave no trace and the doer decides, which feels like a more helpful model than worn out consensus politics. (Burrows, 2018a: 258)

What kind of generosity does this 'foolish and useful' giving speak of, and what relationship does it entertain with notions and mechanisms of community? In his discussion of twenty-first-century performances of friendship,[14] Ramsay Burt (2017: 157) defines Burrows and Fargion as 'generous artists' with reference to their 'human-scale' performances and to how they are 'generous to the audience' in providing the tools with which to sit with their performances. In Burrows' *A Choreographer's Handbook*, the generosity of dance, its 'long history of shared information' (Burrows, 2010: 207) is reflected upon alongside the practice of 'stealing', which always involves a transformation, and which raises the following questions: 'What do you want to own? What might be useful to defend as yours, and what might best reflect on you by keeping your hands open?' Stealing is a mode of engaging with artistic material through the creative process that Burrows and Fargion openly make reference to in *Cheap Lecture*,[15] making the audience laugh: 'everything is stolen anyway', they say. As Ismene Brown (2010) writes in her review of the work, '[t]hey make their thefts clear in their script, no less funny for that'. 'Stealing is how I work' is a statement also made by Fargion in the above-mentioned roundtable discussion on *52 Portraits*, during which he explained that, in creating the series, he would collect all the available material (the videos of the movement sequences danced in silence, the lyrics composed by Burrows which quote the artists verbatim and a piece of music suggested by the artists) and then create the soundtrack by starting with the question: 'what can I steal?'[16]

In this sense, Burrows and Fargion's creative process seems to conflate generosity and stealing, productively confounding practices of borrowing with gestures of giving back. By engaging with the circularity of giving, they short-circuit binary divisions between gift and theft, queering the politics and possibilities of generosity. They borrow from others but also credit their ideas, contributing to their dissemination; they produce collaborative projects which are distributed and marketed in their own names, while also offering platforms on which other artists can present their creative work. I argue that their work both acknowledges and troubles mechanisms of inclusion and exclusion and, in engaging with the practice of giving, finds itself entangled in its ethical paradox as both a generous act and a potential instrument of domination. As such, Burrows and Fargion's work gestures towards the contradictions of *consensus* politics, tapping—not unambiguously—into the question of *dissensus*. I suggest that in doing so, they also unsettle dominant understandings of identity and otherness as based on notions of ownership.

A compelling conceptualisation of alterity and heterogeneity that specifically accounts for relationships based on gestures of giving is formulated in Esposito's political philosophy. Continuing my engagement with Esposito's thinking on subjectivity, which in Chapter 5 I explore through his notion of the impersonal, I propose to interrogate his distinctive understanding of community as based on a constitutive alterity. On account of the etymology of the word, for Esposito (2010) *communitas* is a bond defined by an obligation, a *munus*, a gift which is given (rather than received) and which implies a debt. This supports his conceptualisation of such encounter as a 'subtraction of subjectivity' rather than an 'addition' (Esposito, 2010:

138): the subjects of a community are made 'other' by the gift they have given, which has made them no longer themselves. This conceptual framework inspires me to think of Burrows' collaborations—with Fargion, first and foremost, but also with other artists and thinkers—as relations that, based on the gift that expropriates each collaborator of their own art (dance, music, performance, etc.) as it is conventionally intended, makes them both 'other' and yet truly 'in common'. I suggest that Burrows and Fargion's collaboration stems from what Esposito calls a 'a propensity to open their own individual boundaries' and is constituted not by their sharing their respective gifts but by their mutual loss, which 'exposes [them] to the most extreme of risks: that of losing, along with [...] individuality, the borders that guarantee its inviolability' (Esposito, 2010: 138, 140). Yet what is opened up by this gesture is a different horizon of meaning, 'a meaning that still remains unthought' (Esposito, 2010: 149). I argue that collaboration and plurality generate interruptions in Burrows and Fargion's aesthetics; while, on the one hand, they open the possibility of new signifying registers and of poetic, affective qualities, on the other hand they foreground the collective, political potential of their artistic production. In the next section of this chapter, I engage with recent work by Burrows and Fargion that is openly informed by and, in turn, articulates a rethinking of ideas of community.

AFFECTIVE SOLIDARITY IN *ANY TABLE ANY ROOM* (2017)

I am sitting in the front row of Sadler's Wells studio theatre, the Lilian Baylis, for the first London date of *Any Table Any Room*, in May 2018. Burrows and Fargion sit at a long table, made by joining three smaller ones, alongside Seke Chimutengwende, Tanja Erhart, Jacky Lansley and Alesandra Seutin. In front of each of them lie six clay objects: these, after an initial moment in which the six performers acknowledge and tune in with each other, become the focus of a flurry of activity, so intricately composed and swiftly executed that I soon lose track of who is doing what. I am taking notes, but all I manage to write down is a long list of actions, through which the performers interact with their respective set of objects: lifting, covering, banging, shaking, pulling, trying on, slipping on (as if a glove) shifting, magicking, parachuting, sliding (on the table, on their arms, on their palms), hovering, prodding, caressing, swapping, outlining, blowing, tapping, throwing (pretend to), brushing, stamping, hammering, dabbing on their neck (as if perfume), exhibiting, not looking at, circling, showing the bottom of, dotting, hiding (with their hands, under the table), gathering, rubbing (on their legs), putting to sleep, waving, extracting, weighing, pouring over, stirring, fanning, twisting, folding, pointing at, squeezing, moulding—and more.

These mesmerising sets of gestures, performed in rapid succession and through elaborate arrangements, constitute the primary physical material for the whole piece. Nevertheless, the actions the performers execute on and with the objects are not the only aspect of the work that travels through a myriad of variations. Subtly rich affective modalities seep through the overall impression of a deadpan performance. A variety of moods and attitudes accompany the manipulation of the clay items: engaged, bored, careless, angry, unsure, stubborn, bemused, showy, punctilious, stressed, annoyed, defiant, happy, ecstatic. Similarly, the relationships and interactions between the performers follow many different patterns, from unison to alternate execution, from moving with the group to moving against the group, from isolated gestures to chains of gestures and from giving to receiving. The clay objects each of the performers handles are also unique in shape and no one set is the same as another. Some items are more recognisable than others: a star, a heart, a spatula, a ball, tools, human figures and pots in various styles. Others are less obvious, ranging from thin, tubular shapes to flat objects, to lumps of clay. All are clearly hand-made, and approximate their intended shape with various degrees of accuracy. Towards the end of the piece, after some precise reshuffling of the objects which are passed on between the performers, the terracotta sets of objects are replaced with gold-painted ones. In the final sequences, after the performers have moved position and are now sitting in front of another group member's set of items, each performer's golden objects are pushed off the front of the table and fall to the ground (Fig. 6.1).

Any Table Any Room, which premiered in Brighton in October 2017, is a co-creation by Burrows and Fargion, with Katye Coe and Nicola Conibere collaborating in a dramaturgical role on questions concerning concept, materials, scores, texts and scenography. At each performance, four local artists are invited to join Burrows and Fargion. The first two casts of performers (including Janine Fletcher, Claire Godsmark, Sue MacLaine, Scott Smith, Simon Ellis and Colin Poole, alongside Coe and Conibere)[17] are credited for playing an instrumental role in the development of the piece and in setting its score. The piece continues to address Burrows and Fargion's desire to engage with a larger number of collaborators—a drive that already underpins *52 Portraits* and other recent projects. These include the

Fig. 6.1 *Any Table Any Room*, clay objects (2017)

concept and direction of *Eleanor And Flora Music* (2015), a reinterpretation of *Both Sitting Duet*, commissioned and performed by Eleanor Sikorski and Flora Wellesley Wesley, founders of the dancer-led project Nora, and Fargion's artistic direction and composition of *7 Dialogues* (2016) for Dance On Ensemble, in which six international dance artists engage in a dialogue with six choreographers. As mentioned earlier in this chapter, from 2015 onwards, Burrows and Fargion's collaborative projects have also taken the form of 'salon' events, in which the duo's performances are presented in non-theatre spaces alongside works by other artists; these events are conceived also as convivial occasions on which the host and guest artists share a meal with the audience. Among these are the curatorial projects *Return of the Salon* and *Hysterical Furniture*, held on various dates and in international venues, with invited artists from different disciplines.[18]

The premise of *Any Table Any Room* is an openness to making work for a wide range of formats and settings. The title speaks of an approach to the creation and dissemination of dance work that has underpinned Burrows and Fargion's artistic research for a number of years:

> Matteo and I have had a policy for many years of saying yes to any invitations to perform, and then figuring out how to do it afterwards, whatever the space and conditions of working. Hence the title of the new piece we're making, which is called *Any Table Any Room*. So we might be performing one week in a large proscenium arch theatre, and the next week in a hall without technical equipment. And each of those two extremes requires a different approach to the balance between what is formal and what is informal in the performance, and both qualities must be there in order that the audience members are invited and engaged, and at the same time free. (Burrows quoted in Dunn, 2017: 33)

Before becoming the title of the duo's recent project, the annotation 'any table any room' was already written at the top of the first page of Burrows' score book for *Body Not Fit for Purpose*,[19] to indicate that the piece was adaptable to different performance settings. In reflecting on the significance of this approach, I consider how these logistical considerations also point to the ontological—and, in turn, social—dimension of the work. On one level, the phrase could be seen as an implicit nod to Merce Cunningham's and the Judson Church choreographers' any-movement-whatever approach to dance, or to William Forsythe's choreography that 'starts from any point' (Spier, 2011). More specifically, however, I understand the phrase as indicative of the 'distributive' character of Burrows and Fargion's work in recent years. In particular, as I already discussed in Chapter 3, I suggest that the title speaks of the 'anywhere or not at all' ontology that Osborne (2013) argues is the qualifier of contemporary art—postconceptual art which draws on the legacy of the conceptual art of the 1960s. Contemporary artworks find their unity across the different materialisations and instantiations of the same work: every work is in a sense a series, which takes place anywhere and any time—or does not exist at all. Specifically, in Osborne's theorisation, the transcategoriality and transmediality of contemporary artistic works are accompanied by an engagement with space as socially differentiated, at the same time as 'places increasingly become emptied out of social meaning' (Osborne, 2013: 136).[20] Conceptualising the complex spatiality and temporality of contemporary art and their relational configurations, Osborne (2013: 134) interrogates how 'new forms of social space [... have] manifested themselves within the field of contemporary art, as conditions of its contemporaneity—that is, as conditions of its capacity to articulate, reflect upon and transfigure new forms of social experience'. As contemporary art moves beyond the confines of canonical art spaces into social spaces, the 'ontological structure of art-space [...] must [...] be *reinstituted* by each work, in each instance, *wherever* it is located' (Osborne, 2013: 140, original emphasis).

Positing an 'anywhere' as the location of this collaborative work clearly gestures towards the social premise of *Any Table Any Room*—a project which intends to conjure a space for dance *wherever* it is performed, and in doing so aims to mobilise a community. The programme notes for the 2018 London performance make direct reference to the question of community, with a quote from Jean-Luc Nancy's *The Inoperative Community* (1991: 9):

> Until this day history has been thought of on the basis of a lost community – one to be regained or reconstituted.
>
> The lost, or broken, community can be exemplified in all kinds of ways, by all kinds of paradigms: the natural family, the Athenian city, the Roman Republic, the first Christian community, corporations, communes, brotherhoods – always it is a matter of a lost age in which community was woven of tight, harmonious, and infrangible bonds and in which above all it played back to itself, through its institutions, its rituals and its symbols, the repre sentation, indeed the living offer, of its own immanent unity, intimacy and autonomy.

The idea of community is explored in the piece through the interaction between the individualities of the six performers (and their clay objects) and the formal precision of the score, a complex arrangement that integrates six strands of patterns, producing both a sense of unity of the parts and its inescapable dissolution. According to Burrows' (2017) research notes, the creative process focused on exploring the relationship between the individual and the group; it probed the ways in which the autonomy of each participant was negotiated alongside the sense of togetherness that the overall structure produced. The dramaturgical principle of the piece is guided by the idea that 'the dissolution of any given integration is as important as its coming together'.[21] Because the score is based on an interplay between sustained activity and change, the performers are involved in both working within set parameters and making individual choices. Experiencing 'the freedom to be with or against the dominant activity occurring within the group at any time' (Burrows, 2017), the performers negotiate their relationship with the project and those involved in it and are thus engaged in the politics of collaboration and community.

This modulation between individual autonomy and group cohesion is highlighted dramaturgically through the use of songs. The piece is divided in 51 sections, organised into five larger sections. The beginning of each larger section signals a moment of change, often marked by short songs, mostly sung in unison by the group. The songs explicitly address the topic of community, with lyrics quoting from political or philosophical texts, as well as from popular songs. Song 1 is a line from *Naturally* by the reggae band Reality Souljahs: 'Naturally we're singing this song to help with our community'. Song 2 is a quotation from nineteenth-century political philosopher Pierre-Joseph Proudhon's *What Is Property?*: 'Our principle is good, it is good, it is true, it is social, let us not be afraid to push it to its limit'. Song 3 is from Jean-Luc Nancy's *The Inoperative Community*: 'There is no longer any community or communication, there is only the continuous identity of atoms'. Song 4 quotes again from *Naturally* by Reality Souljahs: 'Help'. Song 5 is a line from David Bowie's single *Memory of a Free Festival*: 'The sun machine is going down and we're going to have a party'. In Burrows' words, 'the texts of the songs [...] both idealise and dismantle notions of community' (Burrows, 2017), occupying a productively ambiguous place between sincerity and humorous distance (Fig. 6.2).

The piece concerns the notion of community also through its dramaturgy: the relationship between the singing and the movement raises

Fig. 6.2 Katye Coe and Colin Poole in *Any Table Any Room* (2017) (Photograph by Hayley Gilbert)

questions about the place of the individual within a group—which also connects to Burrows' own experience of participation in English folk music and dance. This relates to how, as Burrows puts it in his research notes, 'unison activity within dance is widely enjoyed by both participants and spectators, and yet remains questionable because of its association with mechanisms of political coercion and control' (Burrows, 2017). Commenting on early stages of the creative process, Cvejić remarked on what she perceived as a usefully ambiguous interplay between unison and individuality. In an email to Burrows, Cvejić (2016) observed that the performers' 'togetherness was nuanced: certainly no uniformity, but neither a collection of idiosyncrasies. [… S]ometimes when a loud unison emerges, this becomes an event that is soon relativised by the heterophony of approximate togetherness'.

Similarly, the hand-crafted clay objects that the performers manipulate were chosen as the preferred option by the creative team (over other versions such as found objects or coins), who 'were […] looking for a type of object which would state its own individuality, but at the same time be one of an identifiable group of objects' (Burrows, 2017). The hand-made nature of the objects, combined with the use of the same material and colour, points again to the interplay between individuality and togetherness. Following this principle, the movement material was devised by Burrows and Fargion, rather than collaboratively with the other performers. As Burrows (2017) explains,

> Having made six clay objects each, we began to develop 60 possible gestural materials. These gestural materials could have been developed within the group, but Matteo and I wanted the focus of subsequent rehearsals to be on the relationship between the performers, rather than on the development of the materials themselves.

The choreographed gestural phrases here function as the collective structure, the identifiable background activity which enables the interaction between individuals and the personal character of each performer to be brought to the foreground.

The question of the role of the individual within group work is of direct concern to practices of collaboration. The delicate balance between autonomous input and collective structure is the focus of the letter of invitation that Burrows and Fargion send out to all artists taking part in the performance—a letter that, as Burrows says, 'invites the beginning of a sense of negotiation by them of their own autonomy in relation to the co-creators, to the score and to the group' (Burrows, 2017). This is how the letter goes:

> Dear fellow artist who has agreed to join Matteo and me in performing *Any Table Any Room*, here are some thoughts about how the project works, what the project is and how we might perform it.
>
> *Any Table Any Room* grows out of many years of sharing work with a multitude of individual artists in workshop situations, and is a product of our

wish to create a performance which might draw upon some of the collective energies, sharing and generosity we have been privileged to experience in those more private situations. It is a privilege to share the stage with others, and we celebrate it as an opportunity to question the curatorial hierarchies that often separate us as artists.

Our difficulty has been in determining who one might invite to perform the piece in any given situation, because there has perhaps never been a time when there are so many extraordinary dance performers around in any place you happen to visit. It is important to us that the project is neither a constantly changing supergroup, nor a way of exploiting amateur or younger artists. It is also important to us that the project reflects an understanding of the necessity for change within the contemporary dance world, towards a more genuine space, invitation, openness and support for people of all demographics, backgrounds and approaches to working. For reasons of cost but also to keep it personal, the performance invites only four people in each new venue. This number is small to easily achieve all of the above, but our hope is that as the community of people who have joined the project accumulates, then it holds true to its principles and without instrumentalising anybody towards its own success.

Because the piece begins with an idealised notion of the generosity and easy collectivity of dance practice, then it also must doubt and question such things, and our singing will draw upon writing from songs and theory which both celebrate and question community and the impossibility of community. For us these questions are a response to the observation that doing things together is one of the joys of music and dance, but that it risks always the loss of our own ability to choose. [...] Our benchmark is the oddly democratic experience of playing folk music, where a shared resource and understanding create at best a situation which anybody can join, and in which everyone remains both themselves and at the same time loses self into a larger field of action.

These are our starting points then: how to be together, how to resist assumptions about collectivity, how to resist assumptions about individuality, how to face the difficult joy of unison, how much a real being together might need shared knowledge and parameters, and how much shared knowledge and parameters might also allow great licence.

Again for reasons both financial and pragmatic, we have conceived the piece to be made and performed in three days. The time is short and the stakes are high, but the only risk is failure and we find that such failure seems not to erode the joy of the attempt to arrive at these questions. Matteo and I would like to thank you for joining us in this work. There will be a small preparation to do before we meet, to create six small clay objects, and we will be sending you clay and instructions soon. Everything else will be explained and worked upon during the three days of rehearsal together. Please do not hesitate to ask any questions or discuss any thoughts you might have.

Until then with best wishes, Jonathan and Matteo

With this letter, Burrows and Fargion invite collaborators to engage in a negotiation of their own role within a process in which the overarching structure—the 'shared parameters' the letter talks about—is assumed as a necessary vehicle for both individuality and relationality to take place. I suggest that the score that is offered to the participants functions as the Deleuzoguattarian *ritournelle* I discuss in Chapter 4—a configuration that facilitates the coordination between heterogeneous singularities and milieus. Its enthralling gestural patterns act as refrains—rhythmical structures that, as Berardi (2012: 130) puts it, enable individuals to 'find identification points, and to territorialize': '[t]he refrain [...] allows an individual (a group, a people, a nation, a subculture, a movement) to receive and project the world according to reproducible and communicable formats'. In turn, such configuration enables a coming together that is capable of contending with uncertainty and ambiguity: conjoining with the other unfolds through 'unresolved oscillation' and this precarious encounter 'gives rise to the emergence of previously inexistent meaning' (Berardi, 2015: 21).

For Berardi (2015: 14), conjunction is an experience of collectivity based on empathic understanding: it is 'the pleasure of becoming other'. Hence, the community that ensues from the coming together of singularities who converge without a pre-defined finality, who conjoin on a 'path that they share, provisionally, for a time', is not the product of necessity, of 'conventional codes, or marks of belonging': rather, it is 'based on nomadic desire' (Berardi, 2015: 20). To an extent, the nomadism and provisional nature of *Any Table Any Room*, as a project that is recomposed each time it is performed, in each venue, with different participants, qualify the work as a process of conjunction from which singularities coalesce to form what Berardi calls a 'community of desire'. The individuals that make up the community are not brought together by a sense of belonging: rather, moved by 'singular drifts and desires', they join together on 'a pathway from nowhere to nowhere' (Berardi, 2015: 19–20).

For the performance I witnessed at Sadler's Wells Lilian Baylis studio, Burrows and Fargion were joined on stage by artists as distinctive as Seke Chimutengwende (an independent dancer, choreographer and teacher who works with improvisation), Tanja Erhart (a social anthropologist and dancer with Candoco, a UK-based inclusive dance company for disabled and non-disabled dancers), Jacky Lansley (a key figure of British New Dance,[22] founder of X6 Dance Space and Chisenhale Dance Space) and Alesandra Seutin (an independent choreographer whose work brings together Western contemporary dance and African styles). My understanding of this collaboration is that these artists came together not to develop what they had in common, but rather in response to a desire to conjoin. This, in Berardi's (2015: 20) sense of the term, becomes a way to 'express an affective and political solidarity'. Nevertheless, and most importantly, this gesture of coming together also highlights a lack, a void—the absence of a common ground, or rather its transitional quality: a propensity to open one's boundaries and operate in an in-between.

Hence, the community that emerges from their encounter is not one that has been 'regained or reconstituted' to repair a loss—as Nancy argues in the pages that follow the passage quoted in the programme notes of *Any Table Any Room*. Nancy's central thesis in *The Inoperative Community* is that ideas of a lost original community are imaginary projections of the past. 'Nothing [...] has been lost': 'community, far from being what society has crushed or lost, is *what happens to us* [...] *in the wake of* society' (Nancy, 1991: 11, original emphasis). As such, we should be suspicious of claims to shared identity and norms made in the name of community, which are often the basis for exclusionary logics and politics. There is ambivalence in the way in which community is invoked and called upon in the work; this suggests a questioning of ideological views of the common as uncontested positivity—such as the one ultimately underlying Berardi's post-workerist thought.[23] I contend that the idea of community conjured by the nomadic and provisional coming together of distinctively different artists for the rehearsal and performance of *Any Table Any Room* can be most productively understood through Esposito's concept of community, which also engages with the idea of loss.

For Esposito, community is a bond founded on a loss—the loss of its members' respective individualities which, in the absence of something in common and of a sense of belonging (and specifically because of this absence), enhances the possibility of an encounter with the other and opens up a new horizon of meaning. As a piece that exists through transitions and comes to fruition episodically, being transmitted and transformed from venue to venue, from group of participants to group of participants, *Any Table Any Room* emerges as a practice/thinking of togetherness that diverges from ideas of community based on the shared ownership of a collective property—and upholding the ideal of a common good. For Esposito (2010: 138), the members of a community have *nothing in common*, in the sense that what they 'share, based upon the complex and profound meaning of *munus*, is rather an expropriation of their own essence, which isn't limited to their "having" but one that involves and affects their own "being subjects"'. Through their commitment to coming together—the *munus*, the gift they give (rather than receive, according to the etymology of the Latin word)[24]—the members of this community 'are no longer identical with themselves': they become 'other' (Esposito, 2010: 138).

In *Any Table Any Room*, the four distinctive artists who are invited to join Burrows and Fargion in each different venue are not revealed as 'identical with themselves' through the singularity of their dance and movement language; instead, this is, to a certain extent, lost as a consequence of the bond they form with the group. Through their commitment to the score of the piece and to the activity of the group, the participants become 'other', insofar as their subjective stance is subtracted from, rather than added to, the collective practice. Yet, because of this subtraction, they join not as individual subjects, but as a 'chain of alterations that cannot ever be fixed in a new identity' (Esposito, 2010: 138), thus—paradoxically—making community possible. In this sense, the coming together that this collaborative work entails differs from other models of collaborative work, at the level of both its ontology and its political significance. While in Colin and Sachsenmaier's (2016: 13) analysis of collaboration in performance practice collective creation 'maintain[s]' and 'develop[s]' individual identities—as 'the competence of the individual practitioner is both tempered and extended' through collaboration—in Burrows and Fargion's *Any Table Any Room* individual competences are subtracted: the different participants work as a community insofar as the relation that enables their encounter with the others 'separates them from themselves' (Esposito, 2010: 139). If community is the space in-between individuals, this subtraction of subjectivity is what makes it possible.

The specific traits and qualities that make each of the participating artists unique and distinctive in their own work are withdrawn from this collaborative project. Their obligation to the score and to the group means that Chimutengwende's, Erhart's, Lansley's and Seutin's specific movement and performance skills are not brought to the foreground: the communal project is not supported by their individual properties, but rather by their renunciation of their subjective traits in favour of the relation with the other members of the group and with the score. While Colin and Sachsenmaier's (2016: 13) conceptualisation of collaboration acknowledges the idea of a 'whole' as an entity that each collaborator 'seek[s] to progress' by applying their respective disciplinary competence, Burrows andFargion's project does not move towards the production of a totality. The work is not simply *shaped by* the relations between its collaborators: the piece itself *is* the relation between artists who, in coming together, estrange themselves from their respective ways of working. In this sense, the work is collaborative not in the sense of an accumulation of perspectives; it is communal insofar as it coincides with the space and the possibilities that are opened in-between modes of being and working. In Esposito's (2010: 139) words, 'the being of community is the interval of difference, the spacing that brings us into relation with others in a common non-belonging'.

This subtraction of subjectivity should not be understood as an erasure of all personal content and investment. Indeed, the gesture that brings and holds the performers of *Any Table Any Room* together is evidence of their individual commitment to the functioning of the piece as a collaborative process. Through the experience of preparing for the performance—by crafting individual terracotta objects, by learning to work in relation with others, with precise timings and group arrangements, and by finding subtly distinctive ways of embodying the gestural material—each performer is both engaged in deeply personal activities and able to renounce their own individuality in favour of the plurality of the group. Their presence in the work is im/personal in the sense I explore in Chapter 5 through Esposito's philosophy of the third person, arguing that signification unfolds in Burrows' choreography through relationality and plurality, in the space between performers.

What follows from this understanding of collaborative practice is that community implies divergence rather than convergence: it 'is never a point of arrival but always one of departure' (Esposito, 2010: 140). The consequences of this line of thinking/practising are twofold and concern a rethinking of consensus and of mastery. Firstly, if community is not based on shared ownership or a sense of belonging, its politics are not based on consensus. The coming together of distinctive artists in *Any Table Any Room* does not aim to build a consensual harmony of different individual voices—where consensus implies a shared 'knowledge base' and a 'unidirectionality' premised on 'violent politics of exclusion', as political philosopher and practising artist Erin Manning (2007: 62, 70–71) argues. Discussing practices that operate dis-sensually, from a place that 'rejects any pre-constituted communicative subjectivity' (Manning, 2007: 14) and therefore unsettles accepted ways of making sense, Manning draws on Rancière, who conceptualises dissensus as 'not a conflict; it is a perturbation of the normal relation between sense and sense' (Rancière, 2009: 3). While acknowledging Rancière's perspective on dissensus, my understanding of the dissensual dimension of community is specifically informed by Esposito's philosophy of the impersonal, which, without negating the personal, accounts for the heterogeneity of its signification and introduces the idea of an exteriority that prevents sense from being 'circumscribed within a specific subject' (Esposito, 2012: 15).

Secondly, if community unfolds through the 'othering' of its subjects, collective creation does not depend on mastery. By mastery, I mean a practice that, in the pursuit of expert knowledge, strives towards a level of competence and control which implies a condition of strength and a position of power. Here, my understanding of mastery is informed by Julietta Singh's deconstruction of its notion as a practice of exclusion and subordination, a rethinking which advocates 'forms of queer dispossession that reach for different ways of inhabiting [...] ourselves' (2018: 8). In *Any Table Any Room*, the artists that take part in its nomadic iterations are dispossessed of their own distinctive competences and invited to work with unfamiliar media (clay, song) and procedures (repetitive gestures, precise scores). As Burrows and Fargion point out in the letter of invitation sent to each participant, the risk is failure, and yet it is a risk worth taking. As Singh (2018: 8) writes, in order to escape the dominant logic of mastery, 'we must begin to exile ourselves from feeling comfortable at home'. Hence, through the concepts of collaboration as 'conjunction' and 'becoming-other' and of community as the condition of 'nothing-in-common' discussed in this chapter, I wish to trouble the function of disciplinary expertise that dominant understandings of collaboration draw upon. To do so, in the remainder of this chapter, and in the way of a coda, I briefly consider Burrows and Fargion's latest example of collaborative work: the 2018 *Music For Lectures* performances.

DEBUNKING MASTERY IN *MUSIC FOR LECTURES* (2018)

In *Music For Lectures*, Burrows, Fargion, and Francesca Fargion perform together as a rock band, often in non-theatrical spaces, to accompany a lecture on performance by an invited artist. With Burrows at the drums, Fargion at the bass guitar and his daughter Francesca at the synthesiser, they have so far played music alongside two talks, respectively, by the British dance artist Katye Coe and by the Norwegian performance artist Mette Edvardsen, both of whom also hold academic positions. These performances, devised with the dramaturgical advice of Stefan Jovanović, intend to explore choreography in an expanded sense, funnelling ideas about dance through live music and intersecting performance with academic practice and discourse. In her talk entitled *She Dancing*, Coe considers questions concerning the dancer's agency and silent experience, which she reads as the voice of the feminine.[25] In *Every Word Was Once an Animal*, Mette Edvardsen talks about poetry and repetition, reflecting on rhythm, time, memory, digression and translation. During the talks, the band plays music, carefully measuring their rhythm and pauses with the pace and arrangement of the speeches. Although the set-up resembles that of a garage band, the music is kept quiet to allow for the voice of the speaker to be heard.

In these performances, all participants work, to a degree, outside of the comfort of their own practice, inhabiting a place between practices—in a chain of alterations that position them both inside and outside their own artistic remits, but never in a complacent middle. In doing so, they debunk claims to authority and credibility and embrace the risk of uncertainty, reaching outside the space of legitimacy. Dancer Coe comes into the performance space to give her speech having danced for thirty minutes away from the gaze of the audience: what she offers draws on her 'core' practice, while at the same time displacing expectations of masterful artistry, modulating the rhythm and intensity of her talk just as she would with a dance performance. Similarly, Burrows turns musician in this series of works, alongside Fargion and his daughter who choose to play instruments which are not their main ones[26]: yet their playing is 'tightly scored with complex changing rhythmic patterning', drawing upon their 'previous experiences of doing together in time' (Burrows, 2018c).

I suggest that the idea of collaboration underpinning this work diverges from the understanding of collective creativity articulated by Colin and Sachsenmaier (2016). As already discussed, in their framing of collaboration, disciplinary competence and identity are both the starting point and the end result of collaboration, which allows each expert practitioner 'to better understand her or his own disciplinary identity' and arrive at a shared 'whole' (Colin and Sachsenmaier, 2016: 13). In this sense, although Colin and Sachsenmaier acknowledge the importance of 'embracing uncertainty' and 'the unknowable' in collaborative performance making, their idea of collaboration is firmly premised on 'professional performance mastery', which is required for collaborative working to take place and, in turn, will be enhanced by the exchange (Colin and Sachsenmaier, 2016: 15). In contending, with Berardi (2015: 13), that 'there is no design to fulfil at the beginning of the act of conjunction. [...] There is no code to comply with', I understand collaboration as a process that, giving rise to the unexpected, does not submit discrete parts to an overarching rule. Collaboration foregrounds unknowability as both the starting point and the end result of collective practices; as such it must decentre expert knowledge from the process of creation. Here, I take my cue from the Italian writer Tommaso Landolfi's short story *Dialogo dei massimi sistemi* (written in 1937 and translated into English as 'Dialogue on the Greater Harmonies') in which a character named Y, an acquaintance of the narrator, questions the role of mastery with regard to artistic production:

> I reached the precise and incontrovertible conclusion that having at his disposal rich and varied expressive means is, for an artist, anything but a favourable circumstance. For instance, it is in my opinion far preferable to write in an imperfectly known language than in one which is absolutely familiar. [...] Quite obviously, anyone who does not know the right words to indicate objects or feelings, is forced to replace them with circumlocutions, that is with images – with what great advantage to art, I leave it to you to imagine. Thus, when technical terms and clichés are avoided, what else can obstruct the birth of a work of art? (Landolfi, 1961: 30)

As already in the partnership with Fargion, which, as discussed in Chapter 4, develops in the space between the art forms of dance and music, Burrows' collaborations intervene in the fabric and patterns of the artistic languages they engage with, unsettling their rules. They do so not by rejecting the rules altogether, but rather by rearranging and decentring them, through a careful rethinking of their positioning. This brings us back to the thread that runs through this book—the notion of a minor practice which works from within to unthink and undo the masterful authority of a major code. It also gestures forward to the next chapter which, as a way of conclusion, reflects further on the political, subversive implications of choosing an unfamiliar, imperfect dance language that expresses itself through stuttering rhythms and accommodates multiple minor voices.

NOTES

1. Produced by the Nightingale, Brighton, these events comprised pieces by Burrows and Fargion alongside music and performances by invited guests and included a shared meal with the audience. One such date was held at TripSpace's Kitchen, London, on 25 September 2016, and featured *Body Not Fit for Purpose* alongside Francesca Fargion playing Chris Newman's *Piano Sonata No. 1*, and Christine de Smedt and Eszter Salamon performing *Dance#2* (see http://www.tripspace.co.uk/event/167/return-of-the-salon/. Accessed 10 January 2019).

2. I am indebted to Cvejić for drawing my attention to the importance of making a distinction between collectivity, as an ideologically loaded term, and community, as a concept that allows for productive ambivalence in its articulation of togetherness.

3. Conceptualising the category of multitude to capture the plurality and heterogeneity of the social base in the global era, Virno investigates how human activity in post-industrial labour has also moved beyond traditional categorisations: 'to speak/to think are generic habits of the human animal, the opposite of any sort of specialization' (Virno, 2004: 41).

4. Heathfield, '*52 Portraits*: A conversation', talk at Kingston University London, 1 July 2016.

5. See Blades' (2017) and Tomić-Vajagić's (2014) discussion of Cynthia Freeland's definition and analysis of the genre in *Portraits and Persons* (Freeland, 2010). For a discussion of how subjectivity and relationality are articulated in *52 Portraits*, see also Chapter 5.

6. Heathfield, '*52 Portraits*: A conversation', talk at Kingston University London, 1 July 2016.

7. Whatley, '*52 Portraits*: A conversation', talk at Kingston University London, 1 July 2016.

8. In response to these comments, Burrows remarked that he would love it if somebody took the concept of the work and replicated it somewhere else or in future years. Glendinning also added that the project had already started to exist as a new iteration, as his son and Crystal Pite's son had made their own versions of the dances and Glendinning himself had used the format of the work for a project with a primary school ('*52 Portraits*: A conversation', Kingston University London, 1 July 2016).

9. Fargion, '*52 Portraits*: A conversation', talk at Kingston University London, 1 July 2016.

10. Burrows, '*52 Portraits*: A conversation', talk at Kingston University London, 1 July 2016.
11. Whatley, '*52 Portraits*: A conversation', talk at Kingston University London, 1 July 2016.
12. Burrows, '*52 Portraits*: A conversation', talk at Kingston University London, 1 July 2016.
13. De la Fe, '*52 Portraits*: A conversation', talk at Kingston University London, 1 July 2016.
14. I draw on Burt's writing on friendship also in my discussion of rhythm in Chapter 4.
15. For a discussion of *Cheap Lecture*, see Chapter 4.
16. Fargion, '*52 Portraits*: A conversation', talk at Kingston University London, 1 July 2016.
17. Fletcher, Godsmark, MacLaine and Smith formed the first cast, for the premiere of the piece in Brighton (Attenborough Centre, 17 October 2017). Coe, Conibere, Ellis and Poole formed the second cast, although the second performance of the piece (Warwick Arts Centre, Warwick, 21 November 2017) was ultimately performed by Coe, Fletcher, Smith and Poole, alongside Burrows and Fargion.
18. The venues of these projects include *Return of the Salon* dates at The Printworks in Hastings, The Loft in Shoreham and TripSpace's Kitchen in London in 2016; *Hysterical Furniture* at Circolo Ufficiali in Bologna, over three days in 2017, and the Herrenhausen Palace in Hanover in 2018, on the occasion of the Kunstfestspiele Hannover. For further details, see Burrows (n.d.).
19. See http://scores.motionbank.org/jbmf/#/set/score-books/body-not-fit-for-purpose. Digital versions of the score books for a number of Burrows and Fargion's duets can be found on the website of The Forsythe Company's (n.d.) project Motion Bank.
20. Osborne makes reference here to theorisations of new spatial forms, including Maunel Castells' 'space of flows'.
21. My sincere thanks go to Jonathan Burrows for sharing with me the research notes on the piece, which contain reflections on scores, dramaturgy, objects, songs, unison, audience, politics, among other material. The observations quoted in this chapter are from Burrows' own research documents.
22. A recent account of these germinal years of British experimental dance is given by Lansley in *Choreographies* (2017), through autobiographical and archive material.
23. Post-workerist thinkers, such as Berardi, Paolo Virno, Maurizio Lazzarato, Michael Hardt and Antonio Negri, develop the political and philosophical positions of Italian *operaismo*, an autonomist movement that, during the social and political unrest of the 1960s and 1970s, reassessed the Marxist tradition and focused on an analysis of the struggle of the working class.

24. Distinguished from *donum*, the more generic Latin term for gift, the word *munus* indicates a gift that is given, an obligation, a duty, a service. It is upon this distinction, crucial to the etymology of the term *communitas*, that Esposito constructs his conceptualisation of community.

25. The text of the talk is published in Ellis, Blades and Waelde's edited collection *A World of Muscle, Bone & Organs: Research and Scholarship in Dance* (2018): see Coe (2018).

26. In an email exchange, Burrows (2018c) provides some background for the choice of roles and instruments in the band: 'Francesca plays a synthesiser, Matteo plays a bass guitar and I play a drum kit – we are all in some way familiar with these instruments, Francesca from her studies of electronic and digital music forms, Matteo from playing in Chris Newman's art rock band in the 1980s, and myself from playing drums in a band for a long time when I was younger'.

References

Ahmed, Sara (2012) *On Being Included: Racism and Diversity in Institutional Life*. Durham and London: Duke University Press.

Berardi, Franco 'Bifo' (2012) *The Uprising: On Poetry and Finance*. Los Angeles: Semiotext(e).

Berardi, Franco 'Bifo' (2015) *And: Phenomenology of the End*. Los Angeles: Semiotext(e).

Bishop, Claire (2006) 'The Social Turn: Collaboration and Its Discontents', *Artforum*, 44 (6): 178–183.

Blades, Hetty (2017) 'Screendance Self/portraits', *The International Journal of Screendance*, 8: 93–103. http://screendancejournal.org/issue/view/193#.WTqfLTb06t8. Accessed 9 June 2017.

Brown, Ismene (2010) 'Review of *Cheap Lecture* and *The Cow Piece*', *The artsdesk.com*, 14 October. http://www.jonathanburrows.info/downloads/CLCPFI.pdf. Accessed 8 October 2018.

Burke, Siobhan (2016) 'At 52 Portraits, The Stories Behind the Dancers'. *The New York Times*, 24 August. https://www.nytimes.com/2016/08/28/arts/dance/at-52-portraits-the-stories-behind-the-dancers.html. Accessed 9 October 2018.

Burrows, Jonathan (2010) *A Choreographer's Handbook*. London and New York: Routledge.

Burrows, Jonathan (2014) 'Rebelling Against Limit', in Noémie Solomon (ed.) *Danse: An Anthology*. Dijon: Les Presses du Réel: 81–87.

Burrows, Jonathan (2016) 'Talk for Bojana Kunst at Mousonturm, Frankfurt.' http://www.jonathanburrows.info/#/text/?id=188&t=content. Accessed 20 June 2018.

Burrows, Jonathan (2017) Unpublished research notes on *Any Table Any Room*.

Burrows, Jonathan (2018a) 'Politics', in Ellis, Simon, Blades, Hetty, and Waelde, Charlotte (eds.) *A World of Muscle, Bone & Organs: Research and Scholarship in Dance*. Coventry: C-DaRE Coventry University: 252–266. https://www.coventry.ac.uk/PageFiles/276435/AWofMBandO.pdf.

Burrows, Jonathan (2018b) 'What Would Be Another Word for It?' Unpublished text written for a talk with Chrysa Parkinson at Doch Stockholm.

Burrows, Jonathan (2018c) Unpublished email exchange with Daniela Perazzo Domm, 20 November.

Burrows, Jonathan (n.d.) *Jonathan Burrows*. http://www.jonathanburrows.info/. Accessed 20 December 2018.

Burrows, Jonathan, Fargion, Matteo and Glendinning, Hugo (2016) *52 Portraits*. http://52portraits.co.uk. Accessed 10 February 2018.

Burt, Ramsay (2017) *Ungoverning Dance: Contemporary European Theatre Dance and the Commons*. Oxford: Oxford University Press.

Coe, Katye (2018) 'She Dancing', in Ellis, Simon, Blades, Hetty, and Waelde, Charlotte (eds.) *A World of Muscle, Bone & Organs: Research and Scholarship in Dance*. Coventry: C-DaRE Coventry University: 324–331. https://www.coventry.ac.uk/PageFiles/276435/AWofMBandO.pdf. Accessed 9 October 2018.

Colin, Noyale and Sachsenmaier, Stefanie (eds.) (2016) *Collaboration in Performance Practice: Premises, Workings and Failures*. Basingstoke: Palgrave.

Cvejić, Bojana (2004) 'Collectivity? You Mean Collaboration', *Ballettanz*, 7: 34–37. http://republicart.net/disc/aap/cvejic01_en.htm. Accessed 22 December 2018.

Cvejić, Bojana (2016) Unpublished email exchange with Jonathan Burrows, 1 December.

Deleuze, Gilles and Guattari, Félix (1986) *Kafka: Toward a Minor Literature*. Translated by Dana Polan. Minneapolis: University of Minnesota Press.

Dunn, Lawrence (2017) 'Jonathan Burrows + Matteo Fargion: On Making Portraits. Interview with Lawrence Dunn', *Cerenem Journal*, 6: 21–35. https://issuu.com/cerenem/docs/cj6-31jul_final. Accessed 10 January 2019.

Elixir Project blog (2018) *Elixir Ensemble 2014: The Elders Project*. http://rescen.net/blog_elix/. Accessed 9 October 2018.

Esposito, Roberto (2010) *Communitas: The Origin and Destiny of Community*. Translated by Timothy Campbell. Stanford: Stanford University Press.

Esposito, Roberto (2012) *Third Person: Politics of Life and Philosophy of the Impersonal*. Translated by Zakiya Hanafi. Cambridge: Polity Press.

Freeland, Cynthia (2010) *Portraits and Persons*. London and New York: Oxford University Press.

Kunst, Bojana (2015) *Artist at Work: Proximity of Art and Capitalism*. Winchester and Washington: Zero Books.

Laermans, Rudi (2012) '"Being in Common": Theorizing Artistic Collaboration', *Performance Research*, 17 (6): 94–102.

Landolfi, Tommaso (1961) 'Dialogue of the Greater Harmonies', in *Gogol's Wife & Other Stories*. Translated by Raymond Rosenthal, John Longrigg and Wayland Young. New York: New Directions: 29–48.

Lansley, Jacky (2017) *Choreographies: Tracing the Materials of an Ephemeral Art Form*. Bristol: Intellect.

Mackrell, Judith (2016) '52 Portraits: A Year of Solos Capturing Dancers' Fears and Freedom'. *The Guardian*, 9 August. https://www.theguardian.com/stage/dance-blog/2016/aug/09/52-portraits-dancers. Accessed 9 October 2018.

Manning, Erin (2007) *Politics of Touch: Sense, Movement, Sovereignty*. Minneapolis: University of Minnesota Press.

Nancy, Jean-Luc (1991) *The Inoperative Community*. Edited by Peter Connor. Minneapolis and London: University of Minnesota Press.

O'Sullivan, Simon (2005), 'Notes Towards a Minor Art Practice', *Drain: Journal of Contemporary Art and Culture*, 2 (2). http://drainmag.com/index_nov.htm. Accessed 15 January 2017.

Osborne, Peter (2013) *Anywhere or Not at All: Philosophy of Contemporary Art*. London and New York: Verso.

Rancière, Jacques (2009) 'The Aesthetic Dimension: Aesthetics, Politics, Knowledge', *Critical Inquiry* 36 (1): 1–19.

Rancière, Jacques (2011) 'The Thinking of Dissensus: Politics and Aesthetics', in Paul Bowman, and Richard Stamp (eds.) *Reading Rancière: Critical Dissensus*. London: Continuum: 1–17.

Singh, Julietta (2018) *Unthinking Mastery: Dehumanism and Decolonial Entanglements*. Durham and London: Duke University Press.

Spier, Steven (ed.) (2011) *William Forsythe and the Practice of Choreography: It Starts From Any Point*. London and New York: Routledge.

The Forsythe Company (n.d.) *Motion Bank*. http://motionbank.org. Accessed 27 February 2018.

Tomić-Vajagić, Tamara (2014) 'The Self/portrait Effects and Dance Performance: Rineke Dijkstra's *the Krazyhouse* and William Forsythe's *the Second Detail*', *Performance Research*, 19 (5): 82–92.

Virno, Paolo (2004) *A Grammar of the Multitude: For an Analysis of Contemporary Forms of Life*. Translated by Isabella Bertoletti, James Cascaito and Andrea Casson. Los Angeles: Semiotext(e).

CHAPTER 7

Towards a Politics of Poetry, Gesture and Laughter

In dance and performance scholarship, renewed and sustained attention has been given over the last decade to the relationship between performance and politics. From Randy Martin's conceptualisation of the close connection between movement and politics[1] to Bojana Kunst's (2015) critical and theoretical exploration of the relationship of art and performance practice with capitalism, theorists have engaged with notions and questions concerning the politics '*in*' and '*of*' dance practices (Kowal, Siegmund and Martin, 2017: 3 original emphasis). Reflecting on the fragmentary and heterogeneous nature of experimental works by current Western and Eastern European choreographers who create by 'posing questions' in the context of discrete projects, Bojana Cvejić (2017: 199, 200) foregrounds their indeterminacy, understood as 'a consequence of an expanded commodification and subsumption of art and life under capitalism today'.[2] For Cvejić (2017: 215), who thinks with Gilles Deleuze, content and expression are reciprocally articulated, insofar as experimental dancing 'implies a thought that constructs the expression of movement and the disposition of the body to move'.

From these perspectives, as the oft-cited passage from Deleuze and Guattari's *A Thousand Plateaus* puts it, '[t]here is no difference between what a book talks about and how it is made'; as an assemblage, an *agencement*, a book activates relations and horizons of possibility. 'We will never ask what a book means, as signified or signifier; we will not look for anything

© The Author(s) 2019   209
D. Perazzo Domm, *Jonathan Burrows*,
New World Choreographies,
https://doi.org/10.1007/978-3-030-27680-5_7

to understand in it. We will ask what it functions with, in connection with what other things it does or does not transmit intensities' (Deleuze and Guattari, 1987: 4). In this book, by engaging with dance as an *agencement* that opens possibilities, a 'co-functioning' of heterogeneous elements (Deleuze and Guattari, 1987: 69), my writing on Burrows' choreography has attended to—rather than interpreted—the forms of thinking and doing that the work produces. In particular, it has interrogated the ways in which the work mobilises the notion and practice of dance by repeatedly shifting its possible forms of existence and problematising its rules. It has traced the ways in which Burrows and Fargion's poetics articulates movement language, performative presence and collaborative process in a minor register, producing variations of given relations and connections.

Unexpectedly, given the formal logic of his compositional methods, this book has considered Burrows' choreography as a political practice. Previous chapters have discussed examples of work that openly invoke political themes: most notably, *Body Not Fit for Purpose*, one of the duets with Fargion, examined in Chapters 2 and 4, makes direct reference to a number of concerns of international politics. Moreover, Burrows' recent writings openly address the topic of politics, such as the talk entitled 'Politics' written for the European Dancehouse Network conference 'Inventur 2' held at Tanzhaus NRW in Düsseldorf, Germany, in June 2017. Here Burrows (2018a: 253) notes:

> Sigrid Gareis[3] told me last year
> how she felt sad that contemporary dance was not more political,
> and I responded by saying I thought there was an innate politics in much of
> our practice. […]
> I am interested in real politics
> and I'm interested in the social aspects of dance,
> but what interests me most is a more existential question
> of how to go on believing in the ethics of dance,
> and how to interrogate the feeling commonly described by dancers that to
> dance is in itself a political act.

In this sense, Burrows' work sits in close relationship with current choreography that articulates a rethinking of the modes and horizons of dance, questioning accepted understandings of its ontological and political possibilities. Considering dance- and performance-based works presented in recent years on avant-garde stages in New York and across continental Europe, Jenn Joy (2014: 1) constructs the choreographic as a mode of attention and address that 'invites a rethinking of orientation in relationship to space, to language, to composition, to articulation, and to ethics'. Similarly, surveying dance works created over the last decade or so by experimental artists in the USA, Brazil and Europe, André Lepecki (2016: 2) theorises recent dance as a practice of resistance to neoliberalism's capitalist, neo-colonialist and neo-racist power apparatus, for which the meaning of dance today is 'to insist on the social function of the theatre as a gathering place; and to acknowledge that a dancer's labor is inseparable from the conditions of the world'.

Aside from these open declarations of an engagement with politics, this book has framed Burrows' dance as political in the sense of its critical reworking of major codes through a 'minor' practice of choreography, of its disruption of given signifying paradigms towards asignification—an intensive mode of address which operates beyond individual concerns, in a wider sociopolitical field. Chapter 2 has considered the ways in which his work deterritorialises choreographic canons. Chapter 3 has drawn attention to the generative ambiguity of the formalist dance tradition's engagement with content. Chapter 4 has discussed the relational potentialities of rhythm beyond its compositional function. Chapter 5 has emphasised the constitutive plurality of Burrows' articulation of subjectivity. Chapter 6 has conceptualised the ways in which Burrows' work rethinks collaboration and community.

For Deleuze and Guattari (1986: 17), a key characteristic of minor literature is that 'everything in [it] is political': 'its cramped space forces each individual intrigue to connect immediately to politics'. Working with this framework, this book has engaged with Burrows' work as political through an understanding of content and expression as mutually articulated and implicated. In attending to Burrows' dance, this study has ultimately approached it as a Deleuzoguattarian assemblage: it has not asked what it means; it has examined what connections it opens up, what horizons of thought it possibilises. Framing Burrows' dance as a mode of attention, intensity and thought, this book has aimed to trace the political in the interstices of the practice, in the shifts and convergences of the affective and conceptual responses it activates. In thinking towards a politics of Burrows' dance, in this final chapter I wish to offer further—yet brief and somewhat informal—thoughts on three modalities that run through his choreography, highlighting conjunctures between and across the heterogeneous paths of the work. These three elements, which have variously intersected the discussion offered in previous chapters, are: poetry, gesture and laughter. The notes that follow do not aim to provide a conclusion on these aspects of Burrows' poetics. Rather, they have been written in lieu of a conclusion, to return (with no sense of arrival) to modalities that—as in a Deleuzoguattarian —are both possible entrances to and possible exits from the work.

On Poetry

Burrows' dances are precise sequences of movements, with their insistent repetitions, breathing spaces and unexpected changes—a labour of movement and gesture with no ostensible outcome and no recognisable direction. A male duet made of slow, careful movements, uncertain steps which need the guidance of the other, interspersed by pauses, standing still or lying down (*Hymns*), or another choreography for two male performers, this time older, who, walking stiffly across the stage, execute steps that progressively drop into a crouch while emitting a descending cry (*The Quiet Dance*). A flurry of hands that shuffle, pull, hammer and mould an invisible shape, offer it for view and then shake it off in a piece that denounces the corruption and injustice that plague our democracies (*Body Not Fit for Purpose*). They are dances that *stay* with their own workings, with their *being made*—not resting, but not striving for a point of arrival either. In their not looking for an outcome, in their *labouring with* their medium, rather than *towards* a goal, they open up new horizons of signification; they begin to scratch at something, to create a small opening. The audience catches a glimpse of this 'something', a shared affect, an impression of a thought—not a muddled thing, more like a clear image, which nevertheless surprises, like poetry. Burrows (2018b) calls it 'that accident of art arrived at in a moment of almost mechanical fiddling about with a stubborn shape, which itself is not yet art'.

In a roundtable discussion on *52 Portraits* at Kingston University London in July 2016,[4] Adrian Heathfield offered his reflections on the 'transaction' between the concrete 'content' in Burrows, Fargion and Glendinning's video portraits (through the use of lyrics which quote the dancers' autobiographical statements verbatim) and its 'abstract' treatment. In this context, Heathfield proposed an understanding of Burrows' work as a revival of 'abstraction as political', pointing to the generative potential of the 'irresolvable gap' between the 'interiority and exteriority' of dancing— between the experience of dancing and the act of seeing dance. He thus situated the politics of abstraction in Burrows' work in the space between 'something that's known and something that's withdrawn or opaque'.[5] Heathfield's remark about the opacity of danced movement connects for me with an understanding of opacity as a key characteristic of poetry— opacity as 'the mark of the poetic' and of its resistance to hermeneutics (Prinz and Mandelbaum, 2015: 65).

In 'Moving Writing', an earlier contribution by Heathfield in the form of a written exchange with Burrows on the relationship between movement and writing, the two authors engage with the idea—as expressed by the poet Michael Donaghy (1954–2004)—of poetry as a kind of burning that leaves a deeper mark than prose, as a medium that, through its resistance to meaning and signification, generates unexpected intensities (Burrows and Heathfield, 2013). Together, in a conversation conducted through a series of letters, they interrogate understandings of immediacy and spontaneity alongside formality and structure, of freedom alongside tradition, of radicalism alongside orthodoxy. What they explore is the 'shared affect' of dance and poetry and how it may emerge from these ambiguous relationships (Burrows and Heathfield, 2013: 132). In one of the letters to Burrows, entitled 'Freedom and constraint', Heathfield writes:

> I think of you (and of myself) as someone who is very committed to a certain kind of formality – attentive that is, to the crucial way in which an idea takes its shape, manifests itself in the world, and distinguishes itself from other things. Can one consider forms without first considering traditions? It is compelling for me that you invoke tradition as a space of freedom, because it is quite rare to hear an innovative artist express such a sentiment, accustomed as we are to the contemporary incantation of the radical, the unprecedented and the new. (Burrows and Heathfield, 2013: 131).

These ideas conjoin with the perspectives this book has attended to so far. They depict tradition not as a fixed entity, but as a set of traces, of residues—as material that produces rhythmical spacings. They are particularly germane with the Deleuzian concept of how an affective register is afforded by the linguistic 'intensification' employed by a minor practice, in which '*[l]anguage stops being representative in order to now move towards its extremities or its limits*' (Deleuze and Guattari, 1986: 23, original emphasis). In dialogue with the philosophy of Deleuze and Guattari, Franco 'Bifo' Berardi engages with poetry as a language of non-referentiality and excess. Berardi theorises how poetry's emancipation from the logic of semantic exchange becomes a response to the contemporary condition of social and political crisis, which opens the possibility of 'reactivating the emotional body, and therefore [...] reactivating social solidarity, starting from the reactivation of the desire force of enunciation' (Berardi, 2012: 20). As I discuss elsewhere, Berardi takes 'forward the conceptualisations of the interconnection of language, economy, and politics formulated, among others, by the Italian post-workerist authors Paolo Virno, Christian Marazzi, and Maurizio Lazzarato' (Perazzo Domm, 2018: 188), who examine the far-reaching implications of the processes of production introduced by post-Fordist capitalism. By drawing a parallel between the economic changes brought about by 'semio-capitalism', 'based on the loss of relation between time and value' (Berardi, 2012: 86) and the virtualisation of human communication, both of which are characterised by 'immaterial semiotic flows', Berardi (2012: 26) examines the implications of this transformation for linguistic and social processes and the potential of poetic language to reopen the space of singularity, of non-homogenised communication and of excess. In addressing the issue of today's loss of social cohesion, Berardi (2012: 8) foregrounds poetry as a modality of communication capable of overturning the current 'crisis of imagination about the future'. Attending to both the affective qualities of enunciation and the formal and structural aspects of modes of expression, he argues that poetry undermines dominant paradigms of value circulation by escaping the order of exchangeability.

I am drawn to Berardi's conceptualisation of the relation of poetry with finance in advancing a claim about the transformative and political potentialities of Burrows and Fargion's artistic practice and poetics in the age of late capitalism. Attending to the 'opacity' of their pieces—to the ways in which form and content work paradoxically with and against each other to produce intensities and frustrate interpretation—I envision their dance as a compellingly poetic engagement with the world we live in. Theirs is poetry that looks beyond correspondences and yet creates the possibility of a shared space—one where the gaps, the pauses, and the silences enable us to appreciate the plurality of the enunciation, which, even in its repetitiveness (or, rather, because of it), always makes room for the other.

In this poetry, I see an articulation of their politics: their commitment to dance and music and to their mutual dialogue as an interstitial space from which to engage with thinking/doing that resists the dominant logic of exchange and value. Their choreomusical work both materialises and is materialised by an 'infinite slippage' of signification (Berardi, 2012: 21): while foregrounding an unappeasable desire for enunciation, it also refuses to pay a debt to semiotic correspondences. It is here, in this force and this

desire, which contend with and are fed by the endless ambiguity of meaning, that the possibility of 'social solidarity', as Berardi calls it, is reactivated.
I call upon poetry—the language of 'insolvency' (Berardi, 2012: 22)—as
the modality through which Burrows and Fargion's dance-and-music positions itself politically today, in this world.

On Gesture

The material side of Burrows and Fargion's choreomusical poetry is gesture. There is a politics of the hand gestures, which have become the distinctive traits of Burrows' choreography—from the early solo for the camera,
Hands, in which the viewer only sees his hands, to the recent *52 Portraits*
and *Any Table Any Room*, in which hand gestures executed on or above the
surface of a table become the shared medium of these collaborative works.
Gestures also embody the notion of the minor that underpins the argument
of this book. They destabilise the language of dance from within, unsettling
its codes and field of relations and expectations, opening new possibilities.
In *The Minor Gesture*, Erin Manning (2016: 1) writes about how Deleuze
and Guattari's philosophy informs an understanding of 'the gestural force
that opens experience to its potential variation': the minor gesture 'does
this from within experience itself, activating a shift in tone, a difference in
quality'. I suggest that in Burrows' dances, gesture materialises resistance,
differentiation and ethical relationality.

In the context of current choreographic practices, Burrows' gestural
dances operate alongside other movement and dramaturgical modalities
that—for over two decades—have been employed by experimental artists
to expand and shift the practice and concept of choreography. Discussing
ways in which choreography engages with politics by problematising the
Western dance canon, Cvejić has, for instance, analysed the focus on hands
and faces in Berlin-based Hungarian choreographer Eszter Salamon's *Monument 0—Haunted by Wars (1913–2013)* (2015) as an instance of (political) attention to movement that is typically marginalised in the Western
dance tradition.[6] In a similar way, the preoccupation with small movements,
primarily of hands and fingers, of many of Burrows' works since the mid-
1990s, alongside the seated position of several of his duets with Fargion,
as well as of his recent larger collaborative works (from *52 Portraits* to
Any Table Any Room), are explorations of the possibilities of choreography
beyond given paradigms and structures; they reconnect—they *gesture*—
to its most intimately human side. They are instances of what Noémie

Solomon (2014: 20), surveying a range of experimental works created by European and American artists in the first few years of the new millennium, calls the 'movement of dance towards its outside', suggesting that '[i]n this motion, dance gestures *away from* disciplinary formations [...] and moves *toward* broad areas of life'. Solomon (2014: 21) draws attention to the ideas that underpin the recent and current *expansion* of the notion of choreography—an outward movement which reaches towards an *outside*, 'simultaneously incorporating the world while stretching its contours inside out'.

I suggest that what Solomon defines as a movement towards an outside, an elsewhere, is equally a gesturing towards an *otherwise*, a field of transformations and differentiations which materialises as an act both of resistance and of ethical relationality. It exemplifies the gestural modality that Lucia Ruprecht (2017) calls *acting otherwise*. In dialogue with Giorgio Agamben's conceptualisation of gesture and of its inoperativity, Ruprecht (2017: 6) suggests that '[i]t is in the forms, kinetic qualities, temporal displacements, and calls for response which this acting-otherwise entails that a gestural ethics takes shape'. In 'Notes on Gesture', Agamben (2000: 57) writes: 'What characterizes a gesture is that in it nothing is being produced or acted, but rather something is being endured and supported. The gesture, in other words, opens the sphere of *ethos* as the more proper sphere of that which is human'. For Agamben, gesture does not involve either acting or making: it does not move towards a goal nor is it itself the goal. '*The gesture is the exhibition of a mediality: it is the process of making a means visible as such.* It allows the emergence of the being-in-a-medium of human beings and thus it opens the ethical dimension for them' (Agamben 2000: 58, original emphasis).

Thinking with—while also departing from—Agamben, Ruprecht (2017: 6) argues that gesture 'does not evade the act; it possesses an agency that might be called *acting otherwise*'. The inoperativity of gesture makes it open to experimentation and transformation. Yet, while, for Agamben, the inoperativity of gesture is expressed through an 'anarchic' force, a being 'without law, command or origin', Ruprecht's acting otherwise often adopts 'subtler ways of modifying the operative continuum' (Ruprecht, 2017: 8). Similarly, a subtler tone characterises Burrows and Fargion's gestural art. In the broad and varied field of experimental work that has expanded and morphed the notion and practice of choreography, in contrast to strategies of interruption of normative codes and disciplinary borders that employ excess and anarchy to undermine given systems, Burrows and Fargion's choreo-musical performances *act otherwise* in a quieter register. They employ 'quiet dances' and small gestures to mobilise new possibilities of doing and being through dance—not through a lawless engagement with the form, but rather through a gentler, yet resilient, deviation from the canon, a hushed resistance to dominant paradigms.

Thinking and writing 'towards an ethics of gesture', Ruprecht fore-grounds gesture's ethical dimension also by acknowledging its fundamental relationality. Here, she follows Rebecca Schneider, who proposes that 'if bodies are caught in webs of relation, the movements made by those bodies will be relational as well. Gesture is relational, and the ethics of relations haunting our bodies in modes of reiteration make gesture a matter for ethical consideration' (Schneider and Ruprecht, 2017: 114).[7] For Schneider (2018: 286), gestures 'open intervals'—a movement 'in or toward relation' which 'establishes both proximity and distance'. Predicated on an in-between, gestures are relational also insofar as they coincide with a moment of suspension, they possibilise an outcome. Gestures embody a desire for something rather than its achievement. In the words of Daniel Blanga-Gubbay (2014: 130), '[t]hrough gestures, I manifest my ability of being not the one who has to accomplish goals but the one who tries to. [...] Every gesture hence discloses, manifests, and lives in an interstitial space'. In the intervals of sense and of communication, Burrows and Fargion's gestures articulate a desire for relationality and, in their approximation to their goals, possibilise differentiation, thus manifesting an ethical and political engagement with the world.

A politics of gesture also requires that we take into account the way in which the interstitial dimension of gesture—its untranslatability and incommensurability[8]—also '(re)inaugurates duration' (Schneider, 2018: 286), mobilising a different understanding of time and possibilising a different future. As Schneider (2018: 286) puts it, '[a] gesture, like a wave, is at once an act composed in and capable of reiteration, but also an action extended, opening the possibility of future alteration'. Gestures allow us to 'think about, perform, and produce a future "otherwise"' (Schneider, 2018: 289). In this sense, gesture functions politically through its commitment to thinking beyond the present, in its happening between the traces of the past that are inscribed in it and the images it sketches of a possible future.

ON LAUGHTER

Burrows' engagement with minor expressive modalities is a form of 'acting otherwise'. Minor practices often employ humour as a strategy of deterritorialisation of major codes and of affective intensification. Humour is the overriding quality of Burrows and Fargion's gestural poetry, which moves between the precision and composure it is executed with and the laughter it provokes. Audiences often laugh watching Burrows and Fargion perform, responding to the light and playful way in which the duo interact with each other and with the context: the formal conventions of the theatrical event are subtly undermined by the relaxed attitude and conversational tone of Burrows' and Fargion's performances. They laugh at the skilful irony of the odd coincidences—the 'accident[s] of emphasis' (Burrows, 2015: 83)—that can emerge from Burrows' understated performance, and at Fargion's more overtly comical stage presence: chuckles, ripples of laughter, guffaws. Among their duets, *The Cow Piece* has been labelled 'pure, laugh-out-loud, genius' (Brennan, 2015), with a reviewer going as far as saying that the performance caused her 'physical damage' for 'laugh[ing] so hard. Please let me have their *Cow Piece* on my desert island, with its maltreated battalions of toy cows' (Brown, 2015). In the early works, as can be heard from the recordings of live performances, audiences laugh at movement vocabulary that is incongruous with the musical accompaniment and or at unexpected movement combinations that employ absurd gestures or postures, as for example in *Stoics*.

In an interview with Ixiar Rozas, Burrows (2010b) talks about how humour functions in his work:

> The tragic in art always holds prime position in people's sense of what is important, and this is understandable. Sometimes I wish I could find that element in what I do, but the truth is I have a fairly optimistic outlook, and that comes across in the work and it opens the door for a lightness that arrives sometimes at humour. Matteo and I rarely try to be funny, but our most common response to anything we like is laughter, and this is reflected in what we make and how we perform. It's a difficult balance not to go over the top and become slapstick. It happens sometimes and then we have to recalculate and find another way into the performance, something that sustains a greater sense of its underlying seriousness.

Humour is a distinctive aspect of the interstitial place that Burrows' choreographies inhabit. It is the minor key of his compositions, the tonality through which his dances produce poetic ambiguity and relationality, on a human scale—where '[h]uman-scale is one of the most generous things that dance can offer an audience' (Burrows, 2010a: 203).

It is not my aim here to write a comprehensive account of the possible understandings and conceptualisations of humour and laughter. Instead, I wish to highlight the generative possibilities that humour and laughter open up in Burrows' choreography. I engage with this modality as an 'acting otherwise', including when it is discussed under a different name, be it humour, laughter, the comic or irony—although a crucial distinction needs to be made here between humour as minor tonality and humour in the postmodern sense of parody and pastiche.[9] What I refer to here is humour as a relational form which operates through affective intensification and holds transformative potential: humour as an act of suspension which manifests and produces an in-between, a generative interval in a continuum of thinking and doing. For instance, Berardi (2012: 167) writes about a modality of expression and address that suspends signification by relying on 'a common understanding between speakers and listeners', calling it 'irony'. For Berardi, this artistic key 'is an opening of a game of infinite possibilities'—both an artistic mood and a form of positioning which, in calling upon a shared understanding, is politically and ethically responsible and responsive (Berardi, 2012: 169).

Similarly to poetry, with its infinite ambiguity, and to gesture, with its incommensurability, humour inhabits an interstitial dimension between human scale and elusiveness, proximity and distance. If Berardi sees irony as predicated on a common ground of understanding, Henri Bergson's (2005: 2) essay on laughter attributes the comic to an 'absence of feeling', a necessary 'indifference', a detachment from a situation. Accounts on humour and laughter foreground its ineffability: as Bergson (2005: 1) writes, the 'problem' of laughter 'has a knack of baffling every effort [to tackle it], of slipping away and escaping only to bob up again, a pert challenge flung at philosophic speculation'. Yet laughter is also deeply personal: it has 'a timbre, a style, a voice'; laughter is an 'image that Derrida often links with the idea of the rhythmic relation' (Ponzio, 2009: 240). Laughter is poetry. These reflections lead me to draw an analogy between humour and both poetry and gesture. Agamben writes of poetry that it 'lives only in the tension and difference [...] between sound and sense' (Agamben, 1999: 109), and of gesture that it is 'communication of a communicability' (Agamben, 2000: 59). Similarly to both poetry and gesture, humour is a *gag*, 'a loss of memory or an inability to speak', which approximates philosophy in its 'pure mediality' (Agamben, 2000: 59).

Daniel Heller-Roazen (2005: 193) writes that poetry might find its place 'in an indistinct region of speech in which memory and oblivion, writing and its effacement, could not clearly be told apart'. I wonder whether this might be particularly true of the comic, the discussion of which in literary treatises has historically been trusted—quite literally—to the interstice between memory and oblivion. The second book of Aristotle's *Poetics*, on comedy, is lost. Dante Alighieri's essay *De Vulgari Eloquentia* is incomplete and does not include a planned fourth book on the comic genre. The status of humour and the comic, often overshadowed by the overwhelming attention given to serious and tragic art (Street, 2018), is entangled with these histories of lost and abandoned writing. I am intrigued by the idea that these missing books, through their discussion of comedy and of what is funny, might have offered a fitting framework for an understanding of the role of humour in Burrows' poetics. Nevertheless, speculations aside, the existence of the comic in an interstitial space, between memory and oblivion, between actual and potential, already situates humour in a generative place, which opens possible futures.

This place of possibilities and openness is where I leave Burrows' dance, after thinking with it through this book, and over the course of the research that has substantiated it. Burrows and Fargion's artistic work exists in a condition of availability to the future, of readiness to possible variations, of indeterminacy as a generative condition. It is fitting that as I write these 'final' notes, I receive an email from Burrows telling me of how the latest performance of *Any Table Any Room*, presented in Victoria, in the Basque Country, with four local artists in November 2018, has changed, substantially shifting the tone of the piece by stripping off the songs sung in unison, removing the golden objects that were used to replace the terracotta ones at the end and 'calm[ing] the too self-conscious politics' (Burrows, 2018c). Despite the attention to form, the love for precise compositional rules, the written scores, the work is alive and constantly moving. Not an iconic dance—a minor dance which refuses the status of major event and continues to transform itself.

NOTES

1. See for instance, Martin (2012).
2. These discrete projects are understood by Cvejić (2017: 200) as the 'politico-economic' modalities in which 'a distinct quest of means and forces is made around the problem posed':

   > The varied but coherent collection includes the works of Jonathan Burrows, Boris Charmatz, Xavier Le Roy, La Ribot, Vera Mantero, Juan Dominguez, Antonia Baehr, Tino Sehgal, Mårten Spångberg, Eszter Salamon, Mette Ingvartsen, Mette Edvardsen, Thomas Plischke and Kattrin Deufert, Saša Asentić, and others, which have emerged across Europe in the last two decades, most prominently featured in the booming infrastructure of dance and performance venues and festivals in Brussels, Leuven, Berlin, Lisbon, Madrid, San Sebastian, Bologna, Vienna, Tallinn, and Zagreb, to mention but a few.

3. Dance curator and academic, Sigrid Gareis was founding director of Tanzquartier Wien, centre for contemporary choreography and performance (Austria), and general secretary of the Akademie der Künste der Welt, Cologne.
4. This roundtable discussion (with Burrows, Fargion, Hugo Glendinning, Heathfield and Sarah Whatley), which I chaired, forms the basis of my investigation of the *52 Portraits* series in Chapter 6.
5. Heathfield, '*52 Portraits*: A conversation', talk at Kingston University London, 1 July 2016.
6. This was discussed in Cvejić's keynote 'Aesthetic Obfuscations of Conflict in White Western Dance' at the Dance Studies Association conference 'Contra: Dance & Conflict' (Valletta, Malta, 6 July 2018).
7. The connection between relationality and ethics is explained by Ruprecht (Schneider and Ruprecht, 2017) via Walter Benjamin's concept of ethics as always relational.
8. For Agamben (2000: 59), 'the gesture is essentially always a gesture of not being able to figure something out in language; it is always a *gag*'. For Schneider (2018: 289), '[u]ltimately, it is essential to allow the gestures to remain incommensurable, even as they might, from widely variant sides of time and completely different contexts, help us to veer away from linear temporal ideas of futurity.'
9. On humour as an aspect of minor practices, see also Chapter 2.

REFERENCES

Agamben, Giorgio (1999) *The End of the Poem: Studies in Poetics*. Translated by Daniel Heller-Roazen. Stanford, CA: Stanford University Press.

Agamben, Giorgio (2000) *Means Without End: Notes on Politics*. Translated by Vincenzo Binetti and Cesare Casarino. Minneapolis: University of Minnesota Press.

Berardi, Franco 'Bifo' (2012) *The Uprising: On Poetry and Finance*. Los Angeles: Semiotext(e).

Bergson, Henri (2005) *Laughter: An Essay on the Meaning of the Comic*. Translated by Cloudesley Brereton and Fred Rothwell. Mineola, NY: Dover Publications.

Blanga-Gubbay, Daniel (2014) 'Life on the Threshold of the Body', *Paragrana* 23 (1): 122–131.

Brennan, Mary (2015) 'DIG Review: Jonathan Burrows/Matteo Fargion at Tramway, Glasgow', *The Herald*, 27 April.

Brown, Ismene (2015) 'The Associates at Sadler's Wells Reviewed', *The Spectator*, 14 February.

Burrows, Jonathan (2010a) *A Choreographer's Handbook*. London and New York: Routledge.

Burrows, Jonathan (2010b) 'Interview on Voice, Language and Body, with Ixiar Rozas'. http://www.jonathanburrows.info/#/text/?id=45&t=content. Accessed 10 August 2018.

Burrows, Jonathan (2015) 'Body Not Fit for Purpose', *Performance Research*, 20 (5): 81–86.

Burrows, Jonathan (2018a) 'Politics', in Ellis, Simon, Blades, Hetty, and Waelde, Charlotte (eds.) *A World of Muscle, Bone & Organs: Research and Scholarship in Dance*. Coventry: C-DaRE Coventry University: 252–266. https://www.coventry.ac.uk/PageFiles/276435/AWofMBandO.pdf.

Burrows, Jonathan (2018b) 'What Would Be Another Word for It?' Unpublished text written for a talk with Chrysa Parkinson at Doch Stockholm.

Burrows, Jonathan (2018c) Unpublished email exchange with Daniela Perazzo Domm, 28 November.

Burrows, Jonathan and Heathfield, Adrian (2013) 'Moving Writing', *Choreographic Practices* 4 (2): 129–149.

Cvejić, Bojana (2017) 'Problem as a Choreographic and Philosophical Kind of Thought', in Rebekah J. Kowal, Gerald Siegmund and Randy Martin (eds.) *The Oxford Handbook of Dance and Politics*. Oxford and New York: Oxford University Press: 199–221.

Deleuze, Gilles and Guattari, Félix (1986) *Kafka: Toward a Minor Literature*. Translated by Dana Polan. Minneapolis: University of Minnesota Press.

Deleuze, Gilles and Guattari, Félix (1987) *A Thousand Plateaus: Capitalism and Schizophrenia*. Translated by Brian Massumi. Minneapolis: University of Minnesota Press.

Heller-Roazen, Daniel (2005) *Echolalias: On the Forgetting of Language*. New York: Zone Books.

Joy, Jenn (2014) *The Choreographic*. Cambridge, Massachusetts: The MIT Press.

Kowal, Rebekah J., Siegmund, Gerald and Martin, Randy (eds.) (2017) *The Oxford Handbook of Dance and Politics*. Oxford and New York: Oxford University Press.

Kunst, Bojana (2015) *Artist at Work: Proximity of Art and Capitalism*. Winchester and Washington: Zero Books.

Lepecki, André (2016) *Singularities: Dance in the Age of Performance*. London and New York: Routledge.

Manning, Erin (2016) *The Minor Gesture*. Durham: Duke University Press.

Martin, Randy (2012) 'A Precarious Dance, a Derivative Sociality', *TDR/The Drama Review* 56 (4): 62–77.

Perazzo Domm, Daniela (2018) 'Crisis and the Emotional Body: Towards (Another) Freedom', *Performance Philosophy*, 4 (1): 188–205.

Ponzio, Julia (2009) 'The Rhythm of Laughter: Derrida's Contribution to a Syntactic Model of Interpretation', *Derrida Today*, 2 (2): 234–244.

Prinz, Jesse and Mandelbaum, Eric (2015) 'Poetic Opacity: How to Paint Things with Words', in John Gibson (ed.) *The Philosophy of Poetry*. Oxford: Oxford University Press: 63–87.

Ruprecht, Lucia (2017) 'Introduction: Towards an Ethics of Gesture', *Performance Philosophy*, 3 (1): 4–22.

Schneider, Rebecca (2018) 'That the Past May Yet Have Another Future: Gesture in the Times of Hands Up', *Theatre Journal*, 70 (3): 285–306.

Schneider, Rebecca and Ruprecht, Lucia (2017) 'In Our Hands: An Ethics of Gestural Response-ability—Rebecca Schneider in conversation with Lucia Ruprecht', *Performance Philosophy*, 3 (1): 108–125.

Solomon, Noémie (2014) 'Introduction',in *Danse: An Anthology*. Dijon: Les Presses du Réel: 9–23.

Street, Anna (2018) 'Dramatic Measures: Comedy as Philosophical Paradigm', *Anglia*, 136 (1): 75–99.

INDEX

© The Editor(s) (if applicable) and The Author(s) 2019
D. Perazzo Domm, *Jonathan Burrows*,
New World Choreographies,
https://doi.org/10.1007/978-3-030-27680-5

CPI Antony Rowe
Chippenham, UK
2019-12-11 07:37